INSIGHT GUIDES

KENYA

◉ Walking Eye App

Your Insight Guide now includes a free app and eBook, dedicated to your chosen destination, all included for the same great price as before. They are available to download from the free Walking Eye container app in the App Store and Google Play. Simply download the Walking Eye container app to access the eBook and app dedicated to your purchased book. The app features an up-to-date A to Z of travel tips, information on events, activities and destination highlights, as well as hotel, restaurant and bar listings. See below for more information and how to download.

MULTIPLE DESTINATIONS AVAILABLE

Now that you've bought this book you can download the accompanying destination app and eBook for free. Inside the Walking Eye container app, you'll also find a whole range of other Insight Guides destination apps and eBooks, all available for purchase.

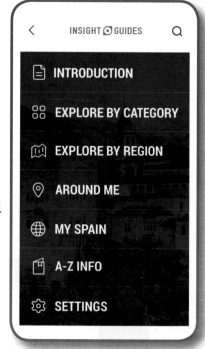

DEDICATED SEARCH OPTIONS

Use the different sections to browse the places of interest by category or region, or simply use the 'Around me' function to find places of interest nearby. You can then save your selected restaurants, bars and activities to your Favourites or share them with friends using email, Twitter and Facebook.

FREQUENTLY UPDATED LISTINGS

Restaurants, bars and hotels change all the time. To ensure you get the most out of your guide, the app features all of our favourites, as well as the latest openings, and is updated regularly. Simply update your app when you receive a notification to access the most current listings available.

Shopping in Oman still revolves around the traditional souks that can be found in every town in the country – most famously at Mutrah in Muscat, Salalah and Nizwa, which serve as showcases of traditional Omani craftsmanship and produce ranging from antique khanjars and Bedu jewellery to halwa, rose-water and frankincense. Muscat also boasts a number of modern malls, although these are rare elsewhere in the country.

TRAVEL TIPS & DESTINATION OVERVIEWS

The app also includes a complete A to Z of handy travel tips on everything from visa regulations to local etiquette. Plus, you'll find destination overviews on shopping, sport, the arts, local events, health, activities and more.

HOW TO DOWNLOAD THE WALKING EYE

Available on purchase of this guide only.

1. Visit our website: www.insightguides.com/walkingeye
2. Download the Walking Eye container app to your smartphone (this will give you access to both the destination app and the eBook)
3. Select the scanning module in the Walking Eye container app
4. Scan the QR code on this page – you will be asked to enter a verification word from the book as proof of purchase
5. Download your free destination app* and eBook for travel information on the go

* Other destination apps and eBooks are available for purchase separately or are free with the purchase of the Insight Guide book

Contents

THE BEST OF KENYA: TOP ATTRACTIONS

Safaris dominate most itineraries, but Kenya's attractions also encompass mysterious Swahili cities, idyllic palm-lined beaches and shimmering Rift Valley lakes.

△ **Lake Nakuru National Park.** Attracting millions of flamingos, Lake Nakuru is also the centrepiece of a compact national park that supports dense populations of black and white rhino alongside water and woodland birds. See page 160.

▽ **Maasai Mara National Reserve.** The northern extension of the Serengeti ecosystem, this world-famous reserve is home to the legendary wildebeest migration for three months of the year, and to the feline stars of TV's *Big Cat Diaries* throughout. See page 165.

△ **Samburu-Buffalo Springs National Reserve.** Northern Kenya's best-known and most-developed safari destination is a good place to see dry-country specials such as Grevy's zebra, reticulated giraffe and the bizarre gerenuk. See page 211.

▽ **Mount Kenya.** Enjoy Mount Kenya's snow-capped peaks gleaming in the sun from one of numerous lodges accessible from the circular road that rings the mountain. See page 277.

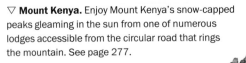

△ **Amboseli National Park.** Kenya's biggest and most habituated tuskers roam the plains and forage in the marshes below the magnificent snow-capped peak of Kilimanjaro, Africa's highest mountain. See page 229.

△ **Watamu.** In addition to its great beach, the tiny Turtle Bay resort town of Watamu offers superb diving and snorkelling, as well as access to the brooding Gede Ruins and endemic-rich Arabuko-Sokoke Forest. See page 264.

△ **Diani Beach.** East Africa's ultimate kick-back-your-feet beach destination is incredibly quiet compared with its Mediterranean counterparts and has plenty of scope for exploring the likes of Shimba Hills. See page 257.

▷ **Kisite Island.** Arguably the best snorkelling site in Kenya, this tiny coral island, south of Diani, supports a mind-boggling diversity of colourful reef fish and is a good place to see larger marine creatures. See page 261.

△ **Ol Pejeta Ranch.** Set in the shadow of lofty Mount Kenya, this is the most accessible of the private reserves that dot the Laikipia Plateau and is home to Kenya's only chimpanzee sanctuary. See page 197.

▽ **Lake Turkana.** Set in the floor of the northern Rift Valley, Lake Turkana is home to the staunchly traditional pastoral Turkana and fisherfolk El Molo, while its shores have yielded some of the world's oldest hominin fossils. See page 222.

THE BEST OF KENYA: EDITOR'S CHOICE

Wild landscapes range from snow-capped equatorial peaks to parched deserts, wonderful hiking opportunities and prehistoric sites dating back to the dawn of mankind.

Mount Kilimanjaro.

BEST LANDSCAPES

Kilimanjaro at dusk or dawn. Kilimanjaro's snowy cap emerging from its cloudy shroud is a spectacle best seen from Amboseli or Tsavo West National Parks. See page 229.
Rift Valley from the Nairobi-Naivasha Road. Close to the town of Limuru, the Rift Valley opens up to offer a stirring view over the volcanic Mt Longonot to silvery Lake Naivasha. See page 157.

Lamu Archipelago from the air. The flight to Lamu culminates in a tantalising view over the turquoise channels, green mangroves, white beaches and craggy atolls that make up the archipelago. See page 277.
Alpine moorland on Mt Kenya and Elgon. The upper slopes of Kenya's two highest mountains support an otherworldly cover of heath-like moorland. See pages 191, 181.

Blue monkeys, Mount Kenya National Park.

BEST FOR BIRDWATCHING

Lake Naivasha. The water birds are the obvious attraction, but the surrounding bush also supports an incredible avian variety, from handsome auger buzzards to brightly coloured lovebirds. See page 157.
Kakamega Forest. Home to dozens of forest species usually associated with the jungles of Central Africa, Kakamega is a must on any serious ornithological tour of Kenya. See page 182.
Arabuko-Sokoke Forest. Although it lacks the immense avian variety of some highland forests, this coastal forest near Watamu hosts several rare endemic birds, such as Clarke's weaver. See page 265.

Flamingos at Bogoria and Nakuru. Up to a million flamingos might be seen aggregated at either of these Rift Valley lakes, tingeing their entire rims pink – a truly inspiring sight. See pages 163, 161.

Flamingos.

BEST HIKING AND WALKING

Mount Kenya. The second-highest mountain in Africa offers some superb hiking opportunities, passing through lush montane forests, beautiful Afro-alpine moorlands en route to the craggy glacial peaks. See page 191.

Longonot National Park. A stiff but rewarding half-day round trip from Naivasha, the perfect volcanic rim of Mt Longonot offers superb views over the surrounding Rift Valley plains. See page 160.

Hell's Gate National Park. Kenya's most pedestrian-friendly savannah reserve offers easy walking conditions in a spectacular valley inhabited by giraffe, buffalo, zebra, baboons and various antelope. See page 159.

Sheldrick Falls. Take the guided walk through forest inhabited by elephants and buffalo to this lovely waterfall in Shimba Hills National Reserve. See page 260.

Male impala

BEST FOR HISTORY AND ARCHAEOLOGY

Gede Ruins. The mysterious brooding ruins of this jungle-bound Swahili city-state, which thrived on maritime trade in the later medieval era, include mosques and a large palace. See page 266 .

Mosque entrance, Gede ruins.

Olorgesailie Prehistoric Site. One of the wealthiest Stone Age tool sites in East Africa, set in a magnificently wild stretch of the Rift Valley. See page 157.

Nairobi National Museum. Kenya's showpiece museum contains some superb ethnographic material along with displays highlighting the country's importance in human evolution. See page 146.

Fort Jesus. This massive 16th-century seafront fortification, now a museum, was the most strategic building on the East African coast for three centuries. See page 250.

The Lamu archipelago seen from the air.

BEST BUSH LODGES AND RETREATS

Solio Game Lodge. Set in Solio Ranch, the best place in Kenya to see serious numbers of rhino, this lodge has vast suites and luxurious bathrooms. See page 203.

Elsa's Kopje. Standing on a small rocky hill in the heart of untrammelled Meru National Park, this is widely regarded to be the most swish lodge in all of Kenya. See page 211.

Kichwa Bateleur Camp. The epitome of safari chic is this ultra-luxurious small lodge set at the forested base of the Oloololo Escarpment bordering the Mara Triangle. See page 173.

Porini Mara Tented Camp. Comprising just six standing tents, this is a wonderfully remote location in an exclusive concession supporting similar wildlife to the bordering Maasai Mara. See page 174.

Porini Lion Tented Camp. One of just three camps in the Olare Orok Conservancy, it offers a truly exclusive game-viewing experience.

Rekero Camp. Classy luxury camp with a perfect location for game viewing in the central Maasai Mara and spacious tents overlooking the Talek River. See page 173.

Satao Tented Camp. Very popular with expats, this wonderfully sited tented camp in Tsavo East overlooks a waterhole that frequently attracts several hundred elephants daily. See page 242.

Maasai Mara tent camp.

Maasai warriors jumping.

White rhinoceros.

Fishing boats, Dunga Bay.

Elephant in Lewa Wildlife Conservancy.

HOME OF THE SAFARI

Kenya is where the first commercial safaris were pioneered, back in the 1930s, and it remains one of the world's top wildlife-viewing and beach destinations.

Maasai warrior.

Tropical beaches protected by offshore reefs, ideal for diving and snorkelling. Vast swathes of savannah, where lions and elephants roam below the snow-capped peaks of Mount Kenya and Kilimanjaro. The spectacular contours of the Great Rift Valley, its floor studded with lakes tinged pink with flamingos. Jungle-bound ruins of medieval trading outposts and lava-strewn badlands inhabited by desert nomads.

Kenya is a land of extraordinary scenic variety. Bordered by Tanzania to the south, Uganda to the west, and Sudan, Ethiopia and Somalia to the north, it owes much of this diversity to the combination of an equatorial location and an altitudinal span that ranges from the sultry Indian Ocean, along its eastern border, to the glacial peaks that cap the central highlands.

Kenya's immense scenery is matched by its rare biodiversity. This was the original home of the safari. And it remains an exceptional wildlife destination, though the modern safari industry emphasises photography rather than hunting, and is increasingly geared towards community-based conservancies.

Kenya's main attraction is its superb game reserves: Amboseli, Nakuru, Tsavo, Samburu and above all the Maasai Mara, where the peerless drama of the

Lesser flamingos on Lake Bogoria.

million-strong wildebeest migration is enacted every year. The country also boasts several more intimate low-key reserves, for instance Meru, Kakamega Forest and Hell's Gate. And these terrestrial wonders are complemented by the spectacular offshore reefs that run along the length of the coast, supporting a mind-boggling diversity of marine life.

Culturally, Kenya is a fascinating country, and one that regularly challenges preconceptions about Africa. On the one hand, there is Nairobi, which ranks among the continent's largest and most modern and industrialised cities. Yet you needn't drive far from the capital to find yourself in areas inhabited by Maasai and other pastoralists whose lifestyle is visibly informed by ancient ancestral values. Somewhere between these worlds are the coastal Swahili, whose rich Islamic legacy, forged by a millennium of international trade, lives on in ports such as Mombasa, Malindi and Lamu.

THE ANCESTRAL PEOPLE

For centuries tribes have migrated into this fertile region from throughout Africa, and today Kenya's population contains at least 30 different ethnic groups.

Culturally and linguistically, Kenya is one of the most diverse countries in Africa. You can walk down Nairobi's main street and in 10 minutes you will pass people representing almost every major language stock in Africa and every other continent in the world – and they could all be Kenyan citizens.

To reconstruct the history of Kenya's various people is not easy, but the research of many scholars in the fields of archaeology, historical linguistics, oral traditions, and Arabic and colonial records has resulted at least in a general idea of how people arrived there.

Language is the most useful common factor in classifying different groups of people, partly because of the close correlation between language and culture, and also because a language can be described accurately and compared with others. This comparison has become a useful tool in reconstructing the history of non-literate peoples and is based on the principle that the more similar two languages are, the more closely the people are related historically.

Linguists have attempted to estimate the dates of language divergence, which usually occur at times of geographical separation. Migration patterns have been reconstructed and word borrowings from other languages have been used as evidence of contact between groups. Archaeology and oral tradition have also both helped in unravelling the intricate weave of Kenya's history.

There are no written sources in East Africa and so the work of linguists and archaeologists has a special importance. In the 1960s, linguists devised a method of measuring not just the extent of the relationship between

Swahili woman wearing a black bui bui, Lamu.

languages, but also the intervals between any changes in the language.

Using their findings, the dates of population movements from north and south can be established, as well as the routes that were taken and the contacts that were made between Kenya's various ethno-linguistic groups, who collectively speak about 70 different languages of African origin.

Of the four main language groups in Africa, three are represented in Kenya. About 65 percent of the population speak one of the country's many Bantu languages, which belong to the Niger-Congo group. Nilotic languages – a subgroup of the Eastern Sudanic language group – are spoken by about 30 percent of the population. Cushitic languages, part of the Afro-Asiatic group, are spoken by only 3 percent of Kenyans. Khoisan is the fourth African language group, but it is no longer spoken in Kenya.

The first immigrants

There has been a long series of migrations, which lasted until the 19th century. This was the ancestral influx of most ethnic groups found in Kenya today. The first immigrant wave was tall, lean nomadic peoples speaking Cushitic languages from Ethiopia. They moved south from Lake Turkana, beginning

centuries. They are represented today by a small and little-known group called the Mukogodo, who live near the forest of Mukogodo, northwest of Mount Kenya.

Over the next millennium, between 500 BC and AD 500, the roots of almost all of present-

An old custom of the Kalenjin was to extract their lower incisor teeth. It is still practised today, on the grounds that it enables victims of lockjaw to be fed milk and medicines.

Turkana women.

Kalenjin girl, Ngomongo Village, near Mombasa.

sometime around 2000 BC. In addition to living off livestock, they possibly cultivated sorghum and made stone tools and vessels including bowls from lava and pumice.

Later, when rainfall began to decrease and the lake levels fell, these Southern Cushitic-speakers restarted their migration in search of better grazing. They encountered little resistance from the indigenous people, whoever they were, and moved leisurely southwards all the way into central Tanzania.

Another group of pastoralists followed their trail approximately 3,000 years ago. These were a group called the Yaaku, a tribe of Eastern Cushitic-speakers, who occupied a large part of Central Kenya for several

day Kenyans spread in from every section of the continent. A tide of Cushitic-, Nilotic- and Bantu-speaking groups arrived in search of fresh territory, and then chose to stay on, attracted by good farming and grazing land, and the abundant water flowing from the forest-clad highlands around Mount Kenya.

The Kalenjin group

The ancestors of the present Kalenjin group, for instance, arrived from the area of the Nile Valley between 2,500 and 2,000 years ago. They began pushing the Cushitic-speakers out of their territories and eventually occupied much of the rich highland area in Western Kenya. Later, this Kalenjin group, who adopted the practice of male and female circumcision from the Southern Cushitic-speakers, developed into the present Kipsigis, Nandi, Marakwet, Tugen and other tribes. They were originally pastoralists, but also cultivated sorghum and finger millet.

Today, the Kalenjin still live mainly in the western highlands around Kitale, Kericho, Eldoret, the Uasin Gishu plateau and the Cherangani Hills. A related tribal group, the pastoral Pokot, occupy the drier lowlands north of Lake Baringo.

One other splinter group of Kalenjin-speaking people are the Okiek, who until very

immigrants and the ancient hunters. Farming has largely replaced pastoralism as the mainstay of the Kalenjin economy, and they produce much of Kenya's tea.

The Bantu

At about the same time as these Nilotic-speakers were entering Kenya from the northwest, different groups of Bantu-speaking peoples were streaming in from the west and south. The movements of these iron-making farmers are still not known with any certainty, but their expansion – which began 2,000 years

Traditional Kikuyu welcome from children at Karunga Primary School, Rift Valley.

Kenya's Bantu-speaking people live mainly on the rich farmland around Mount Kenya, with the Kamba to the southeast. Together they produce most of Kenya's food and export cash crops.

recently were scattered in the mountain forest of Central and Western Kenya. These people, who are called the Dorobo by the Maasai, live by hunting and pot-making, and the gathering of wild plant foods and honey.

Their origins are not known but, most likely, the Okiek are the product of interbreeding between the first Kalenjin

ago in Southeast Nigeria – was explosive. Today, Bantu-speakers occupy a great deal of Central, Southern and Eastern Africa.

In Kenya, the Bantu-speakers were both influenced by and influential upon their new Cushitic- and Nilotic-speaking neighbours, leading to a high level of cultural cross-pollination and fluidity. After many complicated migrations, mixings and splits, some of the Bantu-speakers of Kenya established their present-day territories as late as the 19th century – and movements into new lands are still going on. Today, the main cluster of Bantu-speaking peoples is in central Kenya, and comprises the Kikuyu (about 10 million), the Kamba (about 5 million), the

Meru (about 2.7 million) and many other related sub-groups.

Another group of lacustrine Bantu-speakers lives, as the name implies, near a lake – in this case, Lake Victoria. These tribes, such

The Swahili language, which is essentially Bantu, with an infusion of Arabic, Asian and European words, has become the lingua franca for more than 100 million people in Eastern Africa.

in search of ivory, slaves and skins, and some settled in African villages close to the beach. They built in stone, using coral and lime, and introduced Islamic architecture and culture, eventually developing sizeable townships such as Shanga, Gede and Takwa.

By the 14th century, a new Bantu language and Afro-Arabic civilisation called Swahili were fully developed. (Some think the name Swahili comes from the Arabic word *sahel* meaning 'edge' or 'coast'.) Swahili culture has in effect turned away from the African hinterland towards the sea and the countries of

Giriama drummers in Gede.

as the numerous Luyha (about 6.5 million), the Kisii, also known as Gusii (about 2.7 million) and the Kuria (300,000), have been influenced greatly by the Kalenjin and other Nilotic-speaking people from a long history of close, but not always friendly, interaction. They live to the east of the lake around the towns of Kisii, Bungoma and Kakamega and are famous, or rather notorious, for their high birth rate.

People of the coast

There is no doubt that some Bantu groups had reached the coast when early Arab traders arrived in the 8th century. These Arabs, together with Persian traders, came in dhows

the East, which gave the people their sense of identity, their religion and their markets. Until Kenya's Independence in 1963, the coastal strip was nominally under the authority of the Sultan of Zanzibar.

Another set of coastal Bantu-speakers, distinct from the Swahili mix, are the Mijikenda, made up of nine related tribes (Giriama, Kauma, Chonyi, Jibana, Kambe, Ribe, Rabai, Duruma and Digo). They claim they originated from Shungwaya, which is thought to have been in southern Somalia on or near the coast. It was said to have been a kingdom, with a capital city of stone buildings, where people lived peacefully until the coming of the Galla marauders from the north.

These Oromo-speaking tribesmen had originally moved into southern Somalia in the 16th century, driving away the previous occupants. They then continued as far south as the hinterland of Mombasa and today they are known as the Orma people.

The Mijikenda were casualties of this Boran-Galla drive south, but they held out; their descendants still occupy a long swathe of land inland from the coast, from the Tana River well down into Tanzania. No one knows for sure whether Shungwaya really existed, but it is mentioned frequently in the of northeastern Kenya, with millions living in neighbouring Somalia and Ethiopia.

The Maasai and Luo

To outsiders, perhaps the best known of the peoples of East Africa are the Maasai. Like the Kalenjin, the ancestors of these proud cattle people were Nilotic-speakers who migrated south from the Nile Valley between the 16th and 18th centuries. On arrival in the Lake Turkana region, they interacted with Eastern Cushitic-speakers, and it may have been from them that the Maasai acquired many of their

Maasai mother and child, Selenkay Conservancy.

local oral traditions, in particular those of the Bajun sub-group of the Swahili.

Back in the dry north of Kenya, an Eastern Cushitic language group had developed from the original immigration into the area 2,000 years before. These were the Sam people, the name for some reason derived from their word for 'nose'. They were pastoralists and ranged out to occupy most of Kenya east of Lake Turkana, reaching to the Lamu hinterland and then north into Somalia.

Over time, these Sam have diversified into numerous sub-groups, such as the Rendille nomads and the Aweer or Boni hunter-gatherers of Lamu District. Hundreds of thousands of their kin, the Somali, occupy most

DESERT DWELLER

In the harsh semi-desert and scrub southeast of Lake Turkana live the Rendille, a tribe related to the Somalis. According to their legend, nine Somali warriors once lost their way and wandered for days with their camels until they reached the Samburu region. Before the Samburu elders allowed them to marry women from their tribe, they had to renounce Islam and give up their traditions. They agreed and, as a result of this union, the Rendille tribe was born. They now live in semi-permanent settlements, but spend much of their time herding their camels across the Kaisut Desert, Kenya's most inhospitable terrain.

cultural and social traditions, including possibly the class system, as well as injunctions against eating most wild game, fowl and fish.

The Maasai possess a unique combination of warlike and pastoral traits (see page 176). Their cousins, the Samburu, live in the desert to the north and a third Maa-speaking group, in a small sub-tribe called the Ilchamus or Njemps, lives on the southern shore of Lake Baringo.

The Nilotic-speaking Luo, numbering over 6 million, form Kenya's third-largest group after the Kikuyu and Luhya. Originally from the Bahr-al-Ghazal region of Southern Sudan, now

Maasai warrior, Selenkay Conservancy.

occupied by the related Dinka and Nuer, the Luo began to move into western Kenya through Uganda in the early 16th century. Small groups pushed into western Kenya between 1520 and 1750, displacing or absorbing the resident Bantu speakers. They then spread south around Lake Victoria to occupy and proliferate in their present Nyanza homelands.

At first they were nomadic herdsmen, but as their population increased they settled as farmers and fishermen (they are particularly noted as skilled fishermen with both hooks and floating nets). But the Luo are still itinerant people – they compare themselves to water which flows until it finds its own level – and they have spread across the country in their tens

of thousands, into major cities including Nairobi and Mombasa, north to the shores of Lake Turkana and south to Lake Jipe.

According to the most recent classification, the Maasai, together with other closely affiliated recent arrivals such as the Turkana and Samburu, are East Nilotic-speakers, whereas the Kalenjin are South Nilotic-speakers, and the Luo of the Lake Victoria Basin are West Nilotic.

Group affinity

There is clearly some affinity between the Maasai and the peoples previously referred to as the Galla, but now more widely known as the Oromo. Although the main Oromo territorial focus is southern Ethiopia (with a population of more than 30 million), around 400,000 Oromo-speakers live in Kenya, where they are divided into various subgroups. Of these, there are about 40,000 Gabbra, a tribe of hardy camel nomads who roam the arid northern lands around the Chalbi Desert (over an area the size of Switzerland). Their cousins, the Boran, live to their east, reaching with their livestock well north into their original Ethiopian homeland and also south as far as Isiolo.

Other Oromo-speaking tribes live along the Tana River in arid bush country and can often be seen driving herds close to the coast either to market or in search of pasture. The Sakuye are a small group of mainly camel-herding people who live to the east of Mount Marsabit. Some say that their name derives from the mountain, which in Oromo is called Saku.

All these peoples have complicated age-set systems that strictly control their social and economic life, although to some extent these are now breaking down as a result of the intrusions of modern life.

Later immigrants

In addition to this complex, indigenous African element make-up of Kenya, there are a number of immigrant communities. Some 40,000 Kenyans claim to be Arab, most of them descendants of the early coastal traders but infused with African culture over generations. Many families still maintain contacts with Oman, the Yemen and Saudi Arabia.

Not so well-known or documented are the early arrival and settlement of the coast by people from India and Pakistan. Immigrants from Gujarat and Kutch in southwest India probably began settling in the coastal Afro-Arab trading towns during the 10th and 12th centuries, although there is no evidence that they mixed with the local population as the Arabs did. The Indian influence on Swahili culture is most evident in the architecture and artefacts.

Most of Kenya's present-day Asian community arrived in the late 18th century as labourers on the British railway or as small-scale businessmen. They number more than 100,000 today and are mostly settled in the larger towns and cities, which bear the stamp of their culture in mosques, temples, bazaars and suburbs of squat, pastel-coloured villas. The Asians have also prospered in all sectors of the economy.

percent Roman Catholic). Another 11 percent of Kenyans are Muslim, a religion whose main stronghold is the coast, which was first settled by Islamic Arabs more than 1,000 years ago. A very small number of Kenyans still practice traditional beliefs, with adherents mostly belonging to traditional pastoralist groups such as the Maasai, Samburu and Turkana.

A growing population

Although Kenya has one of the most diverse and successful economies in Africa, it is vulnerable to three major threats – a rapidly

A Swahili woman having her hands painted with henna, Lamu.

There are some 30,000 Kenyans of European descent, mostly descended from settlers who arrived in the late 19th or early 20th century from Britain, South Africa, Italy, Greece and elsewhere to establish farms in the rich highland areas. A substantial community of European and US expatriates is focussed on Nairobi and to a lesser extent Mombasa. Many of them are employed on short-term contracts in commerce, the diplomatic corps, the United Nations and many other institutions.

The influence of these later immigrants has been particularly strong when it comes to religion. Today, over 80 percent of Kenyans identify themselves as Christian (roughly 47 percent of the population being Protestant and 23

increasing population, the HIV-Aids epidemic, and the strong element of tribalism that informs its occasionally volatile political scene. Throughout the 20th century, Kenya's population more or less doubled every 20 years. A government education programme on the need for family planning has slowed population growth from over 3 percent to around 2.5 percent, and the trend has definitely slackened in the post-millennial era.

According to the 1999 census, the country supported around 30 million people at the turn of the 21st century, a fourfold increase since 1960. In 2015 the population estimate stood at nearly 46 million – over 60 percent of it in the under-25 age group. This growing population may mean a growing labour pool, but it also means that the provision of goods and services must rise faster than the birth rate, and it places ever-greater stress on the country's finite natural resources.

Running parallel to the growing population is the devastating effect that HIV-Aids has had on Kenya, which ranks third in Africa (after South Africa and Nigeria) and fourth in the world in terms of number of people infected with HIV. With support from the World Bank, hundreds of Voluntary Counselling Centres have been set up around the country, and the government has also incorporated information on HIV-Aids in the national school curriculum. But while the situation has improved considerably since the 1990s, the statistics remain terrifying: as of 2014 around 1.4 million Kenyans were infected, representing 5.3 percent of the adult population, and the high death toll has left nearly one million Aids orphans countrywide. The short-term economic costs, including care and lost labour, swallow up millions of US dollars every month.

Finally, there is the question of ethnicity, with the cultural diversity that is often one of Kenya's great strengths also being a frequent source

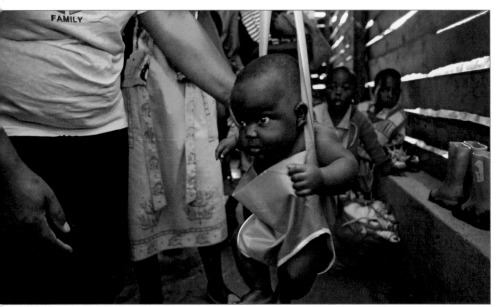

Baby weigh-in at a health clinic.

WANDERING WARRIORS

The nomadic Turkana, a warlike cattle-herding people, were described by a British colonial administrator as 'of gigantic height and extremely savage'. They were certainly aggressive enough in the mid-19th century to drive the Maasai from the area between Lake Turkana and the Rift Valley. They rampaged around the southern and eastern shores of the lake until they were finally subdued by the British in the early 20th century. Following droughts in the 1960s and 1970s, the Turkana have resumed their expansive wandering and can be found both east of the lake and in Samburu country, mingling with their Eastern Nilotic relatives.

of disharmony. The main rivalry is between the politically dominant Kikuyu and the aspirant Luo, and it is no coincidence that the country's Kikuyu founding father, Jomo Kenyatta, appointed as his successor Daniel arap Moi, a member of the smaller Kalenjin tribe who ended up being Kenya's longest-serving president. The post-electoral violence of December 2007 was also ethnic in nature, comprising as it did a flare-up between supporters of the Kikuyu incumbent Mwai Kibaki and his Luo rival Raila Odinga. However, such outbursts are the exception rather than the rule, and the greater trend of Kenya over its first 50 years of independence has been the forging of a proud sense of nationhood from its disparate ethno-linguistic groups.

DECISIVE DATES

6 million BC
The earliest known East African hominin *Orrorin tugenensis* lived in Kenya's Tugen Hills.

1.8 million BC
Emergence of the tool-making *Homo erectus*.

130,000 BC
Homo sapiens active near Lake Baringo.

c. 2,000 BC
Cushitic-speaking nomads arrive from Ethiopia.

500 BC–AD 500
Bantu-speaking migrants arrive in Kenya with metalworking skills.

c. 900
Islamic settlers occupy Mombasa and other seaports, leading to emergence of Swahili civilisation.

1498
Arrival of Vasco da Gama in Malindi signals the start of Portuguese influence.

1500
Portuguese sack Mombasa.

1593
Portuguese begin construction of Fort Jesus in Mombasa.

1699
Omani Arabs capture Fort Jesus, leading to withdrawal of Portugal and long era of Omani rule.

1824
Captain Owen declares Mombasa a British protectorate, a status that is removed three years later.

1832
Seyyid Said transfers his court to Zanzibar.

1830–1880
Slave trade flourishes under Seyyid Said and his successors.

The Age of Exploration

1840s
Missionaries Krapf and Rebmann respectively the first Europeans to see Mounts Kenya and Kilimanjaro.

1856
Burton and Speke discover lakes Tanganyika and Victoria.

1883
Explorer Joseph Thomson travels from Mombasa to Lake Victoria through Maasailand.

1888
Imperial British East Africa Company (IBEAC) builds headquarters in Mombasa.

Jomo Kenyatta.

1890
The Treaty of Berlin brings all Kenya and Uganda under British jurisdiction.

1892
Jomo Kenyatta is born in the highlands north of Nairobi.

1895
The British Government acquires IBEAC's assets, and Kenya and Uganda become 'British East Africa'.

1896
Construction of the railway from Mombasa to Uganda begins.

1899
Nairobi founded as railway headquarters.

1901
The railway reaches Kisumu on Lake Victoria.

1902
First daily newspaper founded in Mombasa.

1918
After World War I, the British Government offers war veterans land in the Kenyan Highlands.

The Nationalist Movement

1922
Nationalist leader Harry Thuku is arrested, leading to the massacre of protesters outside Nairobi police station.

1924
The Kikuyu Central Association (KCA), known as Uhuru, is

formed with Jomo Kenyatta as its secretary.

1929
Kenyatta goes to England to plead the cause of Kenyan liberation.

1939–45
In World War II, Britain uses Kenya as a base for operations in Ethiopia (then Abyssinia). Many Kenyan Africans fight in the British army.

1940
The KCA and other organisations are outlawed and their leaders detained.

1944
The Mau Mau independence movement is founded.

1946
Jomo Kenyatta becomes chairman of the newly formed Kenya African Union (KAU).

1952
State of emergency declared. Kenyatta and 82 other nationalists arrested and imprisoned. War declared on Mau Mau.

Independence Achieved

1956
First elected African representatives in the Legislative Council. Mau Mau rebellion ends.

1959
Kenyatta released from prison, but put under house arrest.

1960
State of emergency ends. Kenya African National Union (KANU) formed by Tom Mboya and Oginga Odinga.

1961
Kenyatta released from house arrest and assumes presidency of KANU.

1963
Kenya becomes independent with Jomo Kenyatta as Prime Minister.

1978
President Kenyatta dies in office and is succeeded by former Vice-President, Daniel arap Moi.

1982
Kenya officially declared a one-party state. Attempted coup d'état by Kenyan Air Force is put down.

1992
First multi-party elections for 25 years, but Moi is returned as president, amid accusations of electoral irregularities.

1997
Police clash with pro-democracy protesters. Moi is re-elected President in widely criticised elections.

1998
Islamic terrorist car bomb at the US Embassy in Nairobi kills 224 and injures 4,500.

2002
Terrorist attacks on an Israeli airliner and hotel in Mombasa leave 15 people dead. Moi's 24 year rule ends with opposition presidential candidate Mwai Kibaki's landslide victory.

2003
Free primary education and anti-corruption measures introduced.

2004
Wangari Maathai is the first African woman to win the Nobel Peace Prize.

2007
Kibaki officially defeats his rival Raila Odinga by a margin of 3 percent in presidential elections. The result is disputed, leading to violence in which 1,133 people are killed.

2008
A Unity Government is installed, with Kibaki as President and Odinga Prime Minister.

2010
East African Common Market allows for free trade with Uganda, Burundi, Rwanda and Tanzania.

2011
Kenya invades neighbouring Somalia in pursuit of the Al-Shabaab insurgents blamed for a string of high-profile kidnappings in Lamu and Garissa Districts.

2012
Crude oil is discovered in Kenya.

2013
Uhuru Kenyatta wins presidential election. 67 people die when Somali Al-Shabaab militants raid a shopping mall in Nairobi.

2014
A series of terrorist attacks throughout the country claims at least 100 lives.

2015
Al-Shabaab fighters kill 148 people at Garissa University in northwest Kenya.

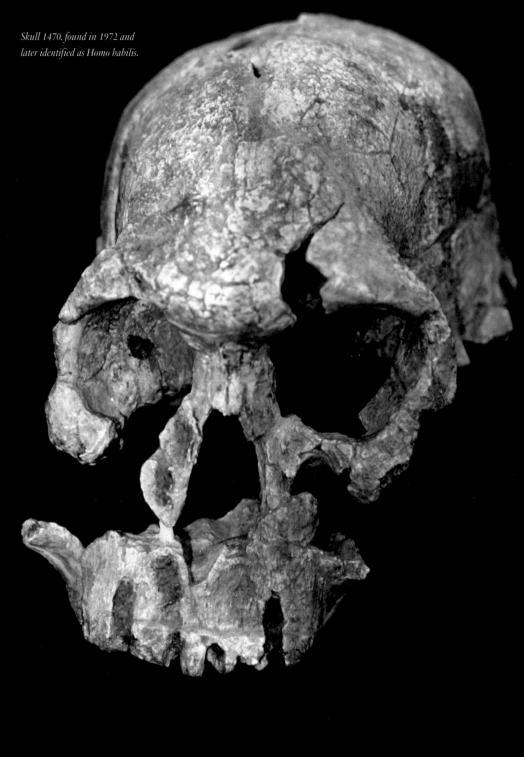

Skull 1470, found in 1972 and later identified as Homo habilis.

THE EARLIEST INHABITANTS

A wealth of unique fossil evidence tells us that the East African Rift Valley has been inhabited by our hominin ancestors for perhaps 6 million years.

The earliest history of human beings is pieced together from a handful of bones and a few broken tools scattered across thousands of miles, from South Africa to the Gobi Desert, and a biological and social study of our nearest relations, primates such as chimpanzees and gorillas. One new find, a skull or set of fossilised footprints, can rewrite the books. At best, it is an inexact science.

Yet one thing cannot be disputed – as things stand at present, most of the key discoveries on which we base our knowledge of the evolution of early hominin primates (essentially, proto-humans) have been made in East Africa's Rift Valley. Koobi Fora, on the Kenyan shore of Lake Turkana, ranks among the most productive locations for early hominin fossils anywhere in the world, while other key sites include Olduvai Gorge in northern Tanzania, the Afar Region of northeast Ethiopia, and Sterkfontein Cave and environs in South Africa.

Richard Leakey with two crucial skull discoveries, Homo habilis and Australopithecus.

First steps

It is now commonly accepted that man's earliest roots do lie in Africa, a theory first postulated by Charles Darwin in the 1870s, and that we are not descended from apes, but share a common ancestor with them. The apes evolved into forest dwellers, while humans, who lived more vulnerably in the open, learned first to stand upright, for better vision, thus freeing their hands to use tools. With no natural defences against predators or weapons for hunting, the use of strategy and tools became essential for survival. And as social creatures, the use of language for communication was an inevitable mark of progress.

It is not known exactly when the evolutionary paths of humans and apes diverged, but molecular studies suggest it was perhaps 6 to 8 million years ago. Two relatively recent discoveries have been put forward as candidates for the title of the world's oldest-known hominin fossil, though neither is universally accepted as such by palaeontologists. These are *Sahelanthropus tchadensis*, discovered in Chad in 2001 and dated to about 7 million years ago, and the arboreal *Orrorin tugenensis*, which lived about 6 million years ago and was first unearthed in Kenya's Tugen Hills in 2000. Some scientists believe that the Orrorin fossils from Tugen represent a common ancestor of all subsequent hominin species, as well as chimpanzees.

Homo habilis was for a long time considered our oldest ancestor but in 2010 scientists working at South Africa's Sterkfontein Caves announced the discovery of Homo gautengensis, more than two million years old.

The Afar region of northern Ethiopia has yielded the world's oldest undisputed hominin remains, thought to be around 5.5 million years old and ascribed to the species *Ardipithecus kadabba*. Ethiopia is also the only place where

South Africa in 1924, as well as *Australopithecus anamensis*, found in northern Kenya, and *Australopithecus afarensis*, identified in Ethiopia. Two sets of footprints discovered by Mary Leakey in 1976 at Laetoli, near Tanzania's Olduvai Gorge, are thought to have been made by *A. afarensis* around 3.6 million years ago.

The oldest Australopithecine fossils, unearthed in northern Kenya, date to more than 4 million years ago, and the genus evidently thrived for several millions of years. Indeed, current palaeontological thinking, subject to regular revision as new evidence emerges, is

Meave Leakey and members of the field crew excavating the Homo erectus skull.

Ardipithecus ramidus, a probable descendent of *A. kadabba* that lived at least 4.4 million years ago, has been located.

First identified in South Africa in 1924, the most widespread of early hominin primates, and possibly the first to be full bipedal, are placed in the genus *Australopithecus* (literally 'southern ape'). They stood 1.2 to 1.4 metres (3ft 8ins to 4ft 7ins) high, and had a chimp-like face. They left no stone tools, but probably used sticks.

Australopithecine fossils have been found all over eastern and southern Africa, and several species have been identified, many of which lived at the same time. These include *Australopithecus africanus*, the species first unearthed in

that the Australopithecines were not necessarily ancestors of modern humans and that they co-existed with our direct *Homo* ancestors until they became extinct around 500,000 years ago.

The first true humans

In 1964, Louis Leakey, Phillip Tobias and John Napier announced another milestone in evolutionary understanding when they found and named *Homo habilis* ('handy' man). Originally thought to be a true ancestor to modern humans, this has now been disproved, with several similar species found at other dig sites. *Homo habilis*, who lived about 2 million years ago, had a significantly larger brain (around 600 cubic cm/36 cubic ins) and was the earliest species known to manufacture stone tools, such as rudimentary choppers, scrapers and chisels.

A more certain candidate than either of the above for one of our direct ancestors is *Homo erectus* ('upright' man), which first emerged on the fossil record about 1.8 million years ago, and went on to become the first human to venture outside Africa, where it survived until some 25,000 years ago. *H. erectus* was tall and relatively upright with a 950 cubic cm (58 cubic in) brain. It had a flatter face than earlier hominines, with an external nose, and a smaller jaw, making it look far more recognisably human. It was also probably the first human to live in a hunter-gatherer society, to make a sophisticated range of purpose-built tools, and to control fire.

Thinking man

Evolution rarely seems to follow a straight line and for a time, H. erectus lived side by side with our own species, *Homo sapiens* ('thinking' man), who first appeared on the scene about 130,000 years ago. Homo sapiens is significantly taller but less bulky than its predecessors, with a much larger brain (about 1,300 cubic cm/79 cubic ins). Our species' success has led not only to total domination of the plant and animal kingdoms, but the eventual extinction, en route, of all other hominid species. Although we now come in all shapes, sizes and colours, these genetic variations are relatively young, and a compelling combination of fossil and DNA evidence asserts that modern man evolved in Africa and spread across the planet from there.

By the Acheulean era, H. Erectus was crafting elegantly designed, highly efficient hand axes, cleavers, scrapers and knives. Fine collections have been found at several sites in Kenya, including Olorgesailie in the Rift Valley south of Nairobi and Kariandusi near Lake Elmentaita. Indeed, the oldest tools of this type, dated to 1.75 million years ago, come from the far north of Kenya, in the vicinity of Lake Turkana. By 10,000 years ago, Acheulean tools had been refined into microliths – small, ultra-efficient flakes of stone used for spears, arrows or as knife blades inserted into a wooden handle. Families lived in rock shelters, their walls frequently decorated with pictures of animals, hunting and dancing.

The Bushmen

Throughout sub-Saharan Africa, the oldest surviving aboriginal people are the so-called Batwa (Bushman), small, relatively sharp-featured, slightly yellow-skinned people whose hunter-gatherer culture and click–based Khoisan language are thought to date back 40,000 years. Even today, the last few groups live as nomadic hunter-gatherers, providing us with a direct link to the late Stone Age. However, as other groups have dominated, they have been integrated, enslaved, exterminated or simply pushed back to the inhospitable fringes

Ogiek man constructing a beehive, Mau forest.

STONE TOOLS: A MILLION YEARS

Homo habilis' first tools were pieces of stone crudely chipped into shape, a class of tool-making known by archaeologists as *Oldowan*. The evolution of *Homo erectus* brought a more skilled style, known as *Acheulian* (after St Acheuls in France, where typical artefacts were first found). Hand axes, cleavers and other tools were now honed on both sides to produce a sharper blade. The basic designs remained unchanged for over 1 million years. The crude hand axe made from a piece of lava at Koobi Fora 1.5 million years ago has the same design as the slim, fine-honed stone axe made 200,000 years ago at Kariandusi.

of the continent, such as the southern Namib and Kalahari deserts.

In Kenya, they are represented by the tiny minority of small tribes who – collectively numbering about 25,000 – are often referred to disparagingly as the Dorobo (literally 'Primitives'). The most significant of these, associated with the forested Mau Escarpment that divides the Rift Valley from the Maasai Mara, are the Ogiek, a loose agglomeration of at least a dozen linguistic groups who total about 50,000 people. Others include the Elmolo fishermen of Turkana and the Dahalo hunter-gatherers that

Maasai woman and her children, Selenkay Conservancy.

inhabit the mainland part of Lamu District. Other than the click, these groups have virtually no linguistic links in common with the better-known Khoisan-speaking 'bushmen' of southern Africa, so if they are related, the split seems to have occurred many thousands of years ago.

Recent Migrants

Over the past 3,000 years, the pace of change has quickened as wave after wave of invaders have arrived and taken root, leading to the complex web of people that now inhabit Kenya.

First to arrive were the Cushitic-speaking tribes, who began to drift south from Ethiopia about 3,000 years ago. With them, they brought agriculture. These were more settled people

than their hunter-gatherer predecessors, living in villages and clearing the bush to plant millet and vegetables, while their herds of domestic cattle, sheep and goats competed for grazing with the local wildlife. The balance between man and nature began to shift.

The most important event in the course of populating modern Kenya was the arrival of the Bantu-speakers from their original home in West Africa. About 2,000 years ago, the Bantu-speakers began to move south and east across the continent, and various tribes have meandered across the continent ever since, to arrive in present-day Kenya is a sequence of staggered waves The massive shifts of 20th- and 21st-century refugees around Africa continues the theme.

Most Bantu-speakers are farmers and cattle herders, living in villages, with a strong family and clan structure. Where they gained superiority over all existing inhabitants was in their ability to work metal. Their iron tools were not only infinitely more effective weapons, but enabled them to cultivate more difficult ground, clearing woodland and invading the less hospitable reaches that had, until now, been the preserve of the hunter-gatherers. Iron was so important that the ironworkers became the local aristocracy, appointing administrators to rule their web of chiefdoms. They were also traders, with the early long-haul trade in salt and iron gradually being joined by gold, ivory and slaves.

Today, hundreds of different Bantu languages and dialects are found throughout southern and eastern Africa, and 70 percent of Kenyans speak a Bantu language. Even Swahili, the coastal *lingua franca* that is also the national language of Kenya and Tanzania, is a Bantu language, albeit one whose vocabulary is peppered with words borrowed or derived from Arabic, English and to a lesser extent Portuguese.

The last major ethno-linguistic group to reach Kenya was the Nilotic-speakers, who came south from Egypt and the Sudan in a sequence of migrations. A relict of the earliest known wave, some 2,000 years ago, are the Kalenjin of the western Rift Valley, whose unverified oral history traces their origin to Ancient Egypt. More recent arrivals are the Luo, Kenya's third largest tribe, who inhabit the area around Lake Victoria. The last to arrive were the Maasai and Samburu, who probably crossed into present-day Kenya as recently as the 18th century. (See page 19)

The Leakeys

The pivotal figure in East African archaeology, Louis Leakey, founded a scientific dynasty that also included his wife Mary, son Richard and granddaughter Louise.

Louis Leakey was born in 1903, in Kenya, the son of English missionaries working with the Kikuyu tribe. Brought up with the local children, he was initiated into the tribe along with his playmates at the age of 13. Always fascinated by early history, he studied anthropology and archaeology at Cambridge in the 1920s, returning to East Africa to conduct digs in several areas. He carried out his first serious excavation of Olduvai Gorge in 1931.

In 1933, he met Mary Nicol, an English scientific illustrator, who was the daughter of a popular landscape painter. Mary had spent much of her childhood in the Dordogne region of France, becoming fascinated by the rich prehistory of the area. She never took a degree, but followed a number of university courses and was, in later life, inundated with honorary degrees. The two married in 1936, after Louis's divorce from his first wife, Frida. Together, they began a serious study of Olduvai, which resulted in a string of discoveries that completely rewrote man's evolutionary history.

International renown

Mary's first major discovery was the first fossil skull of the extinct Miocene primate, *Proconsul*, in 1948. In 1959, she discovered *Australopithecus boisei*, shooting the family to international stardom. In 1964, Louis led the team that found and identified *Homo habilis*.

During World War II, Louis became involved in intelligence work, and in 1945 he became the curator of the Coryndon Museum (now the National Museum of Kenya). In 1947, he organised the first Pan-African Congress of Prehistory. Always a flamboyant man, he was an excellent speaker and fund-raiser who used his increasing international fame to generate finance not only for the family's archaeological expeditions, but a series of other ventures, including the acclaimed primate studies of Jane Goodall and Dian Fossey and his own anthropological work. During the last years of his life he suffered from increasingly poor health, and died in England in 1972, aged 69.

Meanwhile, Mary, who is generally recognised to have been the better scientist but remained in her husband's shadow, continued to excavate Olduvai and surrounding archaeological sites. In the 1960s, she moved almost full-time to Olduvai, living there for the next 20 years. In 1976, she discovered the 3.6 million-year-old Laetoli footprints. In 1983, she retired to Nairobi where she remained until her death, aged 83, in 1996. However, this was not the end of the story. Their middle son, Richard, led his first fossil-hunting expedition in 1964. Two years later, he started work with the National Museum of Kenya and began a series of excavations at Koobi Fora on Lake Turkana, where he added significant new species to the early catalogue of hominids.

Louis and Mary Leakey study fossilized skull fragments.

In 1966, he married an archaeologist, Margaret Cropper, who also began to work in the family 'firm'. In 1970, after their divorce, he married a primate researcher, Meave Epps. Still active in conservation, he became chairman of the Kenya Wildlife Service and a professor of anthropology at Stony Brook University, New York, as well as a stint as a politician in Kenya. During 2016, Angelina Jolie is set to direct a movie about his life, set in Kenya.

However, Meave has continued to work as a palaeontologist, discovering *Australopithecus anamensis* in 1995 and the 3.5-million-year-old *Kenyanthropus platyops* in 2001, the same year their daughter, Louise, completed her PhD in palaeontology. Two years later, Louise married a Belgian anthropologist and primatologist; the dynasty looks set to continue.

A dhow sailboat at sunset off the coast of Lamu.

SWAHILI TRADE

Long before Europeans set foot there, Mombasa and the rest of East Africa's Swahili Coast was a centre of international trade and Islamic culture.

The Indian Ocean, tumbling over the reefs and shores of Kenya, is awash with history. At the centre of this coast, ancient seaports such as Mombasa or Malindi – as namechecked by the 17th-century poet John Milton in *Paradise Lost* – evoke a history of cultural interchange and trade dating back to the Classical era.

It is known that the ancient Egyptians embarked on regular trade with the Horn of Africa, but not whether they explored south as far as Kenya or Tanzania. By AD 60, however, when an anonymous Greek author wrote a guidebook to the Indian Ocean shipping routes entitled the *Periplus of the Erythraean Sea*, it seems that trade between the Mediterranean civilisations and the Kenya coast was well established, a scenario confirmed by Ptolemy's *Geography*, written in about AD 150. Both tracts describe the coast as far south as the island of Menouthesias (thought to be Zanzibar) and the mainland port of Rhapta (possibly Pangani in Tanzania).

It was at about this time that Bantu-speakers first colonised the coast and islands, which were split into numerous small independent kingdoms, each with its own ruler. Following the emergence of Islam in the 7th century AD, Arab traders brought this new religion to the coast, where many settled and intermarried with the local people. Over the years, the local Bantu language and culture became infused with Arabic words and Islamic influences, to form a distinct ethno-linguistic group called the Swahili, a name that is said to derive from the Arabic word *sahel* (edge or coast).

Trade and prosperity

The Swahili Coast entered its golden age of trade in the 8th or 9th century AD. By then,

The ruins of Gede, a great Islamic city in the 14th century, mysteriously abandoned in the 17th.

the Swahili had established a network of Islamic city-states from Mogadishu (Somalia), in the north, to Sofala (Beira) in the south, via Lamu, Malindi, Mombasa and various Tanzanian ports, of which the most important were Zanzibar and Kilwa. In the process, mud and coral houses and stores made way for stone buildings of architectural merit, agriculture flourished and the people were well dressed. The Arab historian Mahsaudi, who visited coastal Kenya in the 9th century, recorded in his *Meadows of Gold and Mines of Precious Stones* that Mombasa and Malindi were rich in ivory and gold – the latter mostly sourced from present-day Zimbabwe, transported overland along the Zambezi Valley to Sofala, and then along the coast via ports such as Kilwa.

After that, the Hegira Arabs began to trade with an empire which spread from the south of France through the Mediterranean, the Red Sea and beyond to the borders of China and India. Trade with the Arab Empire brought substantial benefits to East Africa. Technology, new goods, concepts and business practices brought the coastal towns in line with the cultures the trade connection had to offer.

Life was governed by the trade winds. The Arab dhows, their design little altered today, would head south on the northeast monsoon between October and February, carrying trade goods such as cloth, beads and porcelain, returning north on the southwest monsoon between March and September, laden with gold, ivory and other goods. Towns were thriving; the business of the ports brought stability and much contentment. Narrow streets were crowded with slaves bearing parcels of freight to chanting oarsmen who ferried commodities to and from the vessels riding in the harbours.

Nineteenth-century depiction of Mombasa.

A TRADING CAPITAL

Periplus of the Erythraean Sea is the log of a Greek ship's captain who sailed out of Egypt in the 1st century AD. It provides the earliest known description of trade between Arabia, India and Mombasa:

'There are imported undressed cloth, robes from Aden, double-fringed linen mantles, articles of flint, glass and brass used for ornament and in cut pieces used as coin, sheets of soft copper, iron, olive oil, adzes, swords, girdles and honey from the reed called sacchari [sugar].

There is exported ivory, rhinoceros horn, tortoise shell. In this place are sewn boats and canoes hollowed from single logs.'

This pattern remained in place for six or seven centuries prior to the arrival of the Portuguese, though the focal point of coastal trade occasionally changed, with Mogadishu dominating in earlier days, to be replaced by Kilwa in the 13th century, which in turn had relinquished much of its importance to Mombasa by the late 15th century.

The arrival of the Portuguese

Towards the end of the 15th century, the ordered East was assailed by Western explorers. King John of Portugal and his son, Prince 'Henry the Navigator' inspired the extraordinary record of exploration and conquest manifested by Portugal up to 1700 or so. For the Kenyan coast, the year of the Portuguese was 1498. This was after Vasco da Gama had received orders from Prince Henry to round the Cape and find the sea route to India.

His small fleet reached Ilha do Moçambique, where it found the principal inhabitants to be Islamic. According to the record, 'a few merchant dhows lay in the harbour, laden with rings and a quantity of pearls, jewels and rubies'. The mercantile class at Ilha do Moçambique, possessive of its position in the area, was not pleased to see the Europeans. Dissension broke out and the Portuguese left in a hurry, vowing to return and teach the town a lesson.

As they sailed, a small dhow set off to warn fellow Arabs further north of what might be in store for them. Thus, when the Portuguese fleet arrived at Mombasa, a seaborne guerrilla attack was launched to cut the anchor ropes. To avoid a confrontation, da Gama retreated to Malindi where, finally, he found a friendly Sultan who entertained da Gama and his crew royally.

It was altogether a pleasant visit, according to da Gama's record: 'Malindi houses are lofty and whitewashed and have many windows. On the land side are palm groves and all around it, maize and vegetables are being cultivated. For nine days we had fetes, sham fights and musical performances'. At the end of it, the Portuguese ships were loaded with fruit, vegetables and meat; the Sultan produced a pilot who knew the route to 'Calicut' (Calcutta), and the voyage to India was accomplished.

> *The Swahili language is often described as being a Bantu-Arabic hybrid. In fact, this coastal lingua franca is part of the Bantu linguistic group in terms of grammar, but has also borrowed from Arabic and English.*

The friendly association of the Portuguese and Malindi lasted for almost 200 years, but other ports on the coastline suffered reprisals for the impolite way they had received the first Europeans. Mombasa was sacked in 1500 by Cabral, in 1505 by Almeida and in 1528 by Nuña da Cunha. Other ports, such as Kilwa, were razed, while Ilha do Moçambique was conquered and became the main Portuguese

centre of operations on the southern coast, a position it retained for almost 400 years, only to be displaced by Maputo (or, as it was then, Lourenco Marques) in the late 19th century.

In their chronicles, the Portuguese noted: 'Mombasa is a very fair place with lofty stone and mortar houses well aligned in streets; the wood is well-fitted with excellent joinery work. The men and women go very bravely attired with many fine garments of silk and gold in abundance. This is a place of great traffic and has a good harbour in which are moored crafts of many kinds'.

Vasco da Gama Pillar, Malindi.

Portugal withdraws

In 1593, the Portuguese started to build a fortification overlooking Mombasa harbour, which was to become Fort Jesus. At first it was little more than a walled compound, but it soon developed into the huge fortress that can be seen today. With this massive stronghold, they felt safe. And while the established Swahili sultans fought back to try to regain control, they were unsuccessful, even with Turkish support. Over the course of the 16th century, the Portuguese gradually spread along the coastline, demanding the payment of levies. Every part of the coast suffered under the harsh regime and there was severe retribution for the slightest offence.

The Portuguese were, in fact, in a losing situation. All their supplies to Mombasa, except food, had to be imported from Goa in India. When their soldiers sickened and died from malaria and other scourges, the ships bringing relief and reinforcements had to fight their way into the port. Finally, in 1696, after almost 200 years of Portuguese occupation, the Omani navy launched a siege on Fort Jesus that lasted for almost three years, resulting in thousands of deaths, but that ended Portuguese dominance north of the present-day border of Tanzania and Mozambique. Instead, the region became

coast disappeared. It was not until the early 19th century when a new ruler in Oman came to East Africa that the coast recovered, politically and economically – largely through the establishment of slave caravan routes from the coast through the interior to lakes Victoria, Tanganyika and Malawi.

The mastermind behind this revival was Sultan Seyyid Said, one of the longest-living and influential of the Omani rulers, having come to the throne in 1804, aged 13. Initially based in Oman, Seyyid sent an army to quell Pate, Pemba and Mombasa, then occupied by

Fort Jesus, Mombasa.

part of the Sultanate of Oman, leaving the established Swahili sultanates and their upstart Omani supplanters to maintain an uneasy truce – marked by sporadic outbreaks of violent dissensions – until the coming of the British and Germans in the 19th century.

Oman and the slave trade

Although the Sultan of Oman was the official ruler of the coast following the departure of the Portuguese, he was ineffectual. He appointed governors from the Nahaban family in Pate, the Mazruis in Mombasa and the El-Hathis in Zanzibar. The governors quarrelled among themselves and the people of the coast suffered. Trade dwindled; the wealth of the

the Mazruis. With this began the story of British intervention in the area since the Mazrui chief, Suleiman bin Ali, invoked the protection of England.

The following year, two British survey ships, HMS *Leven* and HMS *Barracouta*, were on a mission to survey the east coast of Africa. When the *Leven* arrived at Mombasa, Captain Owen was begged by the local Mazrui Arabs to raise the Union Jack over the fort and place the island and its surrounding territory in the hands of His Britannic Majesty. Owen agreed to establish a protectorate.

Thus, on 7 February 1824, the British flag was hoisted over the fort. In return, the Mazrui promised to abolish the slave trade. A lieutenant of the *Leven* was appointed Commandant and Captain Owen's decision to assume authority was transmitted to London to await ratification. After three years, London's response was received. Captain Owen's action was repudiated and the British Protectorate over Mombasa was eventually removed. This opened the way for Seyyid Said of Oman to restore his sovereignty, which he did in 1828. He brought in a fleet, placed a garrison in the fort and, in Zanzibar, began to lay out the numerous clove plantations that have since brought considerable wealth to the island.

Britain made genuine efforts to stall the slave trade through the introduction of other forms of commerce. Even before he settled on Zanzibar, Seyyid had signed a treaty forbidding the sale of slaves to Christian countries, and in 1845 he agreed to outlaw the export of slaves south of Kilwa or north of Lamu. But neither treaty was easy to enforce, as canny traders simply relocated to more obscure ports to escape detection, In addition, Britain had no influence over the Omani slave caravan routes into the interior, which had barely been explored by Europeans in the mid-19th century.

Nineteenth-century slave market in Zanzibar.

In 1832, Seyyid transferred his court from Oman to Zanzibar. Within a few years the East African coast, from Cape Guardafui to Cape Delgado, was an acknowledged dominion of the Sultan, and his dreams of an African empire began to materialise. Unfortunately, the fuel for this economic revival was not primarily clove production but human bondage. Under Seyyid, the slave trade out of East Africa, once negligible by comparison to the gold trade or the slave trade of West Africa, increased to the point where an estimated 50,000 slaves were sold annually on Zanzibar alone in the 1840s, and twice as many captives died on the long march from the interior to the coast.

THE LION OF WITU'S BRIEF REIGN

In the 1860s, the sleepy village of Witu became the seat of a sultanate and the capital of the short-lived state of 'Swahililand'. The 'Sultan of Witu' came from Pate in 1862 to escape the powerful Sultan of Zanzibar, with whom he had unwisely quarrelled. Calling himself Simba ('Lion'), the sultan minted his own currency and issued Swahililand stamps.

His sultanate came to an end in 1888 when he signed an alliance pact with the Dendhart brothers from Germany, in effect making Witu a German Protectorate. Two years later the Treaty of Berlin brought the whole of Kenya under British jurisdiction

1908 Uganda Railway poster, showing the track from Nairobi to Mombasa.

EUROPEAN EXPLORATION AND COLONISATION

A combination of missionary zeal, imperial ambition and a simple desire to explore attracted European powers such as Britain and Germany to East Africa.

By 1850, the likes of Portugal, the Netherlands, Britain and Germany had been using the East African coast as a staging point along the trade route between Europe and India for longer than three centuries. With the arguable exception of Portugal, however, none of these European powers had demonstrated any significant interest in territorial expansion beyond a few isolated coastal ports. Likewise, the East African interior, although it was regularly traversed by Swahili slave caravans as far inland as the great lakes, remained a cartographic mystery to European geographers.

All that would change in the second half of the 19th century, an era of terrestrial exploration that resulted not only in the mapping and opening up of the entire African interior, but also in most parts of the continent being colonised by, or entering into treaties as protectorates with, one or other European power.

German school pupil with a Maasai boy, 1938.

Mapping the Interior

In 1846, the German missionaries Johann Krapf and Johannes Rebmann established an evangelical mission in the Taita Hills, and went on to become the first Europeans to see the continent's two tallest mountains, Kilimanjaro and Kenya, though their reports of equatorial snow caps were initially disbelieved back home. However, the main impetus for further exploration of the interior was the so-called slug map produced by another German missionary James Erhardt in 1855. Based on third-hand accounts from Swahili traders, this map was nicknamed for the large slug-shaped lake it depicted at the heart of the continent, which – though wildly inaccurate – generated fresh interest in a mystery

that had tickled geographers since Roman times, namely the location of the source of the White Nile.

Within five years of the slug map's publication, the continent's three largest lakes had all been freshly 'discovered' by Europeans – Lake Niassa-Malawi by the Scottish missionary David Livingstone, Lake Tanganyika by Sir Richard Burton and John Speke, and Lake Victoria by Speke alone. The relationship between these three lakes and the Nile remained a matter of conjecture, with Speke controversially nominating Lake Victoria as the great river's source, while Burton, Livingstone and most other geographers favoured Tanganyika. The controversy was settled only in 1875, when Henry Stanley

> *Joseph Thomson gained a reputation among the Maasai as a great laibon, or 'medicine man'. His repertoire of tricks included frothing at the mouth with the help of Eno Fruit Salts and the removal of two false teeth.*

circumnavigated both lakes and established that Tanganyika was part of the Congo watershed.

Most of the Kenyan interior remained unexplored at this point, largely because these explorers travelled inland along slave caravan routes that mostly left from ports south of the present-day border with Tanzania, but also because of the Maasai's renowned hostility to outsiders. The first European expedition into Maasailand was undertaken in 1882 by Gustav Fischer, who was forced to turn back to the coast when he was ambushed by the Maasai at Hell's Gate near Lake Naivasha. The British explorer Joseph Thomson, who followed in Fischer's footsteps a few months later, became the first European to document the existence of Lake Baringo and Mount Elgon, as well as the waterfall outside Nyahururu that still bears his name.

The first European visitor to northern Kenya was Count Samuel Teleki, a Hungarian aristocrat who hiked to an altitude of 5,350 metres (17,552ft) on Mount Kilimanjaro and 4,725 metres (15,502ft) on Mount Kenya, before heading northwards to Lake Turkana, which he reached in 1888. Arthur Donaldson-Smith became the first European visitor to Mount Marsabit in 1895, and Captain Stigand was the first to cross between these two northern landmarks via the Chalbi Desert in 1909.

The build-up to colonisation

Although hindsight lends the colonisation of East Africa a certain aura of inevitability, it was an unexpected turn of events at the time, one entered into with mixed motives and little premeditation by the concerned European powers, of which Britain was dominant. Nor were British motives for colonisation as entirely self-serving as is often assumed. Indeed, a major advocate of colonisation was the anti-slaving lobby, whose attempts to stop the flourishing coastal trade in human lives were galvanised in 1872 by the emotional funeral of the explorer David Livingstone, an outspoken abolitionist who had ample opportunity to witness the unspeakable cruelties perpetrated by the slavers along the caravan routes he followed into the interior.

Livingstone and his supporters believed that the slave trade could be halted only by opening up the African interior – where murderous slave raids generally resulted in entire villages being razed, as all their inhabitants were either killed or taken captive – to the 'three Cs': Christianity, Commerce and Civilisation. And it was in the wake of Livingstone's funeral that Britain took its first step towards colonisation, formalising its already strong links with the dominant regional power Zanzibar in 1873. A naval

The Victorian explorer David Livingstone led numerous expeditions in Africa.

blockade was placed around the island, and the British consul John Kirk, a former travel companion of Livingstone, persuaded Sultan Barghash (the son of Seyyid) to sign a treaty offering him full British protection against all other foreign powers if he banned the slave trade. As a result, Barghash closed down Zanzibar's notorious slave market, and allowed an Anglican Church to be built on the site.

The partitioning of the East African mainland was initiated by the German premier Leopold von Bismarck, whose main interest in the region was probably to acquire pawns to use in territorial negotiations with Britain and France closer to home. In 1884, based on a series of questionable treaties acquired by the German metaphysician Carl Peters, Bismarck announced claims to a large tract of land between the Pangani and Rufiji rivers in present-day Tanzania. Since large parts of the area claimed by Germany were conventionally regarded to be part of the Zanzibar Sultanate, Britain was bound to protect them in accord with the treaty signed with Barghash in 1873, especially as failure to do so might result in it losing control of Zanzibar's lucrative import and export trade, which generated an annual turnover of two million pounds.

Heliogoland-Zanzibar Treaty

In 1886, as the so-called Scramble for Africa hurtled towards its hurried climax, Britain and Germany agreed to a coastal territorial partition that corresponds to the modern border between Kenya and Tanzania. An administrative and trading concession, covering the whole coast from Vanga to Kipini, was granted to the Imperial British East Africa Company (IBEAC) under a Royal Charter in 1888. However, this agreement didn't set a northern or western border for the British sphere of influence, which allowed Germany to claim a block of territory north of the Tana River (including the Lamu archipelago) in 1890, along with much of what is now Uganda.

By this time, Bismarck had resigned as German premier, paving the way for his successor Leo von Caprivi to knock out the amicable Heligoland-Zanzibar Treaty with his British counterpart Lord Salisbury. This treaty affirmed British protectorateship over Zanzibar, as well as German possession of what is now mainland Tanzania, Burundi and Rwanda. In addition, Salisbury surrendered the tiny but strategic North Sea island of Heligoland (which had been captured by Britain in the Napoleonic Wars), in exchange for which Germany revoked all its claims to parts of present-day Kenya and Uganda, and both parties agreed that the coastline to a depth of 10 miles (16km) should remain part of the Zanzibar Sultanate, a British Protectorate. (It was to stay this way right up until the independence in 1963, when Sultan Seyyid Khalifa ceded his mainland territory to Kenya.)

British East Africa

In July 1895, the virtually bankrupt IBEAC was rescued by the British Government, which bought the company assets for £200,000, and took over

what is now the territory of Kenya as 'British East Africa'. The Sultan in Zanzibar was paid an 'honorarium' of £17,000 a year for British protection of his 16km (10-mile) long strip of coastline. The news that the British Crown had taken over from the IBEAC angered many locals, in particular the prominent Mazrui family, which had never fully acknowledged Omani rule over the Sultanate of Zanzibar, and which led organised attacks on Mombasa and Malindi as part of a unilateral declaration of independence for the coastal strip. These uprisings were dealt with by detachments of the British Army brought over from India.

A confrontation between 19th-century colonials from the coast and local tribesmen.

The people of the interior – few of whom would even have heard of Britain ten years earlier – proved to be equally unwilling to accept their new colonial masters. It took four military expeditions, for instance, to persuade the Kamba tribe to accept the British administration. Further up-country, more troops were garrisoned at Fort Smith to control a territorial expansion of the Kikuyu out of the highland forests. Around Lake Victoria, the Nandi and other tribes began a guerrilla resistance in 1895 which was to last over 10 years until the Nandi *laibon*, spiritual leader and chief strategist, was shot dead at peace talks.

Only the Maasai came into the Protectorate of their own accord. At that time they were having difficulty dealing with predatory raids of the Kikuyu and Kamba since the prophesied plagues of rinderpest and smallpox had seriously weakened them. In the north, a revival was started with food-aid cattle from the Protectorate and a couple of seasons of good rain. The Maasai *moran* (warriors) picked themselves up and replenished the tribe with cattle and women collected in reprisal raids against the Kikuyu, and the Meru and Embu on the eastern shoulder of Mount Kenya.

Economic growth

A Scotsman, Sir William Mackinnon, the former chairman of the IBEAC, brought the first scheduled steamship line to the East African ports and built a road from Mombasa upcountry to Kibwezi. He also advocated the construction of a railway line from Mombasa to Lake Victoria The original purpose of the line was strategic, to get a permanent line of communication into Uganda ahead of the Germans coming up from the south. A vocal opposition group in the British Parliament called it a monumental waste of time and money, 'a lunatic line to nowhere'. But the scheme

Kenya and Uganda Railways freight train, Mombasa.

By the end of 1895, the British rated the Maasai 'a menace and a force to be reckoned with' after they massacred half a caravan of 1,100 men in the Kedong section of the Rift Valley above Nairobi. A passing trader, Andrew Dick, decided to exact retribution on behalf of the Crown. He attacked the Maasai sentries guarding the cattle, made off with a large herd, and was halfway up the eastern escarpment before the main body of the *moran* caught up with him. Trader Dick was thus added to the casualty list, which also included 452 Kikuyu and 98 Swahili. At the official Court of Inquiry, the Maasai were found to have been unreasonably provoked but were charged compensation for the massacre in the amount of the cattle taken by Dick.

went ahead in 1896, with the import of 32,000 Indian labourers from Gujarat and the Punjab.

> *The single-track railway from Mombasa to Lake Victoria covered 935km (581 miles) and cost the British taxpayer £9,500 a mile, which is equivalent to almost £1,000,000 per mile in modern terms.*

In May 1899, a temporary halt to railway construction was called at mile peg 327, and a tented depot was established at the site, now the city of Nairobi, but then a dank, evil-smelling, frog-infested swamp, where wildlife wandered in from the Athi Plains. The Maasai stayed aloof from the new encampment, but the Kikuyu came in to market their crops and livestock. The first coffee was planted by Catholic priests at St Austin's Mission on the outskirts of the township, and tea was started on the wooded uplands of Limuru close to the 600-metre (2,000ft) precipitous drop into the Rift Valley. This, the worst of the natural obstacles in the way of the line, was negotiated first by a funicular system of cables and winches. Later a zigzag slant was cut out on the face of the scarp. From there on it was fairly easy going across the

Sir Charles Eliot, the Commissioner of British East Africa from 1900 to 1904, decided that the huge cost of the railway should be recouped through European settlement along the line, wherever the land could be farmed or ranched. The Scottish-looking Aberdares, with their cool climate and fertile valleys, offered the best prospect for arable development. Several of the first farmer-settlers were the rootless younger sons of the minor British aristocracy. In a sense, these 'White Highlands' became the officers' mess of colonial Africa, with the Asians barred from owning land in the area and the Kikuyu either

White settler and two boys operate farm machinery, c.1940.

Rift floor, up the gentler wall of the Mau Range to an English country landscape around Njoro, and on down to the shores of Lake Victoria. The last spike was driven in at Port Florence (Kisumu) on 19 December 1901, just over five years after construction started.

Boosted by the rail link to the interior, Mombasa rapidly took over from Zanzibar as the main regional trade centre. But while the railway brought prosperity to Mombasa, the companies resident there soon acknowledged that their future lay in Nairobi. As they moved up the line, so did the planters' association, the commercial associations and, finally, the colonial administration, which decided to make Nairobi the colonial capital in 1907.

retained as labourers or asked to remove themselves to a patchwork reserve on the range's lower eastern slopes. Elsewhere, albeit to a lesser extent, local tribes were forced to make way for white settlers, with the likes of Lord Delamere, for instance, being granted a tract of ranchland in the vicinity of Lake Elmentaita, forcing its Maasai residents either to take up employment on the ranch, or to vacate it for a designated tribal reserve.

War in Africa

World War I boosted the colonial economy, with troops and goods from overseas moving through the port of Mombasa. It also had a huge political impact on British and German

East Africa, neighbouring territories administered by the war's two main adversaries. At first the African campaign was a series of minor episodes. The German commander in Africa, Paul von Lettow-Vorbeck, defeated the British embarrassingly at Tanga and then led a hit-and-run campaign against the railway supply line from behind the Taita Hills.

Two-thirds of the British colony's 3,000 male settlers left their wives to manage the farms while they rode after Germans in irregular cavalry units. The colonial government also made strenuous attempts to conscript the

mandate, and began thinking of an economic federation of the three East African territories.

The 'Colony of Kenya'

Another significant consequence of the war was the British Government's decision to offer estates in the highlands to veterans of the European campaign in what was called the 'Soldier Settlement Scheme.' By 1920, when the country was designated the 'Colony of Kenya', the white population was around 9,000. The coastal strip remained detached for a few years on a courtesy lease from the Sultan of Zanzibar.

Lt. Col John Henry Patterson poses with the body of one of the man-eating lions he shot and killed near the Tsavo River, late 1890s.

Maasai and other locals into the regular army. The British successfully attacked the German post at Bukoba, in the west shore of Lake Victoria. Then, led by the South African general Jan Smuts, they drove Vorbeck into a fighting retreat around Central Africa, thereby allowing the German general to achieve his main objective of occupying a large force of the British Army for the duration of the war. He was leading 155 Germans and 3,000 Africans into Portuguese Angola in November 1918 when he received news of the armistice.

Vorbeck ended the war undefeated, but Germany lost Tanganyika in the Treaty of Versailles in 1919. Britain was assigned to govern the larger part of it under a League of Nations

All this advanced the settler community's objective of a permanent white man's Kenya – but they were soon disillusioned. A Government White Paper in 1923 introduced a policy of 'Africa for the Africans'. In what was seen as a Bill of Rights for the black Kenyans, the key paragraph stated that, 'Primarily, Kenya is an African country. H.M. Government think it necessary to record their considered opinion that the interests of the African native must be paramount, and that if and when those interests and the interests of the immigrant races should conflict, then the former should prevail.'

From then on a succession of colonial governors were obliged to apply the paper policy, often facing abusive opposition from a settler community led by Lord Delamere and his National Legislative Council. A takeover attempt by the settlers was always a possibility, but there were never enough of them for any open rebellion or for the political fight, which was probably lost when the administration's power base at Nairobi began a rapid expansion from the mid-1920s. This led to a major social revolution for the adaptable Kikuyu, who flocked to the fledgling city, in the process making a giant leap from a traditional African lifestyle to a more cosmopolitan urban environment with its complex cash economy.

A few young Kikuyu formed community groups as channels for Government protection of their tribal interests. But the fundamental issue was land, and the early associations of the Kikuyu in Nairobi were revivalist meetings for the return of the 'alienated' highlands. About this time, a remarkable former herd-boy called Johnstone Kamau took a job reading water meters for the Municipal Council. He later changed his name to Jomo Kenyatta as he increased his involvement in the political organisation of the Kikuyu in what was to become a long and eventually traumatic struggle with the settlers.

Army Scouts making their way through the forests of East Africa during World War I.

THE MAN-EATERS OF TSAVO

While the railway was being built across the Tsavo plains, a pair of elderly male lions developed a taste for the workforce, killing at least 30 Indian and African labourers, and possibly as many as 135, between March and December of 1898. Several explanations have been put forward for this unusual behaviour, one of the most credible being that it was due to a shortage of normal prey created by a severe rinderpest epidemic. Another theory is that their taste for human flesh was acquired by scavenging improperly buried bodies of malaria victims associated with the railway. Whatever the reason, the two lions – named 'The

Ghost' and 'The Darkness' by terrified railway workers – were legendarily skilled at avoiding traps and barriers, and in one instance they actually boarded a train to drag off their victims.

The lions were eventually shot by Lt Col. John Henry Patterson, whose book about the lion attacks has inspired several movies, notably *Bwana Devil* (1952), *Killers of Kilimanjaro* (1959) and more recently *The Ghost and the Darkness* (1996, starring Michael Douglas and Val Kilmer). The country on both sides of the track was left as a wildlife reserve, later to become Tsavo East and West national parks.

THE STRUGGLE FOR INDEPENDENCE

Kenya's transition from British colony to independent state involved four decades of fervent political debate and, at times, bloody armed conflict.

O n 16 March 1922, a crowd of around 7,000 Kenyans gathered outside the Central Police Station (where the main campus of the University of Nairobi stands today) to protest against the arrest, two days earlier, of Harry Thuku, leader of the East African Association (EAA). This organisation, established by Thuku a year earlier as a multiethnic offshoot of the Young Kikuyu Association (YKU), was the first formal anti-colonial movement of its sort in East Africa, campaigning against the *kipande* system of pass controls, and forced labour being imposed on women and girls.

Suddenly, and for reasons that remain unclear, a volley of gunshots rang out from the police station. A group of settlers gathered outside the Norfolk Hotel reputedly joined in, firing into the dispersing crowd. Officially, 25 protestors were killed, many shot in the back as they fled, but some unofficial sources claim the death toll was more than 100.

This episode marked a turning point in relations between the colonial government and its subjects, initiating the start of a sustained fight for equal political, economic and social rights for all Kenyans. Even at that early date, local leaders such as Thuku and Jomo Kenyatta, who joined the EAA later in 1922, were determined to take over from the British and run the country themselves. Their objective was *Uhuru* – Swahili for 'freedom' – and it was to be a long struggle before they achieved it.

Land grievances

Since the 1902 Land Acquisition Order in Council, white settlers had acquired the most fertile land in Kenya. They had also become politically dominant in a Legislative Council in Nairobi, which allocated more and more land

Jomo Kenyatta celebrates his release from house arrest in 1961.

to Europeans and passed laws that forced Africans to seek employment from settlers. These laws were ruthlessly enforced through an elaborate system of chiefs and headmen established in the early 1900s.

A local newspaper reported in 1922: 'Out at Pangani village [close to Nairobi], the Natives are very busy these days holding meetings of the mass kind. Every Sunday, thousands of *Njoroges* and *Kamaus* may be seen listening raptly to others of their kind holding forth on presumably the question of the hour... And it is fairly apparent that these meetings have a savour of politics about them and that the Natives are discussing matters connected with registration, taxation and so on.'

These meetings were attended by up to 5,000 people and were multi-tribal in character. The main complaints were over the forced labour practices and the imposition of a 'hut tax', which most people couldn't afford. Among the many Africans who attended these rallies of discontent was the young Kikuyu Johnstone Kamau. Born before the

> By 1928 about 26,400 sq km (10,200 sq miles) of Kenya's best arable land had been allocated to European settlers.

British settlement, he grew up as an orphan and was educated by missionaries. As Jomo Kenyatta, his name would leave an indelible mark on Kenya.

Initially, the Colonial Government was not fully aware of the extent to which indigenous Kenyans were prepared to fight for their rights. The first sign of organised resistance had been the formation of the YKU and EAA, and when the colonial government banned these organisations in the aftermath of the crowd massacre in Nairobi on 16 March 1922, local dissidents responded with the formation of the Kikuyu Central Association (KCA), with Kenyatta as its secretary, in

Jomo Kenyatta pleads his cause in Trafalgar Square, London, in 1938.

THE MAU MAU COMPENSATION BATTLE

The full extent of the atrocities committed against Kenyan civilians at the so-called screening camps established by the British colonial administration during the Mau Mau rebellion is an open question. Largely forgotten outside of Kenya for half a century, the issue received fresh public scrutiny in 2005, when Caroline Elkins's controversial Pulitzer Prize-winning book *Imperial Reckoning: The Untold Story of Britain's Gulag in Kenya* detailed the systematic torture that took place in the camps, and claimed a death toll of at least 70,000, possibly more than 100,000.

The issue has received further publicity since 2009, when five octogenarian veterans of the screening camps (one of whom subsequently died) brought a compensation case against the British government. Of the four surviving claimants, two were castrated by their torturers, one was beaten unconscious in an attack that left 11 others dead, and another was sexually abused. Their lawyers have documented 6,000 related cases of human rights abuse by the British administration.

The case is still unresolved, but seems certain to lead to fuller disclosure of events surrounding the Mau Mau Rebellion, following the announcement, in April 2011, of the discovery of 300 'missing' boxes, containing a total of 1,500 files, transported to Britain at independence.

1924. The KCA complained against the Government's policy of dividing the tribes and asked for the establishment of a Central Native Council. Instead, they were fobbed off with Local Native Councils made up of chiefs and appointed members and charged with giving 'the younger and more educated Natives a definite avenue along which to develop'.

Social conflicts

In 1929, there was another complicated social controversy over the custom of female genital mutilation (FGM), a practice that had long formed part of the initiation tradition for the Kikuyu and many other Kenyan tribes. The church decided to expel anyone who supported this practice, a move that many Kikuyu leaders regarded as yet another interference with tribal tradition. The affair led to the formation of independent schools and church movements, and these splinter developments were to become useful to Kenyatta and the KCA, as it was in the independent schools that the Kikuyu sense of identity and African nationalism were inculcated.

Harry Thuku was released from jail in 1930 on the condition that he would cooperate with the government. When he agreed, it isolated him somewhat as a 'stooge'. It was a decision that would undermine his leadership. Many of his supporters joined the KCA. Meanwhile, in 1929, Kenyatta had gone to London to lobby the KCA's cause to the British government and media. He reported back in 1930, but then went off again in 1931 for what would be a 15-year odyssey in the Western world, including some time in Stalin's Soviet Union.

Three years later, a commission inquiring into the disposition of land in Kenya heard views presented forcefully and articulately by the Africans, but nevertheless disallowed all African claims to the 'White Highlands'. As a result, the 'social' organisations proliferated. In addition to the Kikuyu KCA, the Luo around Lake Victoria formed the North Kavirondo Central Association; the Taita Hills Association represented the Taita people west of Mombasa; and the numerous Kamba tribe southeast of Nairobi founded the Ukamba Members Association. In May 1940, 23 leaders of these associations were detained under newly promulgated 'defence regulations'. They were held on suspicion of consulting with the Italian Consulate in Nairobi, a potential enemy of the king. A copy of Adolf Hitler's

Mein Kampf found at the KCA headquarters compounded the felony.

The Kenya African Union

Although the KCA and other associations were banned in 1940, a more potent political organi-

> *The Kikuyu-dominated Mau Mau began in 1948 as a loose but vigorous association of secret societies. The origin of the name Mau Mau is obscure.*

Jomo Kenyatta under armed guard in 1953, following his arrest and subsequent trial by the British colonial administration.

sation came into being following the appointment of Eliud Mathu – a graduate of Balliol College, Oxford – as the first African member of the Legislative Council. Recognising the need to have a base, in 1944 Mathu formed the Kenya African Study Union, with its constitution written by Indian lawyers.

In 1946 the organisation changed its name to the Kenya African Union (KAU). Although it had an intertribal outlook, its leadership was dominated by former KCA Kikuyu members. So it was not surprising that when Jomo Kenyatta returned the same year, after 15 years abroad, he was elected president of KAU. He was the only man who had a chance of uniting the Kenyans against colonial rule.

With Kenyatta at the helm and using the Kikuyu independent schools and churches machinery, KAU grew in strength in Nairobi, Central Province and among Africans working in the 'White Highlands'. It also stepped up confrontation with the government. There was a KAU-supported strike at Mombasa docks, which was ruthlessly suppressed. At Uplands, a few miles north of Nairobi, police shot several strikers at a bacon factory. In the same year, 1947, police fired at Africans demonstrating against the intimidation of a Kikuyu chief.

British soldiers guard Mau Mau rebels after mass arrests in Nairobi.

Oaths of allegiance

As a reaction to the strict enforcement of regulations against squatting in the highlands, the Kikuyu started forming secret societies. New members were sworn in at 'oathing' ceremonies, at which oaths of loyalty to political objectives were often accompanied by vows to kill Europeans and their collaborators.

The authorities, including African chiefs, viewed the oathing as a threat to law and order, and the missionaries and their Christian African followers saw the ceremonies as anti-Christian. This caused a deep social rift, so that when the Mau Mau war started, the Christian Kikuyu were prime targets. Many of them were killed.

As political fervour increased, oathing spread among other tribes – the Maasai, the Luo, the Luhya and, to some extent, the Kamba and the Kipsigis. There was a wave of destruction of settlers' property, as well as murders of chiefs and other Africans loyal to the Government. The 'Mau Mau Rebellion' had begun.

On 21 October 1952, Governor Sir Evelyn Baring declared a 'state of emergency'. Kenyatta and 82 other nationalists were arrested and detained. Military reinforcements were flown into Kenya and war was declared on the Mau Mau. Before the month was over, Kenyatta and five of his colleagues were charged with managing this 'unlawful organisation'. And, despite a spirited defence by a team of international lawyers, Kenyatta was convicted and sentenced to serve seven years in jail.

Walter Odede, a Luo, took over leadership of KAU, but the party was banned soon afterwards and the new leaders detained. By then, according to the Colonial Government, at least 59 leading Africans had been murdered. The reprisal – the arrest of the KAU leaders – only made matters worse. It was followed by an outpouring of Kikuyu from the 'White Highlands' and many urban areas into the forest enclaves of the Mau Mau around the Aberdares and Mount Kenya.

The Government used drastic measures to deal with the rebellion. They herded rural communities together, cramming people into 'protected villages' surrounded with barbed wire. Anyone found outside during a strict night curfew was shot. To augment the police and the army, 20,000 Kikuyu 'Home Guards' were recruited, a move that, along with Christian opposition to the Mau Mau, expanded the rebellion to civil war.

The Lyttelton Constitution

During 1953 and 1954, a number of pitched battles took place between Mau Mau fighters and government troops. After these, the rebels were more or less on the run. The Colonial Secretary, Oliver Lyttelton, turned up in Kenya, and subsequently produced a document known as the 'Lyttelton Constitution'. This created a multiracial Council of Ministers, which infuriated the settlers.

In June 1955, the Government announced that Africans could form political parties at district levels – except in the Mau Mau heartland of Central Province – 'to encourage a simple and orderly development of African political life'. The majority of settlers were far from happy to accept Africans as partners in the

The exact toll of deaths associated with the Mau Mau rebellion is unknown. The minimum figure is 13,000 but some sources place it above 100,000. However, only about 100 of the victims were European settlers.

Government; however, the majority of Africans no longer cared what the Europeans thought. The following year saw yet another Constitution which reserved eight seats in the Legislative Council for Africans – to be elected by all constituents in the country's eight provinces.

These first full representatives of the Kenyan majority included Daniel arap Moi, later President; Tom Mboya, assassinated after independence; Ronald Ngala, who died in a road accident; and Oginga Odinga, an important political figure.

Six months before Kenyatta's jail term ended, the African representatives on the Legislative Council started a clamour for his release. The Government gave way to their agitation and lifted the 'state of emergency' in 1960, although not without initial resistance. But this time, however, it was clear that a settler-dominated Government could no longer be sure of maintaining law and order in Kenya. This, together with the continued agitation of the African elected members, led the British Government to convene the 1960 'Lancaster House Conference' on the future of the colony.

Advising the Africans was a future US Supreme Court Justice, Thurgood Marshall, but as usual, they failed to get what they wanted. Even so, the principle of majority rule and ultimate independence for Kenya as an African – not a white man's – country was endorsed.

At its first meeting as a legal political party, KAU changed its name to the Kenya African National Union (KANU). But there was almost instant division. The coast's representative, Ronald Ngala, with other leaders from the Luhya, the Kalenjin and the Maasai, formed the Kenya African Democratic Union (KADU), with Ngala as president.

Finally, Kenyatta was released in August 1961, and returned to Nairobi to find two hostile groups of African nationalists in the Legislative Council. Apart from their mutual insistence on *Uhuru* (freedom), the two parties had nothing in common. KANU wanted a unitary form of Government with firm control from Nairobi. KADU wanted a federal type of Government

to safeguard the rights of the minorities; it also had support from a considerable number of the settlers. For a while Kenyatta toyed with the idea of forming his own political party. But, because of his long association with the people and ideas that dominated KANU, he eventually agreed to take over as President of the party.

Independence

Jomo Kenyatta led KANU's delegation to another round of talks at Lancaster House in London in November 1961. Haggling, threats and compromise went on for two years until

Maasai elders, displaying anti-Kenyatta slogans, demonstrate at a meeting in Kajiado, 1962.

the Colonial Office finally got KADU and KANU to agree on a date for the end of colonial rule – 12 December 1963.

It rained the night before, but the crowds were impervious to it as they gathered in their thousands near midnight at a makeshift 'Independence Square', which was barely 5km (3 miles) from the site of the 1922 shooting. Men and women all over the country had their ears tuned to their radio sets. Then it happened: midnight and 'freedom' – the embattled, long-delayed *Uhuru*. The lights at the square were dimmed. When they were turned on again, the Union Jack was nowhere to be seen. From the flagstaff flew the black, red and green ensign of the new independent Kenya.

THE MODERN REPUBLIC

The years since 1963 have not been easy for any African state, but Kenya has coped better than most with natural disasters and political unrest.

After a bitter and bloody struggle during which relations with the colonial power had been strained to the limit, Kenya entered its new era as a free nation in a spirit of joviality and positivity. Hardly had Independence been achieved, however, than Kenya found itself in the midst of a region where one neighbouring state after the other was set aflame by revolutions and/or coups, and rumours of communist subversion were rife.

Within a month of Kenya becoming a self-governing state, a bloody revolution in Zanzibar not only ousted the Sultan but also led to a pogrom of Arabs by the African majority. The dust had hardly settled when the army mutinied in neighbouring Tanzania. President Julius Nyerere was forced into hiding and had to call in British troops to overpower the mutineers. Mutinies also broke out in Uganda, and then in Kenya. About 5,000 British troops were stationed in East Africa and some were deployed to quell all three mutinies.

While communists may have been involved on Zanzibar, the mainland troubles showed no such external influences; trade unions were seen as the main instigators. Nevertheless, while Kenyatta was committed to a policy of strict non-alignment, and hoped to exist with both capitalism and communism, several leaders in Kenya became jittery about China and the USSR's ambitions to expand their influence in Africa. Luo leader Oginga Odinga, the first Vice-President of the new republic, was seen as a sympathiser with China and the Eastern Bloc countries, while Tom Mboya, the Minister for Economic Affairs, was accused of being a tool of the imperialists.

President Mwai Kibaki addresses the United Nations General Assembly in 2008.

KANU and KADU parties

Meanwhile, Kenya had become a de facto one-party state under the Kenya African National Union (KANU), with the voluntary dissolution of the opposition KADU (Kenya African Democratic Union) in November 1964. It seemed tribal rivalries had been put aside in favour of a coalition-type government.

Amid allegations that Odinga was plotting to overthrow the government, he was eased out of the KANU hierarchy by 1966. Infuriated, he resigned as Vice-President of Kenya and formed his own rival party, the Kenya People's Union (KPU). Once more the country had an opposition party. A so-called little general election

In the 1966 election, KANU's voting symbol was a cockerel (jogoo) and the KPU's a bull (dume). Accordingly, this was labelled the 'cock and bull election'.

was called the following year to test the newly formed KPU at the polls. It won only nine seats.

But by this time others were sniping at the up-and-coming Mboya, including some influential Kikuyu, who feared that the young and ambitious Luo confidante of Kenyatta might

hospital. A young Kikuyu of the KANU party was charged and convicted of the killing. The murder of one of Africa's most promising young statesmen soon aroused tribal tension, and violence spilled out in the capital, with a near-riot during the memorial service.

There was renewed violence, this time in Kisumu – in the Luo heartland and base of Oginga Odinga – when President Kenyatta paid the town a visit some months later. Eleven bystanders in a crowd were killed when his bodyguards opened fire on what they regarded as a hostile demonstration. Odinga was promptly blamed for the trouble

Prime Minister Jomo Kenyatta arriving at talks in London to discuss the independence of Kenya, 1963.

have ideas about succeeding him as President. It was not long before an amendment was made to the Constitution raising the age limit for a President from 35 to 40, which effectively ruled out young Mboya.

Within a few months of Daniel arap Moi's appointment as Vice-President in 1967, several other important constitutional changes were made, including a provision to enable a Vice-President to succeed automatically on the death of a President, but only for 90 days.

Assassination of Mboya

After a relatively peaceful interval, tragedy again struck Kenya in July 1969 with the gunning down of Tom Mboya, who died before reaching

and was detained, along with most of his leading supporters. The KPU was banned.

In 1973, Kenya celebrated its 10th year of Independence and of Kenyatta's rule. Achievements noted were a doubling of the country's national income, free education up to the first four grades, school attendance up by 150 percent, a tripling of tea production and a 50 percent rise in coffee production. In the 1974 elections, however, more than half the sitting members, including four ministers, lost their seats.

By 1977, the subject of who would succeed Kenyatta had ceased to be academic in view of the President's rapidly failing health. His deteriorating condition caused the cancellation of the KANU party elections – in spite of the fact that none had been held for 11 years. Kenyatta died in Mombasa on 22 August 1978.

Vice-President Moi temporarily took over the running of the country, while making arrangements for the obligatory presidential elections within 90 days. The election became a formality: Moi enjoyed widespread public support and there was no effective opposition. Mwai Kibaki, the Minister for Finance and Planning, became Vice-President.

No significant changes were made in the Cabinet, but there was a major shake-up in the security services and Immigration

Coups and corruption

In August 1982, the official Voice of Kenya radio announced that the armed forces had deposed Moi's government and established a People's Redemption Council in his place. In fact, it was only an attempted coup, by junior personnel of the Kenya Air Force, and was swiftly crushed. In the aftermath, two self-confessed ringleaders and 10 other airmen were sentenced to death for treason, and the entire Kenya Air Force was replaced by a new unit called the '82 Air Force'.

Several civilians suspected of being involved in the abortive coup were thrown into deten-

President Daniel arap Moi addresses members of Kenyan African National Union (KANU) party in 1992.

Department. The new President announced a stern crackdown on corruption, smuggling and nepotism, but promised that political detention would be only 'a last resort'. The new Moi era was known as *Nyayo* ('footsteps') – the implication being that Moi was closely following Kenyatta's policies.

The President made it known in 1980 that all tribal societies would be disbanded immediately. The Kikuyu society's chairman, Njenga Karume, prevaricated, saying it would destroy the tribe's cultural heritage. But the ban was enforced in order 'to stamp out the negative aspects of tribalism', even to the extent of changing household names such as Luo Union and the Luo tribe's soccer team, Gor Mahia.

tion, including former MP George Anyona and a prominent Nairobi human rights lawyer, Dr John Khaminwa. They were detained without trial in June 1982, before Parliament passed a constitutional amendment that made Kenya a one-party state and prohibited the formation of other political parties in the future. Odinga and Anyona were expelled from KANU in the same year following a crackdown on 'dissidents'.

Less than a year later, President Moi startled the citizens with his announcement that a 'traitor' within his government was being secretly groomed by unnamed foreign powers to take over the Presidency. The Minister for Constitutional Affairs, Charles Njonjo, was suspended from the Cabinet, and voluntarily resigned his seat in Parliament only hours before being expelled from KANU.

In 1985, party elections from grass roots to national levels were held in order to rid the party and the government of 'disloyal' and 'anti-*Nyayo*' elements. President Moi then embarked on a wide-ranging re-organisation of the party, turning it into his own power base.

Some 45 members were expelled from KANU for dissent, many others suspended for varying periods – and membership of the party became a requirement for anybody seeking election or appointment to public office. Critical

Parliament Building, Nairobi.

lawyers, clergymen and others were branded as 'tribalists', 'unpatriotic' or 'in the pay of foreign masters'. A number of prominent citizens were picked up by police for questioning. Some were released, others detained.

The growing dissatisfaction with the financial and political mismanagement of the country, under a party that did not allow political opposition, came to a head in 1990. The unexplained murder in February of the Minister for Foreign Affairs, Dr Robert Ouko, was followed a few months later by the death of a government critic, the Rev. Alexander Muge, in a road accident. There were strong rumours of government involvement in both deaths. Meanwhile, Kenya was being pressured

by Western aid donors to set up multiparty elections. Pro-democracy protests in July and subsequent government crackdowns by its paramilitary security forces resulted in 20 deaths and led to the detention without trial of Raila Odinga (son of Oginga Odinga) and two former cabinet ministers, Kenneth Matiba and Charles Rubia.

A multiparty state again

Yielding to external and internal pressure, President Moi released the detainees and rescinded the constitutional one-party status: a handful of new political parties were registered to contest the 1992 election. The principal opposition to KANU came from two branches of the Forum for the Restoration of Democracy (FORD). Using several blatant tactics to ensure success, KANU and Moi were re-elected, with FORD-Asili's Kenneth Matiba as Vice-President. Oginga Odinga, who was the candidate for FORD-Kenya, had played his last political role. He died in 1994 at the age of 82.

In 1995, Raila Odinga succeeded his father as leader of FORD-Kenya, while Richard Leakey entered Kenyan politics for the first time, launching his Safina party. But Moi's acceptance of a multiparty Kenya was thrown into question when Leakey's application to register his party was initially rejected. Amid demands for changes in the constitution, a Constitutional Review Commission was set up. Within months one of the opposition parties, FORD-Kenya, split into two, with Raila Odinga moving to the National Democratic Party of Kenya (NDP).

When Moi opened the final session of the seventh Parliament in March 1997, after five years of a multiparty state, there had been no significant changes. An unlicensed opposition rally held in Nairobi was dispersed by riot police and the main opposition leaders placed under house arrest. The election eventually took place in a fairly orderly manner in December. KANU won again, primarily because the opposition parties remained split along tribal lines.

At the start of the new Parliament in 1998, the President made promises to eradicate poverty and corruption and to stimulate the economy. In a surprise move, he made Richard Leakey head of the civil service and Cabinet Secretary, with the challenging task of clearing up corruption. But in December 2000, the Kenya Anti-Corruption Authority (KACA) suffered a setback when the High Court ruled it was not a constitutionally legal body. The Anti-Corruption and Economic Crimes Bill was thrown out of Parliament – and as a result the International Monetary Fund and World Bank refused to resume funding, which had been suspended in 1997 pending reform. In April 2001 Leakey stood down, not entirely voluntarily, from his role as sleaze-buster.

Meanwhile, Moi's KANU party was not having it all its own way. Its majority was smaller than in previous administrations, and a number of younger parliamentarians were beginning to question the party line. In response, Moi did a deal with the National Development Party, and in June 2001 Raila Odinga and three of his NDP colleagues were given Cabinet posts. But KANU's years as the unchallenged ruling party were nearing an end.

A new regime

With Moi obliged to stand down from the Presidency, the opposition parties saw their chance to seize power in the 2002 election. Most of them combined – for the first time since the multiparty system was introduced – to form the National Rainbow Coalition (NARC), with Mwai Kibaki as its sole presidential candidate. The coalition embraced several former KANU government members, including Raila Odinga, George Saitoti and Kalonzo Musyoka.

In December 2002, Kibaki and NARC won the Presidential and Parliamentary elections by a landslide, giving Kenya its first new ruling party since Independence. The new government promptly implemented one of its election promises – the reintroduction of free primary education – then turned its attention to the long-standing problems of corruption.

The main challenge for Mwai Kibaki's new government was to revive the flagging economy and to normalise relations with and/or meet conditions set by financial institutions such as the IMF and the World Bank, as well as the governments of donor countries. This it did, by drafting new anti-corruption legislations and making a commitment to constitutional reform, as well as securing a three-year Poverty Reduction and Growth Facility (PRGF) with the IMF in November 2003, which in turn led to the release of funds from donors such as the World Bank and the EU, and a new round of debt rescheduling.

There were few in Kenya who objected to this attempt to clean up the corrupt political scene – apart from corrupt officials, magistrates and police officers who lost their jobs in the ensuing purges. But while the early years of the Kibaki administration witnessed a strong economic recovery, reversing the negative growth rate of 2002 to a positive annual growth of 5.5 percent in 2007, they also saw an increase in social inequity, with the wealthy minority being the main beneficiary of the boom. Furthermore, while levels of corruption are inherently difficult to measure, it is widely agreed that,

Activists demand the resignation of government officials implicated in corruption scams, 2006.

after the new broom made its initial sweep, the problem swiftly resurfaced and was soon as widespread as it had been under Moi.

Constitutional reform, which aimed at introducing the executive office of Prime Minister, proved to be equally controversial. Disagreements within the coalition on implementing a pre-election power-sharing agreement were reflected by demonstrations in Nairobi – the first sign of public dissent since NARC was returned to power. On 21 November 2005 a referendum was held on the proposed new constitution. It led to violent clashes between supporters and opponents of reform, and the death of nine people in a campaign that lasted for several months. The voting process was peaceful, but 58 percent of the voters rejected the new constitution, many of them using the referendum as a means of voicing their dissatisfaction with Kibaki's administration.

The referendum result was the main catalyst to the breakup of the already tenuous NARC coalition. Following the referendum, the President promptly dismissed his entire cabinet and set about reorganising his government, sacking all Liberal Democratic Party (LDP) parliamentarians in the process. On 7 December, he announced a glut of new cabinet appointments, but 19 of the appointees immediately turned down the positions, many being members of FORD-Kenya and NPK who constituted the political backbone of Kibaki's regime.

The 2007/8 electoral crisis

The next two years saw Kenya experience a succession of complicated party political manoeuvres. Non-LDP members of NARC loyal to Kibaki founded a new party, NARC-Kenya, while the original NARC was left in under the leadership of chairperson Charity

ODM-Kenya leader Kalonzo Musyoka at a campaign rally in downtown Nairobi in 2007.

SAVE THE ELEPHANTS

In early 2015, Kenya burnt 15 tonnes of ivory to show it's taking a tough stance against poaching. The world's demand for ivory has been constantly on the rise, and slaughter figures reach record highs throughout Africa, with more than 30,000 elephants killed annually. Even celebrity elephants aren't safe; in 2014, conservationists mourned the death of Satao, the world's biggest elephant, who was felled in Tsavo East National Park. Eradicating elephant poaching is now an international issue, and during his 2015 visit to Kenya, President Obama announced new US measures to stem the ivory trade.

Ngilu. The LDP withdrew from NARC and went into coalition with KANU to form the opposition Orange Democratic Movement (ODM), which received the formal backing of Charity Ngilu and the original NARC for the upcoming 2007 election.

In July 2007, only five months before the next general election was due, KANU, led by Uhuru Kenyatta, the son of the former president, pulled out of the ODM. A month later, the ODM split into two factions: Orange Democratic Movement Party of Kenya (still known as ODM) and the Orange Democratic Movement-Kenya (known as ODM-Kenya), respectively led by Raila Odinga and Kalonzo Musyoka. Then, in September, Uhuru Kenyatta publicly declared support for Kibaki, the former nemesis who had led NARC to victory over Kenyatta and KANU in the 2002 election. Furthermore, KANU rallied together with NARC-Kenya and several other minor parties to form the new coalition Party of National Unity (PNU), led by the incumbent president Mwai Kibaki, and with the public backing of the retired President Daniel arap Moi.

As the election date of 27 December 2007 drew closer, it became clear that the presidential race would boil down to a straight face-off between the PNU's Kibaki, of the politically

ECK of rigging the result, claiming that at least 300,000 votes for Kibaki were falsified, and he called for a recount, declaring himself to be the People's President.

The most extensive tribal violence in Kenya's modern history swept across the country in the aftermath of the election. Anti-government rioters clashed with police, while members of differing tribes – in particular the Luo and Kikuyu – set upon each other violently. Particularly badly affected were the slums around Nairobi, the Rift Valley around Naivasha and Nakuru and the port of Kisumu, where over 1,100 peo-

Police stop ODM supporters on their way to central Kisumu for their party's political rally, 2008.

and numerically dominant Kikuyu tribe, and the ODM's Raila Odinga, a member of the Luo, which – as Kenya's second-largest tribe – had long regarded itself to be politically sidelined. An already messy situation was thus further complicated by an inflammatory element of tribalism.

The election was held in a tense atmosphere, and international observers noted a high level of polling irregularities. The result was close and bitterly contested, with early exit polls and initial Electoral Commission of Kenya (ECK) counts predicting a substantial ODM victory, but the final ECK count going in favour of the PNU by about 232,000 votes. Kibaki was sworn in as president, but Odinga accused the

ple died in ethnic clashes, and another 600,000 were forced to flee their homes. Many observers feared that Kenya, a country long regarded to be among the most consistently stable in Africa, was on the verge of total social collapse. Fortunately, however, common sense prevailed, and a power-sharing agreement called the National Accord and Reconciliation Act, brokered by an eminent persons group led by former UN secretary-general Kofi Annan, was signed by the PNU and ODM on 28 February 2008.

Post-crisis Kenya

Following six weeks of detailed negotiations, a new government was named on 13 April 2008 and sworn in four days later. Mwai

Kibaki remained the President of Kenya but his rival Raila Odinga was made Prime Minister, while two Deputy Prime Ministers were named, Uhuru Kenyatta for the PNU and Musalia Mudavadi for the ODM. The Cabinet included 20 ministers from each party, though the PNU held most of the senior portfolios, including foreign affairs, finance, defence, and energy. Despite fears to the contrary, the coalition held solid, and Kenya by-and-large returned to normal.

In 2008, the coalition government appointed a Truth, Justice and Reconciliation Commis-

2010 saw the launch of the East African Common Market, which allows for freedom of movement between the five countries, and is seen as the first step towards implementation

> The massacre at Garissa University carried out by Somalia-based Al-Shabaab in April 2015 was one of the deadliest terrorist attacks in Kenya's history. Over 700 students were taken hostage and 148 people (mostly students) lost their lives.

Then Deputy Prime Minister Uhuru Kenyatta (right) at the International Criminal Court (ICC), September, 2011.

sion (TJRC) to probe human rights abuses since independence in 1963. More significantly, in 2009, it agreed to cooperate with the International Criminal Court (ICC) in The Hague to try key suspects in the post-election violence of 2007/8. Among the six senior politicians implicated as instigators of the violence were then Deputy Prime Minister Uhuru Kenyatta, who appeared before the ICC in a preliminary hearing to deny the charges in September 2011.

On the regional front, the second Kibaki term saw significant expansion in the scope of the East African Customs Union, which came into force in 2005, allowing for free trade between Kenya, Tanzania and Uganda. Rwanda and Burundi joined the union in 2007, while

of a common currency by 2023 and full political federation.

Another important recent development in Kenya has been the long-awaited adoption of a modern replacement for the outdated 1963 independence constitution. Drafted by the coalition government and approved in a referendum held in 2010 (with a 67 percent majority), this document provides for the full separation of powers between the executive, legislative and judicial arms of government, and it includes an advanced Bill of Rights pertaining to all Kenyan citizens. It also has a significant effect on presidential elections, stipulating as it does that that no individual may serve more than two presidential terms, and it also allows for a second round of voting between the top two candidates, should neither achieve an outright majority in the first round.

In 2013, thanks to an incredibly narrow majority, the presidential race was won by Uhuru Kenyatta, the son of Kenya's first president and one of the richest people in Africa (and accused of instigating communal violence after the disputed presidential election in 2007). In late 2014, the ICC dropped all charges against him, saying there was not enough evidence to prove his criminal responsibility. This put an end to the diplomatic isolation of Kenya, and the following year US President Barack Obama visited the country. On the other hand, the deputy president William Ruto's case at the ICC is at an advanced stage and as of 2015 there's a feeling he might not get away that easily, which is a concern for Kenyatta. However, the greatest challenge facing Uhuru Kenyatta as president is dealing with the mounting terrorist attacks, which have devastated the country's tourism sector, leaving thousands distressed and anxious.

> Situated in the remote Garissa District,100km (60 miles) from the Somali border, Dabaab is unofficially Kenya's fourth-largest city, with a population of 350,000 mostly Somali refugees. This figure is actually down from 450,000, following the 2013 repatriation agreement, but is still the world's largest refugee settlement and the refugees are almost entirely dependent on aid.

Al-Shabaab strikes

Late 2011 was marked by the rapid deterioration of relations between Kenya and its northeastern neighbour Somalia. It started with the killing of a British tourist and the kidnapping of his wife in the Lamu Archipelago, followed closely by the kidnapping of a French national in Lamu and of two Spanish doctors in the Dadaab Refugee Camp. This prompted a Kenyan invasion of southwest Somalia in pursuit of Al-Shabaab, the militant Islamic terrorist organisation to which these cross-border kidnappings were attributed. Dubbed 'Operation

Linda Nchi' (literally 'Protect the Country'), the Kenyan invasion of Somalia had the backing of the official government in Mogadishu and was also supported by Ethiopia and viewed sympathetically by the UN, USA and most other outsiders. The invasion is still ongoing at the time of writing, and while the signs are that Al-Shabaab is in retreat, it is questionable whether this cell-based organisation could be eliminated entirely from the East African political scene.

As retribution for Kenya's military deployment in Somalia, Al-Shabaab militants have

Kenyan Defence Forces in Ras Kamboni, southern Somalia, in 2011.

carried out a spate of unprecedented attacks. In 2013, they seized a shopping mall in Nairobi, killing 67 people and demanding that Kenyan troops pull out of Somalia. The following year saw bombings on buses and a market in Nairobi, and several attacks in the northeastern towns of Mpeketoni and Lamu, the death toll of which exceeded 100. Yet, the deadliest attack came in April 2015, when 148 people were killed in a massacre at Garissa University in the Northeastern Province. Desperate for a solution to prevent another Garissa, the authorities announced that they planned to build a 700km (435 mile) -long security wall on the Somali border.

Lake Bogoria.

Mount Kenya.

LIE OF THE LAND

Bisected by a spectacular stretch of the Great Rift Valley, Kenya is home to Africa's largest lake, second-tallest mountain, and a wealth of brooding volcanic landscapes.

Bordered by Somalia, Ethiopia and Sudan to the north, Uganda to the west, and Tanzania to the south, Kenya is a country of rare geological drama and geographic contrast. The country lies entirely within the tropics, and is split by the equator, which runs west between the Somali and Ugandan borders via the towns of Meru, Nanyuki, Nyahururu and Kisumu. Yet its geographic variety embraces the icy glacial peaks of Mount Kenya, the parched deserts that stretch towards its northern borders, cool montane rainforest and their warmer lowland equivalent, seashores and mangrove swamps, as well as the classic East African savannah of the Maasai Mara and similar reserves.

In simple terms, Kenya can be divided into two broad geographic zones: the low-lying coastal belt, which follows some 530km (330 miles) of tropical Indian Ocean frontage between the Somali and Tanzanian borders, and the more elevated interior, whose loftier altitudes peak in the central highlands north of Nairobi. Bisecting the interior, the Great Rift Valley is the country's most important geographic feature, an ever expanding chasm that formed as a result of tectonic activity some 20 million years ago, and which now divides the country along a north-south axis from Lake Turkana in the north to Lake Magadi in the south.

Volcanoes and other highlands

Much of the Kenyan interior, like the Rift Valley itself, is volcanic in origin. Evidence of modern igneous activity within the Rift Valley includes dormant volcanoes such as Longonot and Suswa, whose distinctive outlines

Shetani Lava Flow, Tsavo West National Park.

dominate the skyline south of Lake Naivasha, but there has also been considerable recent activity elsewhere in the country, most spectacularly in the form of the 200-year-old Shetani Lava Flow and Chiamu Crater in Tsavo West National Park.

Kenya's tallest region is the central highlands north of Nairobi. The landscape here is dominated by the 5,199 metre (17,057ft) -high Mount Kenya, an extinct volcano created by the same processes that formed the Rift Valley. Mount Kenya's caldera rim has long since fallen away, leaving the eroded plugs as twin peaks that support several permanent glaciers. A grassy highland saddle links it to the Aberdare Range, one of the few comparably lofty East African mountains whose bedrock is of ancient sedimentary origin, with the blunted peaks of Satima and Kinangop at well over 3,600 metres (12,000ft). Mount Kenya is the second highest mountain in Africa, surpassed only by Kilimanjaro, which dominates the landscape of Kenya's Amboseli National Park, even though its snow-capped volcanic peak actually lies within Tanzania.

The other main highland region is in the far west, around Eldoret and Kitale, where lush slopes are separated from the central highlands by a dramatic lake-studded stretch of the Rift Valley. The largest massif in the west is Mount Elgon, whose 4,321-metre (14,178ft) peak – just across the border in Uganda – makes it Africa's eighth-highest mountain. Rising from the broadest base of any freestanding mountain in the world, Elgon is an extinct volcano that was active between 20 and 6 million years ago, when it stood far higher than Kilimanjaro does today. The far west is also home to the Kakamega Forest, Kenya's largest and most important tract of equatorial lowland forest.

The western and central highlands are the most agriculturally productive part of the country. Some extensive plantations still exist in the area, dating to colonial times, but the majority of the land is parcelled up into smallholdings, known locally as *shambas*, that produce a wide variety of high-quality crops, including beans, peas, tomatoes, grapes, mangoes, bananas, pineapples, avocados, oranges and flowers. Today, tea – much of it grown in the southwest, around Kericho – is the country's single most valuable cash crop. Indeed, Kenya is now the world's third-largest tea producer, after China and India, with a crop of around 400,000 tonnes annually. The country also has a significant but fluctuating coffee industry, one whose output often impacts on the Kenyan economy as a whole.

Lakes and rivers

Kenya contains more than 11,000 sq km (4,300 sq miles) of open inland water (in all, about 2.3 percent of its total surface area). This includes about 6 percent of Lake Victoria, the largest body of water in Africa, the remainder of which lies in Tanzania and Uganda. The largest expanse of water that lies almost entirely within Kenya is the 6,405-sq-km (2,500-sq-mile) Lake Turkana, which is generally regarded to be the world's largest desert lake, set in the arid base of the northern Rift Valley. Other lakes set within the Kenyan Rift Valley include freshwater Naivasha and Baringo, and the more saline Nakuru, Bogoria, Elmentaita and Magadi.

Kenya has very few large rivers. The main exceptions are the Galana and the Tana, both of which rise in the central highlands and drain into the Indian Ocean. The Tana and various tributaries feed the Masinga

Tea plantation, Kericho, Western Kenya.

NORTHEASTERN BADLANDS

By far the largest of Kenya's geophysical zones is the low-lying arid land that extends over the north and northeast. This comprises more than half of the country's surface area, most of it at an altitude of up to 900 metres (3,000ft). It is hot and dry, with sparse groundwater, and is populated almost entirely by nomadic pastoralists who are forever chasing the odd shower of rain and the short-lived green flush that follows it. Although this is the largest part of the country, it is also the most thinly populated, supporting a population smaller than that of the city of Nairobi. It is unsuited to agriculture, so its inhabitants subsist on their livestock.

Reservoir, which is the country's largest artificial lake, and is an important source of hydroelectric power and household water in nearby Nairobi. Another important river is the Ewaso Nyiro, which rises in the Central

Despite hosting numerous volcanoes, the most recent eruption was the Barrier Volcanic Complex in 1921, the natural dam that separates Lake Turkana from its more obscure neighbour Lake Logipi.

the dry lands separating the highlands from the coast. This rainfall, landing on fertile volcanic soil, has been mulched over the centuries by cycles of dense forest, making the eastern highlands among the world's richest agricultural lands. The wettest part of the country is probably the coastal plain, which receives most of its rain over the two Indian Ocean monsoon seasons, and is cultivated in patches with coconut groves, sugar and other crops.

As a rule, altitude rather than latitude determines local climates. The coast is hot and moist, with temperatures and humidity levels peak-

Fishing dhows in Kendu Bay, Lake Victoria.

Highlands, then runs northeast via Thomson's Falls and Samburu-Buffalo Springs, before flowing eastward into Somalia, where it vanishes into the desert sands.

Climate

The East African climate is controlled by two major factors: a meteorological phenomenon known as the intertropical convergence zone, which produces the two main rainy seasons with specific wind directions, and the various ranges and altitudes of mountains in relation to these winds, at different times of the year. The whole mass confronts the easterly winds of the Indian Ocean and drains them of the moisture they have carried – fairly meanly – across

ing from December to March and rainfall over April to June and October to November. The Lake Victoria basin, though a bit cooler than the coast, has a similar rainfall pattern. Nairobi and the surrounding central highland areas are much cooler – unexpectedly so for a region straddling the equator – and have their main rainy seasons from March to May and October to December. The southern Rift Valley is hot and relatively dry, as is the coastal hinterland protected within Tsavo and Amboseli national parks. The vast but thinly populated north graduates from semi-desert to desert conditions, characterised by soaring daytime temperatures, and an average annual rainfall of well under 250mm (10ins).

Black rhinoceros with young,
Lewa Wildlife Conservancy,
Laikipia Plateau.

THE SAFARI EXPERIENCE

The beaches are great and the people fascinating, but for many visitors Kenya's main attraction is its wild places and the creatures that live there.

For longer than a century, Kenya's prolific wildlife has attracted visitors from all around the globe. In early colonial times, most of these tourists were wealthy trophy hunters, who adopted the Swahili word for a long journey – *safari* – to describe their bloodthirsty expeditions into the African bush. That started to change in the post-war era, however, which witnessed the advent of the more populist and sustainable photographic safari, and the creation of a network of national parks, game reserves and other areas where wildlife was protected. Indeed, since 1977, when the Kenyan government placed an outright ban on hunting anywhere in the country, photographs and videos have been the only trophies that safari-goers can take home legally.

In the 1970s and 1980s, photographic safaris to Kenya all followed a somewhat similar formula. Most safari lodges consisted of large hotel-like structures designed to keep the nocturnal bush at bay, and activities were more-or-less restricted to diurnal game drives in the developed areas of the three or four most popular reserves and parks. Since then, however, the industry has diversified in every conceivable respect. A significant trend has been the move away from monolithic brick-and-mortar lodges to rustic (but often very luxurious) tented camps that offer a holistic round the clock bush experience. Meanwhile, outside the established national parks and reserves, there are now dozens of private and community based concessions, where night drives and guided walks are offered alongside the more usual daytime drives. Elsewhere, there are also horseback safaris and camelback safaris, itineraries geared to specialist groups such as birdwatchers and serious amateur photographers, budget camping

Maasai giraffe crossing, Tsavo East National Park.

safaris, and even a few places that independent travellers on any budget can explore on foot.

Choosing a safari

There are plenty of factors to take into account when you plan your safari, several of them partially dependent on your budget, and it is worth researching your options properly, ideally in liaison with one or two recognised operators specialising in Kenya. Perhaps the first question is whether to join a group safari, with the inherent risk of ending up with incompatible travel companions, or to make costlier bespoke arrangements with a more specialised operator. The second is whether to go for the budget camping option (camping in a traditional small

At Hell's Gate National Park, near Lake Naivasha, unguided walking and cycling is permitted, and visitors are almost certain to see buffalo, giraffe, zebra and a variety of antelope – with an outside chance of spotting a cheetah or even a lion!

tent), midrange lodge option (generally staying in large but very comfortable lodges that shut out the bush at night) or upmarket-tented camp option (a more exclusive full-on bush experi-

as most people do, it is also important to ensure that you don't try to compress too much into one safari. For those flying between reserves, at least three nights is advisable for the Maasai Mara or Laikipia, two for the likes of Tsavo East, Tsavo West, Meru, Samburu-Buffalo Springs or Amboseli, and one for Lake Nakuru National Park. Road safaris will need to allow longer for each park, or they risk spending more time travelling between places than on game drives

Not unrelated to this is the choice of which reserves to visit. The Maasai Mara, for instance, is the obvious first choice for neophytes hoping

Watching the sunset from Ruko Community Wildlife Conservancy, Lake Baringo.

ence, but often a little daunting to safari novices). Then, when it comes to getting around, the options broadly break down to the costlier but more time efficient route of flying between reserves and sticking to camps that run their own game drives, or being driven from one reserve to the next and doing all or most of your game drives in the same vehicle.

You should also think about how long you want to spend on safari. There are many repeat visitors to Africa who cannot get enough of being in the bush. Equally, for many first timers, three or four days – enough to stand a good chance of seeing all the Big Five without things becoming too repetitive – is more than adequate. Assuming that you visit more than one reserve,

to see most of Africa's best known safari animals in a compressed time frame, whereas Tsavo East or Meru might appeal to experienced safarigoers who are happy to trade off seeing less wildlife against the plus of a genuine wilderness atmosphere. Other obvious highlights include Amboseli National Park, set in the shadow of Kilimanjaro; Lake Nakuru National Park, with its millions of flamingos and plentiful rhino; Samburu-Buffalo Springs for the presence of several quirky dry-country specialists, from Grevy's zebra and reticulated giraffe to the rubbernecked gerenuk antelope; and the Laikipia Plateau, where a patchwork of superb private conservancies offers great Big Five viewing with the bonus of night drives and guided walks.

Included in the package

Whatever package you choose, it is standard for the price to include all transportation, accommodation, activities (except for balloon safaris), park entrance fees, guiding and meals. Some safaris also include drinks and laundry, but this is the exception rather than the rule. A well-organised safari day will always start just before dawn, ideally with a quick tea or coffee, followed by a morning game drive, leaving as early as possible to take advantage of higher levels of animal activity in the post-dawn cool. After lunch, the convention is to leave at around 3.30pm to 4pm for an afternoon game drive, returning to camp by 7pm at the latest in all national parks and reserves. In private reserves and concessions, afternoon drives often segue into a night drive, where guides use a spotlight to seek out nocturnal specials such as bushbaby, elephant shrew, genet, civet and leopard.

One of the biggest differences between larger lodges and smaller bush camps is that the bush experience at the latter continues into the evening, starting with a long chilled drink around the campfire, accompanied by an aural backdrop of chirruping insects and twittering owls and nightjars. The evening meal, usually at least three courses, is taken under canvas or in the open. After dinner, congenial company and a nightcap around the embers of the campfire is a deeply satisfying experience, particularly if the hyenas, lions, jackals and others are on top vocal form, their eerie serenades creating a richly thrilling – and perhaps just slightly edgy – sense of being miles and miles away from the trappings of civilisation.

Four-legged safaris

If you're an experienced rider, it's possible to view the plains game from the back of a horse. On a typical horseback safari, the tents, camp gear, groceries, horse feed and safari staff are carried by truck along bush tracks while riders go cross-country, led by an experienced guide, covering between 25 and 40 km (15–25 miles) a day. Picnic lunch and water bottles, together with a few personal effects, are carried in saddlebags strapped to cavalry saddles.

After a substantial English breakfast, you head out in the African wilds on a cross-country trek that takes you through mountains, forests, grassy plains, rivers or escarpments filled with a variety of wildlife. There are no fences,

If you don't have the time or budget for a full-blown safari, a half-day game drive in Nairobi National Park – fringing the southern suburbs of Kenya's capital – can be very rewarding, especially with an early start.

telegraph poles or tarmac roads, and the sense of space and freedom is quite overwhelming. You ride among huge herds of plains game, sometimes canter with giraffe or wade across muddy rivers, observed by families of hippo.

Chef preparing a bush breakfast in the Maasai Mara National Reserve.

While you explore the wild blue yonder, staff take down the tents, drive round on bush tracks and then re-erect the whole camp at the next waterhole. After six or seven hours in the saddle (broken by a lunch stop) the party ride into the camp at about 4pm for tea or cold drinks and hot showers before dinner.

It's an extraordinary way to experience some of Africa's most beautiful countryside: the vast open spaces are quite breathtaking, and without a vehicle you really feel on even terms with the wild animals – no other sounds or smells except those of the bush. To enjoy the experience, you must be fit, mentally tuned in, able to face unpredictable situations and confident on horseback at all paces.

On safari, it is undoubtedly the early bird who is most likely to catch lions and other predators in action. So, rather than taking breakfast in camp, ask your driver if you can set off at dawn with a packed breakfast.

An even more exotic way of traversing the bush is to ride on – or walk along with – a camel train, on a safari operated by ex-hunters or ranchers on the fringe of the northern deserts around such places as Rumuruti and Samburu.

Walking safari with Maasai guides, Maasai Mara National Reserve.

These are marvellous expeditions, the best of them with a great retinue of Samburu staff, liveried in red loincloths and carrying spears. There may be a dozen camels, carrying everything from the morning coffee to the evening bath; plus the ex-white hunter, who knows the scientific name for every blade of grass, and a cordon bleu chef in the background organising the bush lunch and a three-course campfire dinner in the evening.

Ecotourism and modern conservation

This is a growing market in Kenya: an increasing number of ranches and local communities are offering safari holidays designed to preserve and foster both the wildlife and the local culture in their area. To raise funds for conservation and social projects, they build small lodges using local materials, and staff them with trained personnel from the area. The fees they charge visitors are all used for local projects – schools, dispensaries, water supply, and so on – which also provide employment opportunities for the area. Many of these community-run eco-lodges are to be found in northern Kenya – in Il Ngwesi, Tassia, Borana, and further north in the Mathews Range. Others exist in Namunyak, Amboseli and Maasai Mara. These lodges are often in stunning locations, with a wide scope for exploring, game drives, walks and birdwatching.

These community reserves and other private concessions reflect changing attitudes to conservation over recent decades. In the mid-20th century, when most of Kenya's parks and reserves were proclaimed, it was often with minimal consultation with local people, and little or no recognition of their traditional claims on the land, or any other rights. As a result, a situation developed where local communities which had always lived alongside wildlife were effectively booted off their land, or denied access to traditional grazing areas or hunting grounds, in order to create the sort of pristine unpopulated tracts of bush that had only very recently existed in the Africa of conservationists' fantasies. Furthermore, the creation of artificially bounded reserves and parks failed to acknowledge the traditional migratory patterns of wide-ranging creatures such as elephants, which frequently range outside parks to make destructive raids on local farms.

Ultimately, this artificial segregation of humans and wildlife proved to be counterproductive, a situation that came to a head during the 'poaching wars' of the 1980s, when commercial ivory and rhino-horn poachers from outside the country paid disgruntled communities on the fringes of parks such as Meru and Tsavo to do much of their dirty work. Today, by contrast, a growing number of communities living on the edge of official wildlife areas have a real stake in conservation in the form of the fees and work opportunities generated by high-cost, low-impact ecotourism on their land, a modern conservation model that works for wildlife, tourists and locals alike.

Spotting Wildlife

Whether you are on an organised or self-drive safari through Kenya's game reserves, you'll see more wildlife when you take a proactive role in spotting it.

Early morning and late afternoon are the best time for game drives. Most predators are largely nocturnal, but they tend to remain quite active for an hour or so after dawn, and may also start moving a short while before sunset. These cooler hours of the day are also when you are most likely to witness action and interaction, such as cubs playing together or adults grooming. Other good reasons to be out and about at this time of day are the high level of avian activity, and superb photographic light (except in overcast weather).

In a sunny climate such as Kenya's, animals generally prefer to lie or stand in the shade. In open country, always scan the ground below isolated trees, and in thicker vegetation make an effort to look into the dense bush rather than letting your eyes follow openings through it. Most animals drink at least once daily, usually from mid-morning onwards, so it's always worth stopping at any accessible watering point to look for thirsty wildlife. Even if things look quiet at first, try switching off the engine and waiting for a few minutes to see what happens.

In some private reserves, or in parks where dangerous animals are thin on the ground, it may be possible to track wildlife on foot. This is the most exciting way to see animals, far more involving than game drives, since the slower pace and silence allow you to pay more attention to sounds, smells and textures, and to smaller creatures such as birds and butterflies.

Animals that are habituated to vehicles might be a lot less relaxed when they encounter human pedestrians, so you'll see more if you try to blend in – wear neutral colours such as green, grey or khaki, removing brightly coloured accessories, avoid applying artificial scents, and above all talk as softly as possible, or better still, keep silent.

Whether in a car or on foot, experienced trackers often locate predators by using indirect clues. Circling vultures often point towards a recent kill, while baboon or impala alarm calls might indicate that a lion or leopard is lurking somewhere out of sight. Likewise, a freshly steaming pat of roadside

dung combined with torn-off branches and other destroyed vegetation is a telltale sign of recent elephant activity. And if you locate a trail of fresh predator paw prints on a muddy or sandy road, it is probably worth following, as lions and other animals frequently follow roads as they would a natural animal trail.

For the novice, picking out a predator's spoor might be easier said than done. Dirt roads are often criss-crossed by a profusion of animal tracks, the majority of which are made by antelopes or other cloven hoofed ungulates. Typically, these look like an inverted elongated heart, split lengthwise down

Cheetah, Ol Pejeta Wildlife Conservancy, Laikipia.

the middle, and they might be anything from 2cm (1.3ins) long, in the case of a duiker, to 20cm (8ins) for a buffalo.

Predator prints also comprise an inverted heart shape, but there is no central split, and it is topped by four oblong or circular toe marks. To identify what made the print, look at the size – 10cm (4ins) or longer, for instance, would narrow the option to a lion or spotted hyena – and check for the triangular claw marks that are present in the case of any mongoose, dog or hyena, but absent in genets and all cats other than cheetah.

For the uninitiated, it is possible to confuse primate and carnivore prints, but the former more closely resemble a human footprint and have five clearly defined toes.

MAMMALS

Kenya is renowned as one of the world's finest wildlife destinations, thanks mainly to an extraordinarily rich array of large mammals.

There are more large mammals in East Africa than virtually anywhere else on earth – more than 80 species in Kenya alone. There are plenty of smaller ones, too, although most of these are nocturnal and can be difficult to spot. Everyone wants to see Africa's Big Five – elephant, rhino, lion, leopard and buffalo – and Kenya contains them all. But in your eagerness to tick them off, don't ignore the less dramatic creatures: the dogs and the smaller cats, the monkeys and the mongooses, and above all the antelopes – dozens of different species, from the imposing eland to the tiny dik-dik.

The list that follows contains more than 50 mammals – the species you are most likely to encounter on safari – with descriptions to help you identify each one, and suggestions as to where you might see them. Many mammals are restricted to one type of vegetation or habitat; others are more versatile and are found throughout the country. Some occur in a variety of subspecies, which we do not have space to describe. For more information, and details of all the Kenyan mammals, you should buy an up-to-date field guide to the region(see page 300).

Lion (Panthera leo)

Tawny or fawn in colour, with manes ranging from gold to black on the male, the lion is the largest of Africa's cats, and also the most sociable. Prides consist of six to a dozen females and their cubs, with one or more dominant males. Most of the hunting is done by females, working as a team usually at night, but males will normally be first to eat at a kill. Some prides specialise in hunting buffalo or giraffe, but most feed on impala, zebra or wildebeest, seizing the prey by the throat and suffocating it.

Leopard (Panthera pardus)

The elegant leopard is larger than the other spotted cats, and distinguished by dark rosettes on the back and flanks and solid spots on the face. The background colour ranges from off-white to russet. It is a solitary animal, except when a pair comes together for mating, or a mother is accompanied by cubs. Hunting mainly at night, the leopard steals up on its prey, then pounces from close range. It is powerful enough to carry an antelope (impala are its favourite food) up a tree to keep it safe from other carnivores.

Cheetah (Acinonyx jubatus)

Much smaller than a leopard, the cheetah is a lithe, long-legged cat with solid dark spots all over its fawn body, a small head and characteristic black 'tear-marks' from the corner of each eye. It prefers open savannah, where it uses its impressive speed – up to 100kph (60mph) over short distances – to run down its prey (typically Thomson's gazelle). Most common in the Maasai Mara, cheetahs are usually seen alone, or in small family groups comprising a female and her cubs. It hunts by day, usually during the cooler hours soon after dawn.

Caracal (Felis caracal)

Similar in appearance to a lynx, the caracal is a medium-sized cat, anything from pale fawn to chestnut in colour, with long, pointed, tufted ears. It is a solitary hunter, preying on mammals from mice to small antelopes, birds and reptiles. It stalks its prey as close as possible, then relies on a pounce or a short run. Its powerful hind legs enable it to leap vertically 3 metres (10ft) to swat a bird. The caracal is widespread in Kenya's drier regions, but is mainly nocturnal and rarely seen.

Serval (Felis serval)

Another spotted cat, smaller than a cheetah, but with a similar build, long legs and a short tail. Its black-on-gold spots give way to black streaks near the head. The serval is usually a solitary animal, but is sometimes seen in pairs or small family groups. It hunts mainly at night, and sometimes in the early morning or late afternoon, preying on small mammals, birds and reptiles. Although it is not uncommon, its favoured habitat of long grass and reedbeds, and its elusive habits, mean it is rarely seen.

African wild cat (Felis lybica)

This small carnivore resembles a tabby cat – in fact, it is the ancestor of most domestic cats – but is distinguished by striped legs and ginger fur on the backs of its ears. It is a solitary nocturnal hunter (except when a female is accompanied by kittens), feeding on small mammals up to the size of hares, and birds, including ostrich chicks. The wild cat is found throughout Africa, especially in areas where rodents are plentiful. This often means the outskirts of human settlements, where it may interbreed with domestic cats.

African wild dog (Lycaon pictus)

Unlikely to be mistaken for any other canid, the wild dog (or hunting dog) has long legs, huge ears, a bushy white-tipped tail and a body covered in black, white and tan blotches. No two animals have exactly the same markings. It is a superb hunter, customarily working in packs of 10 to 15 animals, which can maintain a chase over several kilometres, overwhelming large prey by sheer weight of numbers. Once common, but now IUCN listed as Endangered, it is most likely to be seen in parts of the Laikipia Plateau.

Black-backed jackal (Canis mesomelas)

This jackal is a medium-sized canine, mostly tawny-brown, with a black 'saddle' flecked with white on its back. Unlike most dogs, jackals are not pack animals, and are usually seen alone or in pairs. They are efficient hunters of small mammals, but also scavenge from other predators' kills. Their characteristic call is a scream followed by three or four short yaps. In areas close to man (such as farmland), black-backed jackals hunt mainly at night, but they are commonly seen in daylight in the national parks.

Side-striped jackal (Canis adustus)

Slightly smaller and less common than the black-backed, the side-striped jackal looks uniform grey-brown from a distance. It has a faint pale stripe on its flank, but the white-tipped tail is a better identifier. Usually seen alone or in pairs, it is most active at night and in the early evening. Unlike the black-backed, the side-striped jackal avoids open savannah, preferring wooded areas. It is omnivorous, eating fruit as well as small prey and carrion. A third species is also found in Kenya, the larger and plainer Eurasian jackal *(Canis aureus)*.

Bat-eared fox (Otocyon megalotis)

A small, silver-grey fox with black legs, a bushy tail, pale face, pointed black muzzle and enormous ears – the key to its success as an insect-eater. Its main food is harvester termites, which it can pinpoint up to 30 cm (1ft) underground with acute directional hearing, before digging furiously to unearth them. A resident of dry scrub and grassland, it dens in burrows that it sometimes digs itself, but also occasionally colonises from other creatures. It hides during the heat of the day, emerging to feed in early evening.

Spotted hyena (Crocuta crocuta)

With its sloping hindquarters, coarse spotted coat, round face and broad black muzzle, the spotted hyena, Africa's second-largest carnivore, is unmistakable. It is an opportunistic scavenger, but also an aggressive hunter – of antelope, zebra and even buffalo. It lives in clans, typically of up to 15 animals, led by a dominant female. It is most active at night, when clan members communicate with an eerie whooping call. The striped hyena (Hyaena hyaena), slightly smaller, with dark stripes on a grey coat, is much rarer, but is occasionally seen in parts of Kenya.

White-tailed mongoose (Ichneumia albicauda)

A very large mongoose, dark grey-brown with black legs, a rump that is higher than its shoulders, and a distinctive bushy white tail. Like most African mongooses, it is a solitary creature – though pairs are occasionally seen – and hunts mainly at night, feeding on a wide range of invertebrates, small mammals (up to the size of a hare) and wild fruits. By day, it lies in burrows dug by other animals, in rock crevices or amid dense vegetation. It is widespread in Kenya, mainly in wooded areas and forest margins.

Dwarf mongoose (Helogale parvula)

One of the two social species of mongoose, the dwarf is also one of Africa's smallest carnivores, about 32 cm (1ft) long including its tail, a sleek chestnut-brown creature with short legs and a pointed snout. A family of 10 to 20, led by a dominant male and female, will have up to 20 dens within its territory, often in old termite mounds. From here, they forage as a troop, hunting insects and other invertebrates, reptiles and birds. Usually only the dominant female breeds, but all the troop members care for the young.

Banded mongoose (Mungos mungo)

The most often seen of the mongoose family, and the most social, the banded is dark grey-brown with 10–12 dark stripes on its rump. It lives in family groups of between five and forty individuals, and rarely ventures far from the troop. Sleeping at night in burrows, a troop spends most of the day foraging for food, occasionally pausing to stand upright to look around for danger. It is truly omnivorous, eating insects and other invertebrates, small rodents, lizards, birds, eggs and sometimes fruit and berries.

Large-spotted genet (Genetta tigrina)

Genets are long, agile, feline creatures with short legs and a long ringed tail. The large-spotted species, which grows up to 105cm (41ins) overall, is creamy yellow with distinct dark body spots and a black tip to its tail. Normally solitary and nocturnal, it hunts large invertebrates and small mammals, and is an agile climber. Its close relative, the slender small-spotted genet *(Genetta genetta)*, is greyer with very small spots and a white-tipped tail. Both species are sometimes seen scavenging round camps and lodges.

African civet (Civettictis civetta)

The size of a medium-sized dog, the civet is a stocky, powerful omnivore, its pale coat marked with dark blotches that merge into stripes nearer the head. It is a solitary hunter and may be seen at night (occasionally in the early evening) trotting with its head down in search of insects, rodents, reptiles – including venomous snakes – birds or carrion. It also eats fruit and can even digest poisonous plants. It is purely terrestrial, unlike its relative the forest-dwelling tree civet *(Nandinia binotata)*, which rarely comes to ground.

Ratel (Mellivora capensis)

A powerful, low-slung carnivore, mostly black, but with a silver-grey mantle from head to tail, the ratel is the same size as a badger (its other name is honey badger, after its habit of breaking into beehives to eat honeycomb and larvae). Hunting mainly at night, usually unaccompanied, the ratel uses its massive claws to dig out scorpions, rodents and other burrowing animals. It frequently scavenges round rubbish dumps and camps in parks and reserves, and will attack humans aggressively if threatened.

Cape clawless otter (Aonyx capensis)

Weighing as much as 35kg (77lbs) in exceptional cases, this fish-eating carnivore is dark brown with a bold white collar. Generally associated with freshwater habitats, it sometimes occurs in estuaries and mangroves, being most common in waters where it can easily avoid crocodiles. The smaller spotted-necked otter, which typically weighs around 5kg (11lbs), is absent from aquatic habitats that are alkaline, saline, or offer poor visibility, but it is quite common on the islands and rocky stretches of shore on Lake Victoria.

Elephant (Loxodonta africana)

The largest of all land mammals, the African elephant can grow to 3.4 metres (11ft) at the shoulder and weigh 6,300kg (over 6 tons). Females live in loose-knit herds, in which the oldest cow plays matriarch. Males usually leave the family at around age 12, to drift between herds, roam singly or form bachelor groups. Elephants are active 16 to 20 hours a day, eating, drinking, bathing or travelling in search of food – they can eat up to 150kg (330lb) of vegetation in 24 hours. (See page 95).

Hippopotamus (Hippopotamus amphibius)

This huge mammal (up to 2,000kg/2 tons) is found in most of Kenya's large rivers and lakes, in herds of 10 or more pre-sided over by a dominant male, who defends his territory fiercely. Hippos' skin is very thin and has no sweat glands – which means they can easily dehydrate and overheat, so they spend the day submerged in water, often with only their eyes, ears and nostrils showing. Evenings and early mornings are the time to see them on land, when they follow well-worn trails to and from their nocturnal grazing.

Square-lipped rhino (Ceratotherium simum)

This bulky and peaceable grazer is popularly called the white rhino, a name that derives from the Dutch *weit* (wide) and refers to the square lips that enable it to crop grass so efficiently. It was once rated as Critically Endangered on the IUCN Red List, but intensive conservation efforts in South Africa mean it is now quite common there. Though not native to Kenya, introduced populations have thrived at Lake Nakuru and Laikipia, where the white rhino is more conspicuous than the indigenous black rhino.

Hook-lipped rhino (Diceros bicornis)

Also known as the black rhino, this Critically Endan-gered giant has been poached for its horn of compressed hair, which is used as an aphrodisiac in Asia and as a dag-ger handle in Yemen. Associated with dense thickets, it browses on the foliage with its muscular hooked upper lip. Though solitary, it does sometimes gather in tempo-rary groups, and a calf will stay with its mother for up to four years. Kenya is the world's second-biggest black rhino stronghold, and sightings are reasonably likely in Meru, Lake Nakuru, Tsavo and the Laikipia Plateau.

Buffalo (Syncerus caffer)

Africa's only species of wild cattle, the buffalo is a heavily built bovid (up to 150cm/5ft at the shoulder), with relatively short, stocky legs. Large ears fringed with hair hang below massive curved horns that meet in a central boss. It is gregarious, living in herds from a few dozen to several thousand in number, though it is not unusual to encounter lone bulls (which can be dangerous). It most often grazes at night, and drinks in the early morning and late afternoon, spending the day resting or chewing the cud.

Eland (Taurotragus oryx)

Africa's largest antelope (up to 180cm/6ft at the shoulder), the eland is cattle-like in build, with a large dewlap and relatively short spiral horns. Its fawn coat sometimes has fine white stripes on the sides. The eland is often common in grassland habitats, living in nomadic herds of 20 or more, but it is shy and can be difficult to approach. It is active both diurnally and nocturnally, but spends more time feeding at night in the hottest months. A prodigious jumper, an eland can clear 2 metres (6ft) from a standing position.

Greater kudu (Tragelaphus strepsiceros)

This elegant antelope has slender legs, big ears, a grey-brown coat and 6–10 white stripes on each side of its body. The male has a fringe of hair on his throat and chest, and magnificent spiralling horns. Its numbers were decimated by rinderpest in the 1890s, but small herds still occur in some areas, usually in woodland or thickets and never far away from cover. It browses on seeds and shoots, but also eats seed pods, and occasionally grazes. The smaller lesser kudu *(Strepsiceros imberbis)* is found in arid areas, mostly to the east of the Rift Valley.

Bushbuck (Tragelaphus scriptus)

A medium-sized antelope that appears in various hues: males are often dark brown and females paler chestnut, but there is much variation. Both sexes may have white spots and/or stripes. The male has straight, sturdy horns. The bushbuck is both a browser and a grazer, preferring woodland and bush, always near water. It is mainly nocturnal, but often feeds in the early morning and late afternoon. The closely related sitatunga *(Tragelaphus spekei)* is a localised splay-hoofed aquatic antelope most commonly seen in Saiwa Swamp National Park.

Bongo (Tragelaphus euryceros isaaci)

Weighing up to 400kg (882lbs), this is the second-bulkiest antelope after the eland, and though mainly associated with lowland forest in western Africa, it is represented in Kenya by a montane subspecies. It has a chestnut coat, a dozen white vertical stripes, and heavy black ivory-tipped horns. Classified as 'Critically Endangered', the wild population of this species amounts to perhaps 100 individuals that inhabit montane forest pockets in the Aberdares and Mau Escarpment.

Sable antelope (Hippotragus niger)

Both the male and female of this species possess magnificent curved horns and distinctive black-and-white faces, but the male's body is jet black and the female's chestnut brown. The sable avoids dense woodland, preferring to live in wooded savannah, such as exists in Shimba Hills, its one remaining stronghold in Kenya. A herd of 10 to 30 individuals will be controlled by one dominant bull. The related roan antelope (Hippotragus equinus) also has a very limited distribution, occurring only in the remote Ruma National Reserve.

East African oryx (Oryx beisa)

This statuesque antelope has a grey body, a striking black-and-white face and unmistakable long, straight horns. Kenya hosts two subspecies, the fringe-eared oryx (O. b. callotis), which occurs in Tsavo and has curious long tufts of black hair growing from its ear tips; and the Beisa oryx (O. b. beisa, which is common in Samburu-Buffalo Springs and farther north. An oryx can live for months in dry open country without access to water. It is predominantly a grazer, but eats fruit and acacia seedpods. It moves in herds of up to 30 led by a territorial bull.

Waterbuck (Kobus ellipsiprymnus)

This large, robust antelope (up to 135cm/4.5ft at the shoulder) with a shaggy grey-brown coat has a pronounced rump. It the case of the nominate race, known as the common waterbuck, this takes the form of a white ring on its rump. By contrast, the Defassa subspecies (K. e. Defassa), which is more common to the west of the Rift Valley' has a solid white circle on its behind. The males of both races have gently curving, lyre-shaped horns. The waterbuck is a grazer, generally seen in family groups of five to ten individuals in grassy areas, always near water.

Blue wildebeest (Connochaetes taurinus)

East Africa's most abundant antelope is an ungainly creature, dun-grey with a straggly black mane, black face and buffalo-like horns. It generally congregates in herds of around 30, but huge concentrations take part in annual migrations centred upon the Maasai Mara following the rains and the fresh young short grass that is their sole diet, with the largest concentrations being in Kenya from July to October. Breeding is synchronised so that hundreds of thousands of calves are born in the Serengeti (Tanzania) in February and March.

Topi (Damaliscus lunatus)

The topi is a distinctive antelope: its shoulders are higher (125cm/49ins) than its rump, and its glossy reddish coat has dark patches on the upper legs. Both sexes have a dark face and stout ridged horns that curve backwards and upwards. The topi is a grazer, found on open grassy plains in the Maasai Mara and elsewhere, usually in small herds of five or six individuals, controlled by one dominant bull, who defends his territory against other males. It is one of the fastest antelopes, and uses its speed and endurance to outrun predators.

Hartebeest (Alcelaphus buselaphus)

Similar in build to the topi, Coke's hartebeest or kongoni (*A. b. cokei*) has a longer, pointed head, narrow ears and a white rump. Both sexes have smallish lyre-shaped horns set very close together at the base. Fleet of foot, the hartebeest prefers open plains and medium and tall grassland and is often found in small family groups in the Maasai Mara, where it sometimes posts sentinels on termite mounds to watch for predators. They are relatively sedentary animals.

Hirola (Beatragus hunteri)

Also known as Hunter's hartebeest, the Critically Endangered hirola has a similar shape to other hartebeests, but is smaller and more lightly built, with impala-like horns and distinctive white 'spectacles'. It is now endemic to Kenya, where the population has dropped from more than 10,000 in the 1970s to fewer than 500 today. Herds introduced to Tsavo East in 1963 and then in 1996 have adapted well to this semi-arid habitat, and are most likely to be seen in the vicinity of Aruba Dam.

Grant's gazelle (Gazella granti)

Grant's gazelle is between the impala and a Thomson's gazelle in size. It has a white belly, a pale side-stripe and a chestnut back, with black lines flanking white buttocks. Both sexes have long, elegant horns, particularly striking in the male. It lives in herds of about 30, controlled by an adult ram, who performs elaborate displays when confronted by a rival. Herds are mostly nomadic and can last long periods without water, but when food is plentiful, they stay in a small territory, both browsing and grazing.

Thomson's gazelle (Gazella thomsoni)

The most abundant gazelle in East Africa (with numbers around 550,000), the dainty 'Tommy' is distinguished by a broad black horizontal stripe on its flank, with chestnut above and white below. Both sexes have upright, almost parallel horns, shorter and slimmer on females, and short black tails. Tommies graze on open savannah, preferring short-cropped grass, and often follow the wildebeest herds around the Serengeti. When threatened, they bounce around stiff-legged (known as 'pronking').

Gerenuk (Litocranius walleri)

An unusual gazelle, the gerenuk is unmistakable for its long legs, elongated neck and huge ears. Males have fairly short, lyre-shaped horns. Equally distinctive are its feeding habits: the gerenuk is the only antelope habitually to stand on its hind legs to browse on new leaf growth, buds and flowers high up on trees and bushes. It is often solitary, but is also sometimes seen in small mixed groups with a single ram. It occurs in arid areas such as Samburu-Buffalo Springs, where it can live without drinking water.

Impala (Aepyceros melampus)

Common throughout southern Kenya, this slender, elegant, chestnut-coloured antelope is distinguished from gazelles by unique black-and-white stripes on the rump and tail. Males have impressive lyre-shaped horns. Impalas prefer wooded savannah, where they feed on fruits, seedpods, leaves and sometimes grass. They live in two kinds of groups: 'bachelor herds' (all male) and 'harems' of females and young. In the breeding season, a ram will take over a harem – and then battle with challenging males to preserve his breeding rights.

Bohor Reedbuck (Redunca redunca)

The bohor reedbuck is a fairly nondescript reddish-brown antelope, identified by bare patches behind the ears and (in the male) smallish horns that turn forward at the point. Reedbuck are mostly active at night, but may be seen during the day, singly or in small groups, grazing in open grassland, always near water. In some montane areas, the bohor's place is taken by a close relative, the mountain reedbuck (*R. fulvorufula*), which is very similar in appearance, but more commonly seen in daylight.

Grey duiker (Sylvicapra grimmia)

Also known as the common or bush duiker, this small antelope can be anything from grey to chestnut in colour, but it always has a distinctive tuft of black hair between its ears. Rams have short, pointed horns. It is the most widespread of all the duiker species, found (singly or in pairs) in savannah woodland or open bush, and has a remarkably wide diet, feeding on shoots, leaves, fruits and cultivated crops, digging for tubers and roots with its front hoofs, and even taking termites and other insects. Several other duiker species occur in Kenya.

Kirk's dik-dik (Rhynchotragus kirkii)

This tiny, delicate, grey-brown antelope is easily identified by a crest of dark hair on its head, large eyes and an elongated nose like a small trunk. The ram's short, spiky horns may be hidden by the head crest. Usually seen in pairs or small family groups, dik-diks favour dry bush country and scrub, where they browse on leaves and also feed on flowers and fruit knocked to the ground by larger animals. Pairs mate for life and live in permanent territories, with regular paths between resting and feeding sites..

Oribi (Ourebia ourebi)

A graceful, small, reddish-brown antelope with a long, thin neck and a short, black-tipped tail. Rams have short, straight horns. The oribi is usually seen in pairs or small groups of one ram, which is vigorously territorial, and several ewes. It occasionally browses but is mainly a grazer, preferring short grassland with longer grass patches to provide cover. When disturbed, it gives a sharp whistle or sneeze, and runs off with stiff-legged jumps. Alternatively (and unusually for antelopes), it lies down to hide in the long grass.

Giraffe (Giraffa camelopardalis)

The giraffe prefers open country to woodland, although its main food is leaves, especially from the tops of acacia trees, which it grasps with its amazing 45cm (18-ins) -long tongue. Giraffes are non-territorial, roaming around in loose herds of up to 15, of both sexes. The Maasai giraffe, characterised by ragged edges to its blotchy markings, is common in the south, while the striking reticulated giraffe, with straight edged markings, is found in the north, and the intermediate Rothschild's giraffe is only common in Lake Nakuru National Park.

Plains zebra (Equus burchellii)

The plains or Burchell's zebra (by far the world's most common and widespread wild equid species) is an unmistakable striped horse with a long erect mane. A zebra's stripes are as individual as a human fingerprint, and serve to break up the animal's outline and so confuse predators. A typical zebra herd consists of one stallion and half a dozen mares with their foals. Zebras mingle happily with other herbivores, but can eat long, coarse grass that is unpalatable to other grazers, so they are often the first to arrive in grazing areas.

Grevy's Zebra (Equus grevyi)

The world's largest wild equid, standing 1.5 metres (5ft) tall at the shoulder and weighing up to 430kg (948lbs), is a dry-country specialist whose global population of around 2,500 is practically confined to northern Kenya in Samburu-Buffalo Springs and on the Laikipia Plateau. It is distinguished from other zebras by its larger size, narrower striping, white belly and rounded bear-like round ears. It moves in smaller herds than the plains zebra, and a stallion generally enjoys exclusive mating rights with all females that enter its territory.

Golden-rumped elephant shrew (Rhynchocyon chrysopygus)

These peculiar rodent-sized creatures have bizarrely elongated, twitchy snouts (hence their elephant reference). Endemic to Kenya, it is confined to the Arabuko-Sokoke National Park and nearby forested habitats. The golden-rumped elephant shrew is the largest and most threatened of roughly 15 described species, red-brown in general coloration, but with a bright yellow-gold rump and throat. It is a terrestrial feeder, scratching through the litter to locate its insect prey with its sensitive nose.

Warthog (Phacochoerus aethiopicus)

The only African wild pig that is commonly seen by day, the warthog has a grey body sparsely covered with bristly hairs, a dark coarse mane and upward-curving tusks. It is named after the wart-like growths on its face (the male has four, the female two). It grazes on a variety of grasses, and in the dry season it also roots for bulbs and tubers, kneeling down and digging with its tusks. It lives in family groups of females and young with one dominant male, sleeping and hiding from predators in networks of burrows.

Bushpig (Potamochoerus porcus)

This hairy pig varies in colour from grey to reddish brown, and has a characteristic crest of hair along its spine, tufted ears and a 'beard'. The bushpig prefers thick vegetation and is mainly active at night, snuffling around for roots, fruits and fungi. It is a favourite prey of the leopard and spotted hyena, and is also hunted as food by people. The much larger and hairier giant forest hog *(Hylochoerus meinertzhageni)* is a localised forest dweller, likely to be seen only after dark at Serena Mountain Lodge.

Chimpanzee (Pan troglodytes)

This agile, muscular ape, standing about 120cm (4ft) tall, is covered in black hair except for its bare face, hands and backside. Chimps live in woodland areas, in large communities of up to 100 individuals, usually dividing themselves into smaller family groups of six to eight. Their diet is varied, including fruit, leaves, bark, insects, eggs and animals such as bushpigs, guinea fowl and monkeys. It does not occur naturally in Kenya, but an introduced population lives in semi-wild conditions in the Ol Pejeta sector of the Laikipia Plateau.

Greater galago (Galago crassicaudatus)

Galagos are small nocturnal primates, distant relatives of the lemurs of Madagascar. The greater or thick-tailed galago is by far the largest (80cm/2.5ft overall), silver grey-brown with a darker bushy tail and large leathery ears. It is omnivorous but prefers fruit, especially figs. It has a loud screaming call, like a human baby in distress. The bushbaby *(G. senegalensis)* is the commonest of the smaller galagos. It has huge eyes and ears, and forages by night, usually alone, feeding on sap and insects.

Baboon (Papio cynocephalus)

Africa's largest monkey has a distinctive dog-like black muzzle and a permanently kinked tail. It is active during the day and largely terrestrial. Baboons climb trees to gather fruits, to take refuge from predators or to sleep at night; otherwise they are found on the ground in complex social groups of up to 100, foraging, fighting, playing, grooming, nursing or courting. They feed on all kinds of plants, including crops, and also take insects, eggs and small mammals. The 'typical yellow baboon' and olive baboon *(P. anubis)* both occur in Kenya.

Vervet monkey (Cercopithecus aethiops)

The vervet or green monkey is small and slender, with a long tail, grey-green fur, a white belly and black face and hands. It is common throughout Kenya, living mainly in savannah and sparse woodland rather than thick forest, in troops of up to 30. The vervet is agile in trees, where it eats fruits, leaves and flowers, but is equally at home on the ground, foraging for seeds and insects. It is a very social creature, communicating with a wide variety of calls, gestures and facial expressions.

Blue monkey (Cecopithecus mitis)

This medium-sized primate (also called Sykes' monkey) has a dark blue-grey coat, with darker patches on the crown and limbs, and sometimes a white throat patch. An inhabitant of riparian woodland and forest, it lives in troops of 10 to 20, controlled by a single adult male. It is active during the day and spends most of its time in the trees, where it feed on leaves, fruits, seeds, gum and bark, and occasionally insects and birds. It has a wide range of calls, including a very loud, far-carrying bark to warn of danger.

Black-and-white colobus (Colobus polykomos)

This distinctive forest monkey lives in troops of 10–20, which often catch the sun in the canopy in the early morning, but might be seen leaping athletically between trees later in the day. Exclusively leaf-eaters, the colobus are unique among monkeys in that they have no thumb. On the coast, the very similar Angola colobus *(C. Angolensis)* is widespread. The Tana River area is home to red colobus *(Piliocolobus rufomitratus)* and mangabey *(Cercocebus galeritus)*, both on the IUCN endangered list.

Rock hyrax (Procavia capensis)

Hyraxes look like large rodents, brown, round and short-legged, but are in fact distant relatives of the elephant. The rock hyrax lives in small colonies on rocky hillsides or kopjes, where it is often seen basking in the early morning. It feeds on leaves, flowers and fruits, never moving far from the shelter of rock. It often becomes tame when accustomed to people, for instance around lodges. Its relative the tree hyrax (*Dendrohyax arboreus*) is a solitary, nocturnal forest animal with an eerie shrieking call.

Spring Hare (Pedetes capensis)

Despite its name, this is not a member of the rabbit family and, despite its appearance, it is not related to the kangaroo. The spring hare is a true rodent, around 80cm (2.5ft) long, yellowish-fawn above and paler below, with large ears and eyes, a long bushy tail and enormous hind legs. It propels itself with these, in a series of leaps or hops, and uses its tiny forelegs solely for feeding or digging. It is a solitary animal, living alone in a burrow, and largely nocturnal, feeding on roots, grass and other plants.

Porcupine (Hystrix spp.)

Easily recognised by its covering of long, black-and-white-banded quills, the porcupine grows up to a metre (3ft) in length. Two species are found in Kenya, both very similar in appearance and both sharing the same habits. Both live in burrows (often several animals in the same network) in all types of habitat except thick forest, emerging only at night to forage for roots, bulbs, tubers and tree bark. A porcupine makes use of regular pathways: its quills are easily detached and often found along these trails.

Aardvark (Orycteropus afer)

An unmistakable creature, the aardvark is vaguely pig-like, but with a long tail, a long tubular snout, and huge ears. Digging is its speciality, using its powerful forelegs and massive front claws to excavate extensive burrows where it hides during the day. The aardvark is a solitary animal, and active only at night, when it may wander for several kilometres in search of termites, ants or larvae. When it finds a colony, it digs into it vigorously, lapping up insects with its long, sticky tongue.

The Elephant Herd

Strictly matriarchal and highly gregarious, the African elephant usually moves in herds of up to 30 females and youngsters.

African elephants display intriguingly complex social behaviour that can be fascinating to watch. The typical elephant herd consists of a core family group, led by the oldest female, whose wisdom and memory of landmarks is vital in lean times. This family group typically includes about 10 elephants, but it has strong links to bond groups of extended family, which spend up to 50 percent of their time together. The large herds formed by 5 to 15 bond groups are called clans, while unrelated elephants using the same area are known as a sub-population.

Gathering of the clans

During the wet season, elephants can gather in herds of up to 500. Great excitement is displayed when two families meet. Trumpeting, growling, rumbling, defecating and urinating accompany the greeting ceremony. Trunks are entwined, with much touching and caressing as the elephants renew their acquaintance. As the water dries up and food resources shrink, the group splits up, but will stay in touch. Elephants can communicate over remarkably long distances using very low frequency infrasound, below the level of human hearing.

Research undertaken in Kenya's Amboseli National Park has shown that this low-frequency sound enables elephants to maintain contact over a distance of 10km (6 miles) even through heavy vegetation. The deep rumble we hear from time to time is a contact vocalisation, which only just enters the range of human hearing. Elephants use their trunk to produce the classic trumpeting sound, both in anger and exultation.

Mother love

It is particularly moving to see how gently elephants nurture their young. Calves are born at night, weighing about 100kg (220lbs), and can fit under their mother's bellies until they are six months old. A mother will use her trunk and feet to guide her baby under her tummy to shelter from the sun, or to her teats between her front legs. When on the move, she'll hold the baby's tail, guiding it forwards, crook her trunk around its rump to

help it in steep places, lift it out of a wallow and spray it to keep it cool. As the baby grows, its older sisters help to look after it, preparing themselves for motherhood.

When a baby elephant is in trouble, its core family encircles it protectively. Similar concern is also seen if an elephant is injured, its companions using their tusks to support or lift it. When an elephant dies, family members display evidence of distress and sometimes cover the body with branches.

Adolescent males, driven from the matriarchal herd when too boisterous, find companionship and safety in loosely knit and continuously changing

Calves are cared for by the whole herd.

bachelor herds of up to 20 males, who might move together for a day, a week or a season.

When bond groups unite in the rainy season, they are often joined by a breeding bull in musth – a condition recognised by a copious, pungent secretion from the temporal gland, the dribbling of urine and bouts of aggressive behaviour. Young bulls come into musth for a few days; in a prime breeding bull, it can last four to five months.

Females come into oestrus for two to six days, every three to five years. The bull chases the cow briefly, lays his trunk along her back and rears up on his hind legs. Penetration only takes 45 seconds. Immediately after mating, the cow will scream, with her family group gathering around and trumpeting loudly, as if sounding their approval.

Agama lizard, Taita Hills Wildlife Sanctuary.

KENYA'S REPTILES

From ferocious giants that can kill and consume a zebra to tiny fly-eating lizards, Kenya has a wild abundance of scaly, cold-blooded beasts.

The richness of Kenya's reptile fauna compares favourably with any other part of the world. Since most species have no significant commercial value, poaching is not generally a problem, though crocodiles are sometimes killed for their skins. A far greater threat to many reptile species is habitat loss and the expanding human population, especially as it is customary for many locals to kill snakes and larger lizards on sight.

Crocodiles

The Nile crocodile *(Crocodylus niloticus)*, a ferocious inhabitant of rivers and lakes, can grow to 5 metres (16ft) or longer. It was once ubiquitous in suitable aquatic habitats, and while its range has been substantially reduced through uncontrolled trapping and shooting, it is still common in many areas. It feeds mainly on fish, but it will also attack larger mammals that venture into the water, or close to its edge, and is responsible for many human deaths, particularly among local people using the rivers.

Nile crocodiles.

In Tsavo East, there is often a spectacular concentration of crocodiles at a lookout point on the Galana River below Lugard Falls, and they are also plentiful in Lake Baringo. During the last decade crocodiles have been on the increase in the Ewaso Ngiro River (Samburu); and a few can usually be seen at Mzima Springs, at the Hippo Pools of Nairobi National Park, and on the Mara and Tana rivers. One of the world's last great crocodile sanctuaries is Lake Turkana.

Secretive snakes

Visitors to Kenya are often surprised at the apparent scarcity of snakes, which tend to be secretive creatures and are particularly shy of humans, whose approach they can sense through seismic vibrations along the ground. Despite this, snakes are by no means uncommon, though most species are harmless to humans.

There are three species of mamba, the largest being the black mamba *(Dendroaspis polylepis)*, which can grow up to around 3.2 metres (10ft) long, and is not black but olive-brown in colour. It can inflict a lightning-fast bite, injecting immense quantities of exceedingly powerful venom, and it has a reputation for aggression when pursued or otherwise annoyed. In Kenya this species is uncommon.

The coastal green mamba *(Dendroaspis angusticeps)* and its western counterpart Jameson's mamba *(Dendroaspis jamesoni)* seldom reach over 2 metres (6ft) in length. Both are brilliant green and deadly, but their venom is only about one-fifth as toxic as that of the black mamba.

The widespread puff adder *(Bitis arietans)* is considered the most dangerous of Kenya's snakes. Relying on its mottled brown camouflage, it does not generally take evasive action, but remains motionless, so a person walking through scrub or high grass can easily step close enough to be struck.

The black-necked spitting cobra *(Naja nigricollis)* ejaculates its venom when cornered, aiming at the eyes. If washed out quickly, the

The distinctive Leopard tortoise.

A KALEIDOSCOPE OF CHAMELEONS

Notable for their prehistoric appearance, independently swivelling eyes, rapidly unleashed body-length tongues, and capacity to change colour according to mood and background, chameleons come in many sizes and shapes. At least a dozen species occur in Kenya, ranging from the massive Kikuyu three-horned chameleon *(Chamaeleo jacksoni)*, which inhabits highland forests around Nairobi, to the mouse-sized Kenya pygmy-chameleon *(Rhampholeon kerstenii)*, which lives on tiny insects. The flap-necked chameleon *(Chamaeleo dilepis)* and slender chameleon *(Chamaeleo gracilis)* are savannah inhabitants and can be seen on safari.

effect is only temporary but acutely painful; if neglected, permanent damage can result.

The largely arboreal boomslang *(Dispholidus typus)*, though highly venomous, carries its poison fangs so far back in its jaws that a human being, in order to be bitten, would have it put a finger into its mouth.

Kenya's two species of rock python *(Python natalensis and Python sebae)* are heavy bodied snakes that often attain a length of 5 metres (16ft). They are non-venomous and kill by strangulation, making them harmless to adults, though they do very occasionally attack children. Although widely distributed, habitat tolerant, and not uncommon in some places, these impressive creatures are not often seen.

A number of small vipers are endemic to Kenya. The Kenya horned viper *(Bitis worthingtoni)*, restricted to the central Rift Valley, is an attractive little snake with black, brown, lilac and white markings, and horns over its eyes. The diminutive Kenya mountain viper *(Montatheris hindii)* – so different from any other snake that it is placed in a monotypic genus – is unique to the upper moorland zones of Mount Kenya and the Aberdare Mountains. The Mount Kenya bush viper *(Atheris desaixi)* is a striking black and yellow snake first discovered in 1967 and known from only two localities in western Kenya.

There are too many harmless snakes to mention in detail, including specialist feeders such as centipede-eaters, slug-eaters, egg-eaters and even a little shovel-nosed snake that lives off gecko eggs. Others are more general feeders, such as the sand snakes *(Psammophis)* which, despite their name, never live in sand.

Tortoises and turtles

Only four species of tortoise are found in Kenya. The leopard tortoise *(Geochelone pardalis)*, named for its distinctive yellow-on-black shell markings, is the largest, with some individuals weighing in at 40kg (88lbs), and also the most common.

From the rocky areas comes the strange pancake tortoise *(Malachochersus tornieri)*, which is quite flat and has a flexible papery shell. Unlike most tortoises, which retire into their shells when threatened, these gallop off at speed to hide among the rocks, and wedge themselves in so tight that they are difficult to extricate.

In addition to the land-dwelling tortoises, half a dozen species of freshwater terrapin occur in Kenya, most being flattish with a rubbery shell and a narrow pointed head. Five of the world's marine turtle species also occur off the Kenyan coast, including breeding popula-

> Snake fans should visit the Nairobi Snake Park in the Nairobi National Museum, or join a day's snake safari at the Bio-Ken Snake Farm in Watamu (www.bio-ken.com).

can be found in dry bush and savannah country, at a considerable distance from any water.

Many kinds of agama lizard, some with bright red, orange or purple heads, can be seen around lodges and camps, especially in rocky areas. It is the males that have the coloured heads, and the colours intensify when they are agitated.

Geckos are widespread in Kenya, and often a welcome sight, due to their taste for household bugs. Though typically quite dull in colour, most of the country's 40-odd gecko species have adhesive toe pads that allow

A male Jackson Chameleon.

tions of hawksbill turtle *(Eretmochelys imbricata)* and green turtle *(Chelonia mydas)*.

Lizards

Almost 200 lizard species, all harmless to humans, are known from East Africa, varying in size from the giant monitors to the tiny cat-eyed coral-rag skink *(Ablepharus boutonii)* that lives on outcrops of coral-rag (petrified coral in limestone) and maintains an osmotic balance by having very saline blood.

The 2-metre (6ft) Nile monitor *(Varanus niloticus)*, mainly found along rivers, is known to dig up crocodile's nests and to eat the eggs. The similarly proportioned, but duller savannah monitor *(Varanus albigularis)*

them to run up and down walls and walk on ceilings.

Giant plated lizards *(Gerrhosaurus major)*, named for their reddish-brown scaling that looks like chain mail, are mainly fruit-eaters, but will devour insects and mice if they get the chance. These can become very habituated and sometimes will hang around campsites begging for scraps.

Of Kenya's multitude of lizards there is one other that deserves a special mention: the serrated toed lizard *(Holaspis guentheri)*. These are small lizards of the high primary forest, conspicuously marked with bright yellow longitudinal bars. They can glide from tree to tree like the Asiatic dracos.

Greater flamingos on Lake Nakuru.

KENYA'S BIRDS

Kenya's equatorial location, coupled with diverse habitats ranging from jungle and lush highland areas to savannah grasslands and desert, supports a corresponding abundance of birdlife.

The enormous variety and concentration of bird life in Kenya makes it one of the world's top ornithological destinations, with more than 1,100 species recorded. Compare this figure with the 250 or so species recorded in Great Britain, or the 850 in Canada, Mexico and the United States combined, and you will understand why Kenya is a birdwatcher's delight. Aside from their aesthetic value, birds perform an essential function in controlling insect numbers, and their relative abundance is a strong ecological indicator of the state of the environment.

Age-old migrations

The vast majority of Kenya's birds are breeding residents – that is, they live there all year round – but a significant proportion are non-breeding or breeding migrants. Some are intra-African migrants, for instance dividing their year between the Congo Basin and East Africa, but a far greater number are Palaearctic migrants, which means that they spend the northern summer in Europe, Asia or the Arctic, but head southward to Africa when the harsh northern winter depletes their food sources – meaning that the best time for ornithological tours of Kenya is from September to April.

It is estimated that up to six billion individual birds – including many species of wader, raptor, waterfowl, warbler, along with the likes of barn swallow and white stork – undertake the annual migration to East Africa from as far east as the Bering Straits and as far west as northern Scandinavia, with some birds flying on to the southern tip of the continent. Those that survive make the return journey each spring to breed in their chosen latitudes.

Brown-hooded kingfisher, Shimba Hills National Reserve.

Bird migration is not learned behaviour, but largely instinctive. Many species that breed in the northern latitudes and migrate to Africa each year actually leave their young to find their own way south, or perish in the attempt. A perfect example of this is the Eurasian cuckoo (*Cuculus canorus*), which lays its eggs in the nests of foster parents. The young cuckoo, even when totally blind, instinctively and forcibly ejects any other egg or even young chick from its nest. Foster parents spend the next 20 or so days feeding this voracious monster until it can fly and feed itself. By now its parents have long since left for Africa, often weeks before the European weather turns miserable. The young cuckoo starts the long journey south with no guidance, following its instinct to fly or die.

Many ducks and geese exhibit similar behaviour. Once breeding is over adult birds go into 'eclipse', when they moult their flight feathers and cannot fly until new feathers have grown. In the meantime their new brood has learned to fly very well and they disappear south, well ahead of their parents.

Those that survive the long journey over harsh deserts, flying mostly at night, find rest and feeding grounds in the amenable climate of southern Kenya. There is a sudden influx of birds almost overnight as huge numbers appear in the bush country, forests and even suburban gardens.

The ability of migrant birds to navigate several thousand miles unaided by technology, and to return repeatedly to the same breeding site, is a remarkable phenomenon, and ornithologists throughout the world have cooperated to study ringed birds in order to build up a picture of migration patterns. Nevertheless, even though we know why birds migrate, and where, much research needs to be done before we fully understand the

Lesser Flamingos in flight over Lake Oliedon, off Lake Naivasha.

TRANSCONTINENTAL FLIGHTS

Bird-ringers trap birds in nets, identify and weigh them, record wing length and other data, then attach a small numbered ring to one leg before the bird is released. Recording the time and place of the encounter means that if the bird is recovered elsewhere, a rough estimate can be made of its migration route and flight pattern. The proportion of ringed birds recovered is very small, but every instance adds to knowledge of bird movements. One ringed shore bird that was picked up dead in Kenya's Rift Valley turned out to have been ringed by Russian enthusiasts just west of the Bering Straits – only 18 days before.

complexity of their highly tuned navigation systems.

Water birds

The coastal climate is hot all year round, and the beaches, with wide tide differentials (up to 4 metres/13ft), provide massive food supplies for waders or shore birds. At low tide thousands of these birds can be seen feeding along the beaches, coral pools and mud flats, particularly from September to April, when numbers are boosted by migrants.

Among the migrants that live and feed here, storing up energy for the long spring flight back to their northern breeding grounds, are the sanderling (*Calidris alba*), whimbrel *(Numenius phaeopus)*, ringed plover *(Charadrius hiaticula)*, ruddy turnstone *(Arenaria interpres)*, common greenshank *(Tringa nebularia)* and Eurasian oystercatcher *(Haematopus ostralegus)*.

Resident birds are also much in evidence. The grey heron *(Ardea cinerea)* feeds in the shallow pools, several species of gull are ever-present, and in the evening large flocks of terns come to roost on the coral cliffs. Breeding colonies of the roseate tern *(Sterna dougallii)* establish themselves on offshore islands, and there is a confusing variety and large numbers of egrets.

> *The blacksmith plover is so named because its repetitive 'tink-tink' call sounds like a hammer being struck on metal.*

bill into shallow water, and snapping it shut the moment it touches something edible.

Along the rivers

The great rivers that rise in the mountains of central Kenya flow east across semi-desert country to the ocean, not only providing a pre-

Tawny Eagle in the Maasai Mara.

In shallow water without coral cliffs, mangrove swamps develop. Here the mud attracts the habitat-specific mangrove kingfisher *(Halcyon senegaloides)*, black-crowned night-heron *(Nycticorax nycticorax)* and other species of heron, including the strange black heron *(Egretta ardesiaca)*, nicknamed the 'umbrella bird' for its unique method of hunting. It paddles in the mud with bright yellow feet and then brings its wings up over its head in umbrella fashion to shade the water underneath.

There is also the crab-plover *(Dromus ardeola)* and yellow-billed stork *(Mycteria ibis)*, which feeds by sweeping its partially opened

cious source of freshwater in an otherwise arid environment, but also supporting a ribbon of greenery known as riparian or riverine forests. Many bird species take advantage of this narrow strip of permanent water where food supplies are always available, not least the various species of yellow weaver that build nests in the overhanging trees.

Large raptors such as tawny eagle *(Aquila rapax)*, martial eagle *(Polemaetus bellicosus)* and the migrant Wahlberg's eagle *(Aquila wahlbergi)* nest in the treetops and feed off small mammals, dry-country game and birds such as guinea fowl and francolin, which come to the water to drink. Blacksmith plovers *(Vanellus armatus)* nest on the sand bars and huge flocks

Vultures gather with astonishing speed at the scene of a kill. But their nests are in treetops or on rocky cliffs many miles from the open plains that supply their food.

of sandgrouse *(Pterocles spp.)* come to quench their thirst and bathe.

On each side of these rivers stretch vast areas of semi-desert and scrub. This is harsh land at relatively low altitude, but when the rain does fall, life blossoms, and every living thing takes

by man. Here are the true dry-country birds that have evolved to take advantage of their environment: the large Heuglin's bustard *(Neotis heuglinii)*, various sandgrouse that fly 30 to 50km (18 to 30 miles) each day to scarce waterholes, and the tiny crested lark *(Galerida cristata)*.

Vast areas of Kenya are covered by savannah – great open grass-covered plains, where rainfall is erratic, but usually good when it does fall. Watercourses, some permanent, others only seasonal, create tree-lined valleys that slice through the plains where various long-

Lilac-breasted roller, Maasai Mara National Reserve.

advantage of the vast increase in food supply, including the bird life. Every tree is suddenly full of nesting birds: red-billed buffalo-weaver *(Bubalornis niger)*, white-headed buffalo-weaver *(Dinemelalia dinemelli)*, many thousands of red-billed quelea *(Quelea quelea)*, yellow-necked francolin *(Francolinus leucoscepus)*, many types of hornbill *(Tockus spp.)* and those that prey on this new abundance. The secretary bird *(Sagittarius serpentarius)* nests on the top of flat trees, while the black-chested snake-eagle *(Circaetus pectoralis)* hawks lizards and snakes.

Arid regions

In the north of Kenya lie extensive areas of almost true desert, most of it uninhabited

claws and pipits *(Motacillidae)* breed and live alongside numerous almost indistinguishable species of lark and cisticola *(Cisticola spp.)*. The scavenging marabou stork *(Leptoptilos crumeniferus)*, also known as the 'undertaker bird' due to its macabre cloaked appearance, is often seen at kills, while overhead might soar half-a-dozen species of vulture.

Along the valleys cutting through this region, heavier growth of trees and scrub provide shelter and nest sites for other birds, who feed on the plains: colourful barbets *(Lybiidae)*, fruit- and seed-eating birds, bush shrikes *(Malaconotidae)*, game birds such as francolins and guineafowls *(Phasianidae)* and many species of pigeon and dove *(Columbidae)*.

Birds of prey, notably the pale and dark chanting-goshawk *(Melierax poliopterus* and *metabates)*, find this environment much to their liking, while the bateleur *(Terathopius ecaudatus)* – a striking black, white and red eagle – might soar effortlessly overhead for hours at a stretch.

Birds of the mountains

The immense equatorial mountains of the Kenyan interior – Elgon, the Aberdares, and of course Mount Kenya itself – support a series of isolated attitudinally determined habitats rang-

> The endangered Clarke's weaver often moves in 100-strong flocks within the forested Arabuko-Sokoke National Park – but it probably breeds elsewhere and its nests have never been found.

The lower slopes of Mount Kenya are covered with dense evergreen forest, which thrives best on east-facing slopes, since they tend to have a higher rainfall and more morning mist. The forests grow all year

Helmeted guineafowl, Meru National Park.

ing from evergreen montane forests to Afro-alpine grassland and moorland.

Although the number of species associated with the latter habitat is limited, many are very specific to it, notably the impressive Mackinder's eagle-owl *(Bubo capensis mackinderi)*, the beautiful scarlet-tufted malachite sunbird *(Nectarinia johnstoni)* and the somewhat drabber alpine chat *(Pinarochroa sordida)*. The birds confined to this alpine zone, despite its harshness, probably could not survive elsewhere, but they are sometimes joined by more wide-ranging species. Vultures, for instance, have been recorded on the snowline of several East African mountains, although there is no good explanation for why.

KENYA'S ENDEMICS

Subject to certain taxonomic disputes, Kenya is home to at least nine endemic species, including Clarke's weaver. Williams' lark *(Mirafra williamsi)* is known from two areas of black lava desert in the north, Sharpe's longclaw *(Macronyx sharpei)* is associated with high-altitude grassland in western and central Kenya, while Hinde's babbler *(Turdoides hindei)* inhabit the southeast foothills of Mt. Kenya. The Taita Thrush *(Turdus helleri)* and Taita white-eye *(Zosterops silvanus)* are forest birds of the Taita Hills bordering Tsavo, while the Kulal white-eye *(Zosterops kulalensis)* is known only from Mt Kulal (overlooking Lake Turkana).

round so they are always green, lush and cool, and provide a permanent home for bird life.

In the treetops, insect-loving shrikes *(Laniidae)* and helmet-shrikes *(Prionopidae)* feed in noisy family parties, often accompanied by starlings *(Strunidae)* of various different species.

At lower levels, nearer the moist, cool earth, plant and insect life are abundant. Robin-chats *(Cossypha spp.)* and thrushes *(Turdus spp.)* of several kinds find this perfect. So does the confiding common bulbul *(Pycnonotus barbatus)* and many more secretive

Golden palm weaver, Diani Beach, south of Mombasa.

species of closely related greenbul *(Pycnonotidae)*. In the treetops, the raucous but spectacular Hartlaub's turaco *(Tauraco hartlaubi)*, with its long blue tail, brilliant scarlet wings and green torso, feeds on the abundant fruit.

Overhead, the crowned eagle *(Stephanoaetus coronatus)*, possibly Africa's most powerful bird of prey, soars in display – sometimes appearing as only a speck in the sky, its piercing call drawing attention long before it is seen – before swooping down on its favoured prey of forest monkeys.

This is a place to sit quietly and watch. If the wild fig trees are fruiting, sit under one for a while and wait, because the ripe fruit may well attract Hartlaub's turaco, African

green pigeon *(Treron calvus)*, silvery-cheeked hornbill *(Bycanistes brevis)* along with colourful starlings and barbets of many kinds. When the fruit becomes overripe, it attracts insects, which are followed by a huge influx of insect-eating birds.

Low forest and swamp

True lowland African jungle does not really exist in Kenya, though the Kakamega Forest in the west, at an altitude of over 1,500 metres (4,920ft), approximates this habitat, and provides a unique Kenyan stronghold for several dozen bird species more normally associated with Uganda or West Africa, making it a favourite haunt of dedicated birders. The most spectacular of Kakamega's specials is undoubtedly the great blue turaco *(Corythaeola cristata)*, which looks somewhat like a psychedelic turkey, but other eagerly sought species here include the blue-headed bee-eater *(Merops muelleri)* and familiar African grey parrot *(Psittacus erithacus)*, a wonderful sight in its natural habitat.

The coastline of Kenya supports the sparse remains of a once vast forest, created by unique local conditions. Typically situated about 5km (3 miles) inland from the sea, this forest evolved to take advantage of fertile coral-based soils, an erratic but heavy annual rainfall, and zero altitude.

Although much of this forest has now been destroyed by people, a substantial tract is protected within the Arabuko-Sokoke National Park, near Malindi and Watamu, which supports three very localised bird species. These are Clarke's weaver *(Ploceus golandi)*, a Kenyan endemic confined to this one forest (though it evidently vanishes for the three-month breeding season), the tiny Sokoke scops owl *(Otus irenae)*, which is only otherwise known from Usambara Mountains in Tanzania, and the near-endemic Sokoke pipit *(Anthus sokokensis)*.

Swamps appear in deserts in years of unusual rainfall and immediately attract the attention of birds not generally found there. Since the swamp holds water long after the surrounding country has returned to normal, the birds will stay. Other swamps are more permanent. Water-loving birds always appear where there is food and disappear when the water dries up.

Insects and Arachnids

Home to more than 100,000 species of insect, Kenya has much to excite entomological collectors and photographers alike.

Ants, beetles and locusts are among the better known representatives of the class *Insecta*, members of which can be distinguished from other invertebrates, such as arachnids (spiders) and crustaceans, by their combination of six legs, a pair of frontal antennae, and a body divided into a distinct head, thorax and abdomen. Insects are also the only winged invertebrates, though some primitive orders have never evolved these appendages, and other more recently evolved orders have discarded them. The tropical forest and savannah habitats of Kenya are particularly rich in insects, which range from vividly coloured dung beetles that use their hind legs to push along the dung balls in which they lay their eggs, to the columns of army ants that march single-mindedly along the forest floor, attacking anything that gets in their way.

Kenya's immense diversity of insect life is epitomised by the presence of more than 1,000 species of butterfly, as compared with roughly 650 in the whole of North America, and a mere 56 on the British Isles. Many individual forests in Kenya harbour several hundred species; indeed, a visitor might easily see a greater variety of butterflies in the course of a few hours sitting quietly at a forest pool than one could in a lifetime of exploring the English countryside. The most spectacular of Kenya's butterflies are the large and colourful swallowtails *(Papilionidae)*, named for the streamers that trail from the base of their wings. The African giant swallowtail *(Papilio antimachus)*, a powerful flier with a wingspan of up to 20cm (8ins), is the largest butterfly species on the continent, but it is seldom seen due to its preference for foraging on forest canopies.

Not all flying insects are as benign as butterflies. Kenya is home to numerous species of mosquito, including the genus *Anopheles* – some species of which transmit malaria. Likewise, locusts, though strictly vegetarian, seasonally irrupt in numbers that can wreak total destruction on crops. However, the importance of insects in the food chain – being the main source of nutrition for many bird and small mammal species – cannot be overstated. And many insects are not only harmless but fascinating to observe: take the praying mantises that are still held sacred by many African peoples, for instance, or the giant armoured rhinoceros beetles that march determinedly along forest verges.

Predatory arachnids

Distinguished from insects by having eight legs rather than six, arachnids are a class of mostly terrestrial and predatory invertebrates that include spiders, scorpions and ticks. Spiders are particularly well represented in Kenya, with some several thousand species identified to date, among them the spectacular golden orbs whose huge webs are often seen in game reserves, and the scarily hairy baboon spiders.

It is hoped that the mosquito-eating Evarcha culicivora spider could be used in the fight against malaria.

Few Kenyan spider species are dangerous to humans, and fatal bites to adults are almost unheard of. The jumping spider *Evarcha culicivora*, first discovered in Lake Victoria in 2005, is evidently partial to feeding on human blood. Fortunately, it isn't capable of preying directly on people, but rather hunts down the blood-sucking *Anopheles gambiae* mosquito, preferring those that have recently fed on a vertebrate. As the spider kills this malaria-transmitting mosquito in the process, it is arguably more ally than foe to man.

Of the other arachnids, certain tick species transmit tick-bite fever, while scorpions, though seldom seen unless actively sought by turning over rocks or dead logs, are known for their painful and sometimes strongly venomous sting.

KENYA'S AVIAN GIANTS

Among Kenya's 1,100-plus bird species are some of the world's largest and most dramatic feathered creatures – and most of them are easy to spot.

Most of Kenya's largest birds live in open country, and are seldom seen on the wing, though only one species is truly flightless. Others simply prefer to spend their days on the ground, such as the ground hornbill, a turkey-sized creature that can be seen lumbering around in small family groups, rooting for grubs and insects.

Other large ground feeders include the secretary bird (whose head feathers resemble the quill pens of old clerical workers), the guinea fowls (helmeted, crested and vulturine), various cranes and bustards, francolins and spurfowl. All are capable fliers that usually roost in trees at night, but spend their days feeding terrestrially.

The same goes for large birds associated with water – the likes of great white egret, Goliath heron, yellow-billed stork and saddle-billed stork only take to the air when necessary. Another large stork, the marabou, sometimes feeds on frogs, but often abandons the water to scavenge carrion along with vultures.

Kenya's seven species of vulture, of which the largest is the lappet-faced, always feed on the ground, where they sometimes seem ungainly and clumsy. But they spend most of the day gliding elegantly and effortlessly above the plains, employing thermals to reach a height of up to 900 metres (3,000ft) above the ground. Even at this height, their astonishing eyesight can discern a likely kill kilometres away.

The greater (white and red) and lesser (pink) flamingos sometimes number up to two million on Lake Nakuru. They feed on tiny organisms by sieving water through their bills.

The kori bustard is the world's heaviest flying creature. During its extraordinary mating display, the male stands erect, flattens its tail along its back and inflates its throat.

White pelicans breed in vast colonies around the Rift Valley lakes. They catch fish by hunting as a team and use their beak pouches as dip-nets.

THE LARGEST BIRD ON EARTH

The ostrich is the world's biggest bird, standing up to 2.75 metres (9ft) tall. Weighing up to 150kg (330lb), it is simply too heavy to fly, and it has thus evolved long, powerful legs as its main form of defence. One kick from an ostrich's two-toed foot is enough to kill a person. The ostrich is also the fastest runner in the bird family, capable of attaining a maximum of 70kph (45mph) and maintaining a speed of 50kph (30mph) for 30 minutes, making it faster than any predator other than a cheetah. Its long neck allows it to spot enemies from a distance and it often sxerves as an early alarm for other animals. If approached, an ostrich may flatten its heads to the ground, but contrary to legend, it does not bury it. An ostrich egg is 15cm (6ins) long and weighs as much as 36 hen's eggs. Kenya is one of the few countries where the common ostrich (*Struthio camelus*) and rarer Somali ostrich (*Struthio molybdophanes*) both occur; the former has pink and the latter blue-grey legs.

The male Somali ostrich is noted for its flashy plumage, while the female is a pale brown colour.

...e crowned crane, with its crest of bristly feathers, is a ...mmon species.

The black-headed heron feeds in shallow waters, spearing frogs and fish with its long, sharp bill.

The secretary bird is the only bird of prey that walks to work. It kills snakes, lizards, rodents and insects by stamping them to death. Its scaly legs protect it against snake bites.

Although not a native species, bougainvillea are a common sight in Kenya.

PLANT LIFE

Kenya contains an astonishing variety of plants, each perfectly adapted to its habitat, from alpine peaks to humid coastal swamps.

The diversity of flora in Kenya reflects the country's wide range of ecological and climatic conditions. Rainfall and altitude are the two major factors affecting the distribution and growth of different plant species – and this is a country that rises from sea level to nearly 5,200 metres (17,000ft), and varies in rainfall from 125mm (5ins) to 2,500mm (100ins) a year.

Above 3,650 metres (12,000ft) lies the alpine zone, where a relatively small number of hardy floral species has adapted to the extreme conditions. Below that, between 1,800 and 3,650 metres (5,900 and 12,000ft), the highland areas contain open Afro-alpine moorland and grassland, while dense evergreen Afro-montane forests flourish in areas of high rainfall.

Areas with medium to high rainfall at altitudes of 1,100 to 2,000 metres (3,600 to 6,560ft) are usually covered with wooded grasslands of *Acacia*, *Albizia* and *Combretum* trees. Grasslands are medium to low rainfall areas at altitudes of 760 to 1,800 metres (2,500 to 5,900ft). Bushland is generally found below 1,650 metres (5,450ft) and is sometimes interspersed with grasslands. Finally, Kenya's semi-desert areas, where rainfall is generally below 250mm (10ins), are often covered with arid bushland or dwarf shrub grasslands.

Plant families

Many families of plants – such as the *Malvaceae* (mallows), *Asteraceae* (a large varied family including daisies and asters) and *Orchidaceae* (orchids) – have a wide tolerance of different ecological conditions and can be found throughout the region.

For example, orchids, both terrestrial and epiphytic (growing on another plant), can be found from sea level to altitudes of around 3,600 metres (11,800ft) in conditions ranging from warm and humid to dry and cold.

An epiphytic orchid.

Where ecological zones have marked characteristics, flora has adapted itself to meet them. For example, in East Africa's vast grassland areas, the various thorn trees of the genus *Acacia* have evolved to cope with both fire and drought. In many species the seed actually germinates more easily after fire; and leaves are thin, often turning their narrower margins towards the sun to limit transpiration (loss of water vapour).

In all drier areas the true grasses of the family *Poaceae* produce an unusually large quantity of seed to enable them to survive long periods when no rain falls and when germination is either doubtful or impossible. Similarly, the flowers of many plants have a higher than average nectar content to attract bees to stimulate fertilisation. Others, such as the distinctive spiky succulents of the genus *Aloe*, have bright orange or red flowers to attract birds, since the dry conditions inhibit much of the insect life that normally performs the pollination. Many plants in semi-desert and bushland regions have grey and aromatic foliage: the colour limits transpiration and the scents attract pollinating insects.

In the medium altitude zones of grassland and wooded grassland there are numerous genera of *Malvaceae*. Notable among them are *Hibiscus*, *Abutilon* and *Pavonia*, which are found mainly in

Hibiscus are found in medium altitude zones.

grassy plains and, strangely enough, in rocky terrain and lava flows.

Fabaceae, the pea family, is also prominent in open and wooded grasslands and highlands. Represented strongly by the genus *Crotalaria*, of which there are probably more than 200 species in the region, they are widely distributed and can often be seen in considerable drifts of colour, mainly with yellow or yellow and orange flowers, though there are one or two species which are predominantly blue.

The carpet flowers

A notable feature from sea level to more than 3,350 metres (11,000ft), the convolvulus family (*Convolvulaceae*) is represented by at least 20

East African genera and 170 species. Prominent everywhere is the genus *Ipomoea*, whose myriad flowers scramble over coral at the coast and also thrive in semi-desert scrub, in wooded grasslands, forest glades and even on the moorlands.

Cycnium t. tubulosum, a member of *Scrophuliaraceae* with white 'pocket handkerchief' flowers, is dotted all over the grassland plains, especially on black cotton (soft clay) soils. A near relative, *Cycnium. t. montanum*, has large pink flowers and extends to slightly higher altitudes. Both these plants are parasitic on the roots of grasses and speckle the countryside for huge areas where grasses have been burnt or grazed heavily.

In dry, open bushland is another parasitic plant from the *Orobanchaceae* or broomrape family, *Cistanche tubulosa*. An erect, unbranched spike of yellow flowers like a large hyacinth springs out of a bare patch of soil, drawing its nourishment from the roots of neighbouring shrubs or trees.

Throughout shady and damp places in Kenya's higher rainfall regions, nestling in banks or decorating the sides of streams, you can find members of the *Balsaminaceae* family, related to the busy lizzies or impatiens of gardens in temperate zones.

The desert rose (*Adenium obesum*) is found in semi-arid areas, often among inhospitable rocks. From the family *Apocynaceae*, this succulent has magnificent long red to pink tubular flowers and fat fleshy branches: it appears a glowing mass of colour in a semi-lunar landscape.

Lilies

Among the *Liliaceae* (lily family) are three outstanding species. *Gloriosa superba*, sometimes known as the flame lily, is a particularly beautiful plant with a red, red and yellow or red and green striped flower with its outside petals bending abruptly backwards. It is widespread in the area below altitudes of 2,500 metres (8,200ft). There is a singularly fine variant at lower altitudes with lemon-coloured segments and a deeper violet meridian stripe. The plant grows from a V-shaped tuber and can reach 5 metres (16.5ft).

Albuca abyssinica is the most common of all the lilies in East Africa. This robust plant, up to 1 metre (3ft) tall, has bell-shaped flowers rather widely spaced on the stalk. Though they never open fully, these flowers are yellowish-green in colour with a darkish stripe down the middle of each petal and off-yellow on the margins.

Aloes are among the *Liliaceae* most widespread in the middle and lower altitudes. Red, orange or

No-one knows just how many plants exist in Kenya, but when botanists complete their survey into the flora of East Africa, it's probable that more than 11,000 species will have been noted.

yellow with green spotted or striped leaves, they form dense groups of beautiful colour, especially in grassland areas where grazing has reduced competition. Elephants are particularly fond of the aloe.

found up to an altitude of 3,000 metres (10,000ft), has yellowish-brown to orange flowers and is a relative of the garden varieties derived from *G. primulinus*. Above that altitude, the finest species of them all, *G. watsonioides*, with bright red flowers, grows in stony soils only in alpine and sub-alpine regions on Mount Kenya. *Gladiolus ukambanensis* is a delightful species with white, delicately scented flowers, produced copiously but capriciously in wet years. It is restricted to stony soils in the Machakos district and in the Maasai Mara. For a comprehensive photo feature on Kenya's trees, see page 188.

The exquisite flame lily.

In the amaryllis family (*Amaryllidaceae*) are two beautiful species. *Scadoxus multiflorus*, the fireball lily, is an arresting sight. Growing from a deep-rooted bulb in rocky places, riverine forest and open grassland, often in the shade of trees or on the side of termite mounds, the flower spike arises before the leaves and is crowned with up to 150 small flowers, making a single magnificent red to pink head that looks like a gigantic shaving brush. Crinums often flower at the same time, notably *Crinum macowanii*, named the pyjama lily after the pink stripes marking the long tubular flowers. It grows throughout East Africa and is often seen at the sides of roads and in ditches.

In the iris family (*Iridaceae*) the genus *Gladiolus* has three beautiful species. *Gladiolus natalensis* is

HIGH ACHIEVERS

In high montane and alpine areas there are three curious evolutions, all growing to extraordinary heights. The tree groundsels of the genus *(Dendrosenecio)* reach up to 10 metres (33ft), with a flower 1 metre (3ft) long. The giant *lobelias (Lobelia telekii* and *L. deckenii)* grow to 4 metres (13ft) high or more, with an inflorescence (cluster of flowers) 3 metres (10ft) long and an exaggerated deep calyx in which the blue flower is almost hidden, as protection against the dramatic variations in temperature at these altitudes. The giant heather *(Erica arborea)* has evolved up to 7 metres (22ft) tall with white flowers at the end of its branches.

Hot air balloons over the Maasai Mara at sunrise.

ACTIVE PURSUITS

A holiday in Kenya need not involve just looking at
animals or lying on a beach. There's plenty to do for
the more energetically inclined.

ount Kenya, the second highest mountain
in Africa, provides a variety of challenges
to mountaineers, trekkers and rock
climbers. The main summit peaks of Batian and
Nelion should be undertaken only by mountaineers experienced at climbing steep ice and rock
at altitude. By contrast, no technical skills are
required to reach Point Lenana, the third-highest
peak, though the climb should be attempted only
by reasonably fit travellers – for whom the effort
is justified by the beautiful Afro-alpine scenery.

The most popular base for climbing Mount
Kenya is at Naro Moru, 171km (106 miles) from
Nairobi on the main road to Nanyuki. The track
from here is the shortest way up, and most tourists ascend the mountain this way, neglecting the
more involved routes, of which there are seven.

It's also possible to climb Point Lenana from
the east, by way of the Chogoria Track, which starts
at the town of Chogoria, 228km (141 miles) from
Nairobi, on the road to Meru. Either way, three
days should be allowed to reach Point Lenana.
A good trek is to climb the Chogoria Track to
Lenana then descend the Naro Moru Track, so
completing a full traverse of the mountain.

Another challenging hiking area is the relatively infrequently visited Mount Elgon, on the
Uganda border. Good destinations for less strenuous day walks include Longonot and Hell's
Gate national parks, both readily accessible from
the myriad resorts around Lake Naivasha, and
the coastal forest of Arabuko-Sokoke National
Park near Watamu.

Freshwater fishing

The freshwater angler may not give Kenya a passing thought when seeking out productive waters.
Yet the country offers the expert ample and varied reward for his or her skills. In the Central

Freshwater fishing.

Highlands there are innumerable trout streams
of a quality that would command formidable fees
if they were in Europe. In Kenya, however, they
are available for locals and visitors for no more
than the nominal cost of a sports fishing licence.

Fly-fishing came to Kenya just before World
War I, when the European settlers became
nostalgic for their native lochs and moorland
streams. The rainbow trout they imported
from South Africa are doing exceptionally well
in the parasite- and predator-free streams that
flow through the forests of Mount Kenya and
the Aberdares. Below the forests, the rivers are
larger, deeper and muddier, but still offer an
occasional heavyweight trout.

South of the highlands in the Central Rift,

Deep-sea fishing

The abundance and variety of game fish, together with well-equipped boats and professional crews, make the coast of East Africa a paradise for sports fishermen. From Pemba Channel on the Tanzanian border all the way north to Kiwayu, there are efficient charter operators available during the eight-month fishing season (August to March). The high winds of the *kusi* (southeast monsoon) make waters unfishable between late March and late July.

The most challenging sport fish of the ocean – black, blue and striped marlin, broadbill sword-

> For the intrepid adventurer, one- to three-day whitewater rafting trips on the Tana, Mathioya or Athi rivers are organised by Savage Wilderness; http://savagewilderness.org.

Lake Naivasha contains plenty of small tilapia for a good day's sport, but the angler's favourite quarry is the largemouth or black bass, a native of the southern United States introduced to Naivasha in 1930, which ranges from a modest 500g (1lbs) to 3kg (6lbs) or more.

Fishing boats, Turtle Bay, Watamu.

HIGH-ALTITUDE TRAINING

Founded in 1999 by four-time World Champion Lornah Kiplagat, the High Altitude Training Centre (www.lornah.com) is set at around 2,400 metres (7,900ft) in the small town of Iten, in the highlands west of Lake Baringo. It has become a popular training centre for world-class athletes and the construction of a 25-metre swimming pool has also made it very popular with top triathletes from all around the globe. However, you do not need to be an Olympic contender to enjoy the facilities at this superb training centre – it also offers regular holiday packages allowing dedicated amateurs to train alongside some of Kenya's top runners.

fish and Pacific sailfish – all abound in these waters, as do the powerful yellowfin tuna and a wide variety of game fish including barracuda, kingfish and bonito.

Fishing tackle and boats run by Kenya's dedicated professional operators are based at points along the 400km (250-mile) coastline. At Malindi there are charter operators who have become especially skilled at light tackle and fly casting for sailfish, marlin, broadbill and other smaller species of game fish.

Other water sports

Windsurfing has not bypassed the shores of the Indian Ocean. Already the venue for international windsurfing competitions, the Kenyan coast, with its constant breeze and comparatively placid and warm waters, is ideal for the sport. The sheltered lagoons are interlaced with sailboards tacking, beating and running before the wind – a brilliant array of colour splashed across the blue water. Tuition and board hire are available at virtually every hotel and beach resort, and a nucleus of windsurfing enthusiasts also ply their hobby on the lakes and dams in up-country Kenya.

The ability to swim a little, or simply to float, permits the less athletic to snorkel. Simply by donning a glass mask, the wonders beneath the crystal-clear waters are revealed in all their brilliance. The shark-free coral gardens and inner reefs are a paradise of colour and movement – brilliant coral, fish and plant life combine in a spectacle no photograph can adequately reproduce.

The more experienced can scuba dive, spending longer periods underwater, but this is a pastime that requires training. Scuba schools abound, all professionally run and offering first-rate equipment for hire. The Kenyan coast has achieved a reputation in scuba circles for the quality of its diving, and the sport competes with windsurfing for popularity.

There is an opportunity for sailors to tack, reach and run with the wind on lakes Naivasha and Victoria. Water-skiers can enjoy jumping the waves at the coast and at lakes Naivasha and Baringo.

Scenic golf

The golfer who brings his clubs to Kenya will find some superb scenic courses to choose from – from sea level all the way up to a course which claims the highest tee in the Commonwealth, at over 2,400 metres (7,800ft). New arrivals in Nairobi, driving in from the airport, are often startled to see a golf course within a nine-iron lob of the Parliament Buildings in the city centre. This is the Railway Course, the junior of three within the city limits.

The Royal Nairobi, built in 1906, claims seniority (the 'Royal' was bestowed on the Nairobi Golf Club in 1935 by King George V). Muthaiga Golf Club, which usually hosts the annual Kenya Open, is also within a 10-minute taxi ride of Nairobi's central hotels. North of the city is the Windsor Golf and Country Club, which is home to one of the top courses on the continent and certainly the best in Kenya. In the suburb of Karen is the scenic Karen Country Club course on land that was once part of Karen Blixen's coffee estate.

Visitors are welcome at all Kenyan golf clubs. Green fees are moderate and caddies are always on hand. At the more popular and crowded courses there are restrictions on visitors at weekends.

A round of golf on a Kenyan course can have diversions. Exotic and sometimes noisy bird life is profuse, and a number of clubs have rules that may appear strange to players from overseas. The course rules at Kisumu, on the shores of Lake Victoria, states that: 'If a ball comes to rest in dangerous proximity to a hippopotamus or crocodile, another ball may be dropped at a safe distance, but no nearer the hole, without penalty.'

Water skiiing on Lake Naivasha.

THE BIG ONE

The ultimate freshwater fishing adventure in Kenya is arguably the search for the giant Nile perch on lakes Turkana or Victoria. The largest freshwater fish anywhere, growing to well over 100kg (220lbs), it's underrated as a fighter by the heavy-tackle brigade, but it will fight a rare battle on a light line. The catch is not returned, except for the 13kg (30lbs) infants, since these huge fish are excellent for eating. Choicest cuts like the cheeks are grilled and taste like rock lobster. Part of the catch may be salted and sun-dried and the larger fillets packed in ice for eventual transport home. The debris is abandoned for the crocodiles.

SPORTING KENYA

Kenyan runners are internationally known in the athletics stadium, but there are also many other fields in which the country performs with vigour.

With fine and usually predictable weather, Kenya affords endless opportunities for the sports spectator. The country's enthusiasm for varied sporting activity is indicated by the existence of more than 40 different associations and management bodies controlling a diverse range of sports and pastimes, from athletics to windsurfing. Sport is an important part of the Kenyan way of life, and newspapers devote many pages to local and overseas sporting events.

The Safari Rally

Every year, for three days, usually between March and June, some of the world's finest rally drivers converge on Kenya to face the multiple challenges of dust, mud, fatigue and diabolical roads in one of the world's greatest motoring events: the Safari Rally. Along with the rally crews come top mechanics, team managers, journalists, photographers and ordinary rally watchers who cannot resist the event's magic.

Competitor in the annual Safari World Rally Championship.

The rally began simply enough in 1953, when 57 local drivers, in ordinary cars, struggled round Kenya, Uganda and Tanganyika (then still under British rule). Originally known as the East African Coronation Safari, it was a delightfully amateur event: no winner was declared, no service crews were allowed, and repairs had to be done by the participants themselves (although it was permitted to use a dealer workshop en route). The race's glamour soon attracted professional interest, however, along with the attention of the international motoring press, and after it was granted international status in 1957, an increasing number of drivers from outside East Africa participated on an amateur basis.

Today, although the Safari Rally no longer has the status of a World Rally Championship event, its reputation as the world's toughest rally ensures it attracts a fair quota of professional drivers. Historically, however, overseas drivers seem to find it difficult to win, probably because they lack experience of driving in East African conditions. More often than not, the rally has been won by local drivers, particularly in its early years, but also since 2003, when the only person to break the Kenyan monopoly on the trophy has been the Zimbabwean driver Conrad Rautenbach in 2007.

The most successful driver in the event is the late Shekhar Mehta, who won the rally five times between 1973 and 1982, a record most closely threatened by Carl Tundo, who won in 2004, 2009, 2011 and 2012. In both 2013 and 2014, the winner was Baldev Chager.

Football frenzy

While Kenya's athletes make sports headlines abroad, it is Association Football, or soccer, that commands the attention within Kenya. Though it never reaches the fervent support that accompanies the game in South America or Europe, soccer is played by thousands on any level ground with anything that reasonably represents a ball. Thousands of supporters cram

Kenya's Humphrey Kayange tackles Argentina's Lucas Amorosino in the Rugby World Cup Sevens in Dubai, 2009.

the stadiums for the weekend league and cup matches – although (as elsewhere) over-exuberance from the crowds occasionally requires police intervention.

The showcase of domestic football is the 16-club Kenyan Premier League. Below this is a 16-club Nationwide League Division One, a two-zone Nationwide League Division Two, and various provincial leagues. Historically, the Premier League's most successful club ever has been Nairobi's Gor Mahia, which garnered 15 titles, including most recently in 2013, 2014 and 2015. Another most awarded team of all time is AFC Leopards, which won 13 times, but none since 2000. The major annual knockout

tournament is the FKF President's Cup, which has operated under several different names since it was established in 1956. No team has dominated this event as comprehensively as Gor Mahia and AFC Leopards, which lead the all-time winners' table with ten and seven titles respectively. Gor Mahia has also been the most successful Kenyan club internationally.

The Kenyan national team, the Harambee Stars, have hardly distinguished themselves in international competition. In 2004, they returned to the African Cup of Nations after an absence of 12 years, and were swiftly eliminated (despite scoring their first-ever victory in the competition – a 3-0 win over Burkina Faso). They haven't qualified for the competition since.

In 2004, the national team was at the centre of an international controversy: the Government sacked the executive committee of the Kenya Football Federation, accusing its members of incompetence and corruption. FIFA, football's ruling body, objected to government interference in the administration of the game, and suspended Kenya from all international competition – including the qualifying games for the 2006 World Cup. The suspension was lifted in 2007.

In 2006, Dennis Oliech became the first Kenyan to play in one of Europe's top leagues, making his debut for FC Nantes in the French First Division. In 2007, following Nantes relegation from the top division, he transferred to Auxerre, then to Ajaccio and Dubai CSC, for whom he still plays today. Recent years have seen many more talented Kenyan footballers follow suit.

Fast and furious rugby

Kenyan rugby players favour a fast, open game, with plenty of running and handling, which makes for excellent spectator entertainment. The main competition run by the Kenya Rugby Football Union is the Bamburi Super Series, which comprises two pools of four teams apiece, with names such as the SDV Transami Cheetahs and Mumias Sugar Buffaloes. The majority of the clubs are based around the Nairobi area, but the game is played as far afield as Nakuru, Kisumu and Mombasa. The season runs from late March until early September. As well as the leagues, the club sides also compete in the end-of-season Enterprise and Mwamba knockout cups, regional tournaments that also include teams from neighbouring Uganda and Tanzania.

Internationally, the standard of the 15-man game still lags behind many rugby-playing nations, although the Rugby Football Union of East Africa is working to build a team that might one day qualify for a Rugby World Cup. Meanwhile, Kenya's Sevens rugby team is growing in popularity and prestige. The national squad has competed around the world, gaining its first significant success in 2004, when it pulled off a surprise victory against Australia in the IRB International Sevens tournament in New Zealand. Kenya is now one of the 15 core teams to feature in the international sevens series, and its overall record places it tenth on the all-time table of wins, ahead of 29 other teams, including Scotland, Canada and the US.

Started in 1996, the Safari Sevens is a seven-a-side competition held in Kenya that attracts teams from all over the world. Kenya excelled itself in the 2013 event, beating Australia 'Renegades' 40-7 in the tournament final.

Competitive cricket

Cricket has a strong place in the country's sporting calendar. On the world stage, the Kenyan national team has yet to be admitted into the elite circle of Test-playing nations. However, it achieved official One Day International (ODI) status in 1997, entitling them to compete regularly in ODI competitions. Kenya competed in the Cricket World Cup since its start in 1996, memorably reaching the semi-finals in South Africa in 2003. Unfortunately, the national side has declined in standards since this impressive feat, as epitomised by the heavy defeats inflicted in all six games at the 2011 World Cup. In 2014, Kenya lost its ODI status.

At club level, Kenyan cricket is fiercely competitive, with volatile temperaments sometimes gaining the upper hand of reason. Watching a league match, the result of which may decide the destination of the trophy, is not for the faint-hearted. The domestic season is between June and March, with a large number of league matches at national and provincial levels, and also international club games against visiting overseas sides, such as provincial teams from South Africa and Bangladesh.

The Kenya Cricket Association is undertaking a major development programme starting at grassroots level, with better organised instruction in schools and coaching courses for teachers.

Several Kenyan-born cricketers have played at the top level abroad: Derek Pringle for England, Qasim Omar for Pakistan and Dilip Patel for New Zealand.

Sticks and racquets

Kenya's hockey teams, both men and women, have won gold medals at the All Africa Games, and have also competed in the Commonwealth Games and the Olympics. Hockey is enthusiastically played by men and women at a social

The Kenyan Women's Field Hockey team battle South Africa at the finals of the African Olympic qualifiers in Nairobi, 2007.

level, mainly on murram or grass pitches.

Three major tennis competitions, including the Kenya Open, are held at the beginning of the year, with many smaller tournaments around the country throughout the year. Kenya has hosted Davis Cup group competitions on a number of occasions.

Squash is a rapidly growing sport and one in which Kenyan teams have done remarkably well in international competitions, including the World Junior Championships and the Commonwealth Games.

A select number of sports clubs cater for lawn bowls and croquet, with top-class facilities and standards. Kenyan teams regularly compete in international tournaments such as the Commonwealth Games.

Equestrian sports

Kenya's climate and open spaces provide limitless scope for a range of equestrian activities, the envy of those who dwell in more constricted surroundings. Throughout the year, apart from a short break in August, horse racing is held every Sunday and on most public holidays at the Ngong Racecourse, which opened in 1954 on the outskirts of Nairobi. The picturesque course is well patronised on racing days, and the standard of racing is high. The most prestigious annual event is the Kenya Derby, which was first held elsewhere in 1914, and now takes place at Ngong every April.

During the British winter, several professional jockeys enjoy a working holiday by riding in Nairobi. The legendary Lester Pigott has ridden the course – inevitably on a winner with his first ride – and commented most favourably on the course and its facilities.

Run right-handed, the entire course is visible from the stands. With an eight-race card, the entrance fee also gives access to the stands

A polo match at Nairobi's polo ground on the outskirts of the city.

COMPETING ON HORSES

Polo has a small following in Kenya but is played regularly at weekends in Jamhuri Park, Nairobi, and up-country at the likes of Nanyuki and Gilgil. Standards vary, with a few good players and a remarkable number of new players taking to the game. An annual international tournament attracts well-known high-handicap players from overseas.

A number of equestrian events – including dressage, show jumping and cross-country jumping – are held throughout the year at various venues around the country, culminating in the Horse of the Year Show held at Nairobi's Jamhuri Park in February.

and clubhouse. Catering and other facilities are splendid, and with both tote and bookmakers on hand to take care of the gambling urge, there can be few more enjoyable ways of spending a Sunday afternoon. Racing is run professionally, with stipendiary stewards and a qualified handicapper, and Kenya racing has rid itself of its slightly unsavoury reputation of years gone by.

Good-quality breeding stock has been imported into Kenya over many years and there is a flourishing bloodstock industry, with horses exported to other African countries. There is a tendency for horses to grow rather more 'leggy' than their northern counterparts, but there is remarkable quality to be seen throughout the 300 or so horses in training.

Running for Gold

When Kenya won a bronze medal in the 1964 Olympics, few guessed it was the first step towards becoming a dominant force in the world of long-distance running

Kenyan athletes – especially long and middle-distance runners – have been a powerful presence in world athletics since the 1960s. Yet Kenya did not appear in any international athletics meeting until 1952 and did not win any medals until the 1958 Commonwealth Games. It was in the 1960s that Kenyan runners began to attract worldwide attention – particularly two outstanding athletes, Kipchoge Keino and Naftali Temu.

Wilson Kipruget won Kenya its first Olympic medal – a bronze in the 800 metres event – at Tokyo in 1964. The first of many international gold medals was won by 'Kip' Keino in the 1,500 metres at the first All Africa Games in Brazzaville in 1965. The next year he picked up two golds at the Commonwealth Games, where Temu also won the 6 mile race, and followed that with the 5,000 metres title at the World Games in Helsinki. The world was then stunned by a dazzling team performance at the Mexico Olympics of 1968. Represented by only 18 athletes, Kenya collected an astonishing nine medals in total, including three golds, and returned home to a heroes' welcome.

Some critics claimed that their unexpected success was due to the altitude of Mexico City – similar to that of their Kenyan homeland. However, at the 1972 Munich Olympics they proved that altitude had nothing to do with it. Kip Keino picked up a gold and a silver, Benjamin Jipcho a silver, the Kenyan team won the 4x400 metres relay, and there were two bronze medals into the bargain.

World records

So it continued throughout the 1980s and 1990s, with Kenyan athletes consistently beating the world at long- and middle-distance events. By the mid-1990's other African nations such as Ethiopia and Morocco had started to follow Kenya's lead and were producing world-class distance runners.

Even so, Kenyans won seven medals in the 2004 Athens Olympics, including claiming the gold, silver and bronze medals in the men's 3,000 metres steeplechase. And it had its best Olympic haul ever at

Beijing in 2008, collecting five gold, five silver and four bronze medals. Four years later in London, it took home 16 medals in total, including seven gold. In 2015, Kenya topped the table at the World Athletics Championships.

Furthermore, Kenyan athletes hold or have held innumerable outdoor running world records in recent years. Famously, Kenyan-born Wilson Kipketer (now a Danish citizen) set a record of 1:41.11 for the men's 800 metres in Cologne in 1997, a time that remained unbeaten for 13 years until another Kenyan, David Rushida, ran 1:41.01 in 2010, and then in 2012 he beat it himself, running 1:40.91. In

The Safaricom Marathon is the only marathon in the world staged inside a game reserve, the Lewa Wildlife Conservancy.

addition to Rushida, outdoor world records are currently held by Kenyans in 21 other distances. Some of these records are long-standing indeed, notably the 3,000 metres held by Daniel Komen since 1996, but others are very recent, suggesting that Kenya's athletic future is as rosy as its past.

Is the Kenyan landscape, climate or altitude an explanation for this seemingly endless stream of distance runners? Although that is a matter for sports physiologists to argue over, it is interesting to note that all of Kenya's world-beating stars are mostly from a very small number of tribes, the Gusii and three Kalenjin groups – the Nandi, the Sabaot and especially the Kipsigis, and all of these tribes have their homeland in the Great Rift Valley.

Cooking fish on the beach.

EATING AND ENTERTAINMENT

There's no shortage of restaurants in Nairobi and on the coast – and the cuisine has a richness and variety that reflects Kenya's cosmopolitan culture.

Kenya is not first and foremost a culinary destination. Which does not mean that you won't eat well there – almost certainly you will, especially in Nairobi, along the coast, and at the top safari camps and lodges – but rather that it offers limited options in terms of a unique national cuisine, so that eating out, even in the very best restaurants and hotels, tends to be a cosmopolitan culinary experience rather than one that feels distinctively East African.

Swahili cuisine

The most important exception to the above is Swahili cuisine, which reflects centuries of coastal trade with Arab and Asian merchants, who first sailed into ports such as Mombasa, Malindi and Lamu in medieval times, bringing with them an array of sweet and spicy condiments ranging from dried and fiery chillies. And the Arabs and Asians were followed by the Portuguese, who introduced a range of foodstuffs from newly discovered Brazil to East Africa – maize, bananas, pineapples, peppers, sweet potatoes and manioc – most of which were destined to become local staples.

As a result, coastal cooking has a definite Asiatic influence, with a favourite dish being Swahili chicken curry, whose distinctive creamy texture and tangy aftertaste derive from two main ingredients: fresh coconut milk and Swahili curry mix, the latter a golden-brown blend of ground cinnamon, roast coriander, cumin and fennel seeds, and fresh chilli and coriander. It is usually eaten with *wali na nazi* (rice boiled in coconut milk) or chapatis (a variant on roti bread), and is also often accompanied with a spinach-like vegetable called *sukuma wiki*.

The coast is also renowned for its fine quality seafood. This is often served in a curry,

Homemade pickles and sauces.

similar to the chicken dish described above, but is also superb grilled or fried. Popular dishes include whole line fish stuffed and grilled over charcoal, or grilled prawns smothered in a garlic or peri-peri (chilli) sauce. Of the various coastal ports, Lamu has the most limited selection of upmarket restaurants, but it is a great place to try inexpensive Swahili cooking at any of half-a-dozen unpretentious local eateries that line the historic waterfront. Lamu is also famed for its fresh fruit juices, notably the lip-puckering tamarind. After your main course, ask for a *kaimati*, a Swahili-style doughnut flavoured with cardamom, or for a hunk of sticky halva, an Arab sweetmeat made with almonds and ghee.

Upcountry style

One measure of how little the East African coast and interior had to do with each other in pre-colonial times is the limited extent to which the cosmopolitan influences absorbed into Swahili cuisine spread inland. Where Swahili cooking tends to be richly flavoursome and spicy, the people of the interior traditionally subsisted on a stolid diet of sorghum, millet or *ugali* (a stiff maize porridge), supplemented by bland vegetable or bean stew, or *nyama choma* (grilled meat), or – in the case of the Maasai and related pastoralists – a fermented blend of cow's blood and milk.

It has to be said that the British colonial influence did little to make upcountry cuisine more exciting, and while rice, chips and bread (usually pre-sliced and rather stale) are now served in most *hotelis* (as small local eateries are known), the food still tends to be on the bland side. Indeed, it could be argued, convincingly, that the colonists greatest contribution to Kenya's culinary scene was the importation of thousands of Indian railway workers, who brought with them the curries, chapatis and chutneys that are now as traditional for Sunday lunch in Kenya as roast beef is in England. Nairobi is particularly well served by Indian

Fresh seafood.

TO DRINK WITH YOUR MEAL

Local beers have always been good value. White Cap and Tusker are among the more popular lagers. In good hotels, lodges and restaurants they are served ice cold, but many local bars will go with the common Kenyan preference for warm beer (after a long dusty day on safari, the two most useful words in the Swahili language are undoubtedly '*baridi sana*' – very cold.)

Attempts to grow wine-producing grapes near Naivasha were abandoned when South African and European wines began to flood the market. Imported wine in restaurants is expensive by Kenyan standards. Wine in supermarkets is more reasonably priced, considering how far it has travelled.

Carbonated soft drinks are widely available in Kenya, but the most widely drunk local beverage is *chai*, a sweet tea where all ingredients are boiled together in a pot, flavoured with spices such as ginger. In Kenyan hotels, tea is served in the more familiar way, and is generally preferable to filter coffee, which tends to be burnt, over-stewed or insipid. The one exception is the Swahili *kahawa* – a thimbleful of black coffee topped with a pinch of ground ginger – sold by street vendors and in traditional eateries along the coast.

Tap water cannot be recommended, but mineral water is widely available. A refreshing, healthy alternative is coconut milk, drunk straight from the shell.

restaurants, but there are also plenty to choose from in Mombasa, and often one or two to be found in smaller towns away from the major tourist centres, all invariably with a good selection of dishes for vegetarians.

> The local equivalent to doughnuts are maandaazi, sweet deep fried doughballs that make a tasty breakfast snack when freshly cooked, but tend to go stale quickly. Mahamri is a coastal variation made with coconut milk.

the City Market, to see the wonderful quality and variety of vegetables and fruits grown in Kenya. The market will prepare you for the country's limitless choice of fresh foods – from asparagus to tree tomato, pineapples to strawberries – and is an ideal shopping place for picnics.

In the bush

Once on safari, it's customary to eat all meals at your lodge or camp. Indeed, almost all safari lodges automatically provide full-board packages, for the simple reason that there is generally no alternative within reasonable driving distance

MacKinnon Market, Old Town, Mombasa.

If the coast excels when it comes to seafood and Swahili cuisine, Nairobi unquestionably boasts Kenya's most cosmopolitan contemporary restaurant scene. Almost every major international cuisine is represented in the capital, from Italian and French to Thai and Mexican, but the capital is best known for its red meat, in particular steak sourced from the cattle that range freely across Kenya's open ranch land. This meat fetish is taken to self-explanatory extremes at The Carnivore, Nairobi's most famous restaurant, whose set menu comprises one great roast of meat after another – as much as you can eat of Molo lamb, skewered chicken, beef, impala, gazelle and ostrich.

It isn't all about meat, however. Before you visit any Nairobi restaurant, try to take a quick trip to

(and, in any case, driving after dark is generally forbidden in reserves). Overall, the standard of food provided at these lodges ranges from good to exceptional. Larger lodges mostly serve up expansive but unadventurous buffets.

By contrast, most smaller camps offer set menus comprising three or four courses, with a choice of at least two dishes for each course, and the more upmarket camps often come up with genuinely creative and delicious concoctions belying their remote location. Particularly when staying at smaller camps, vegetarians and those with special dietary requirements should specify their needs well in advance, and are strongly advised to confirm arrangements upon arrival for every overnight stop.

Reticulated giraffe, Ol Pejeta Wildlife Conservancy.

Camels on Diani Beach.

Lesser Flamingos in Lake Oliedon, off Lake Naivasha.

Blue wildebeest migration, Maasai Mara National Reserve.

INTRODUCTION

A detailed guide to the entire country, with principal sites clearly cross-referenced by number to the maps.

A dhow on the Lamu Archipelago.

The main gateway to Kenya is Nairobi, East Africa's largest city and site of its busiest international airport. This sprawling modern city provides an unrepresentative introduction to a country best known for its outdoor attractions, but it has excellent facilities, and the likes of the informative Nairobi National Museum and the genuinely wild Nairobi National Park ensure it has plenty to keep visitors occupied – as does the scattering of craft markets and shopping malls in its green suburbs.

Nairobi is the main hub for air and road safaris to Kenya's diverse national parks and reserves. These divide up into several circuits. To the east of the capital, towards the coast, lie the vast arid tracts of bush protected in Tsavo East and West National Parks, as well as the smaller Amboseli National Park, famed for its elephants and views of Kilimanjaro. West of Nairobi, the floor of the Great Rift Valley, studded with dormant volcanic cones and shallow sump-like lakes, is home to Lake Nakuru National Park, renowned for its immense flamingo flocks and easily located rhinos. The western Rift Valley also offers access to the peerless Maasai Mara National Reserve, which peaks in activity from July to October, when the wildebeest migration crosses into it from neighbouring Tanzania.

Maasai giraffe, Nairobi National Park.

North of Nairobi, the sentinel Mount Kenya, its peaks scattered with snow and protected within the country's highest altitude national park, stands over the agricultural heartland of the country. The great mountain's footslopes are home to another cluster of fine safari reserves: the untrammelled Meru National Park, the arid Samburu-Buffalo Springs National Reserve, and the private conservancies of the Laikipia Plateau.

Further north lies the spectacularly remote Lake Turkana, while the far southwest comprises the densely populated basin that holds Lake Victoria, the world's second-largest freshwater body. Finally, there is the 480km (300-mile) coastline, where ancient Swahili ports such as Mombasa, Malindi and Lamu are complemented by some lovely Indian Ocean beaches and several marine parks famed for their snorkelling and diving.

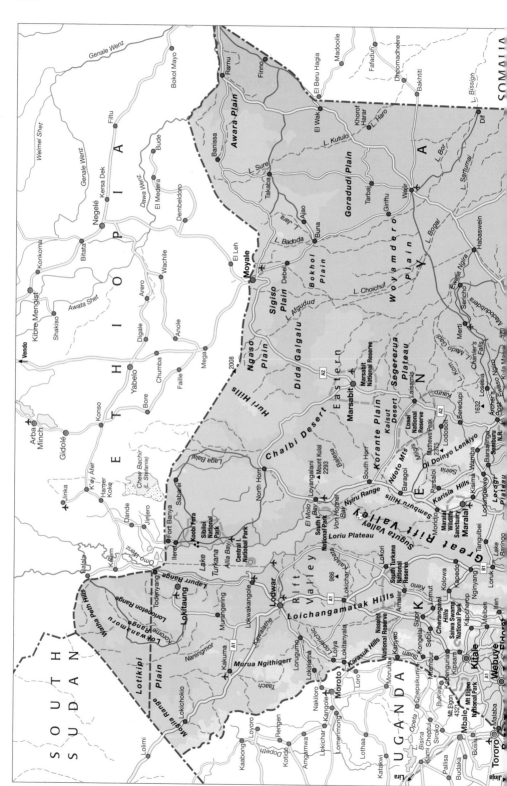

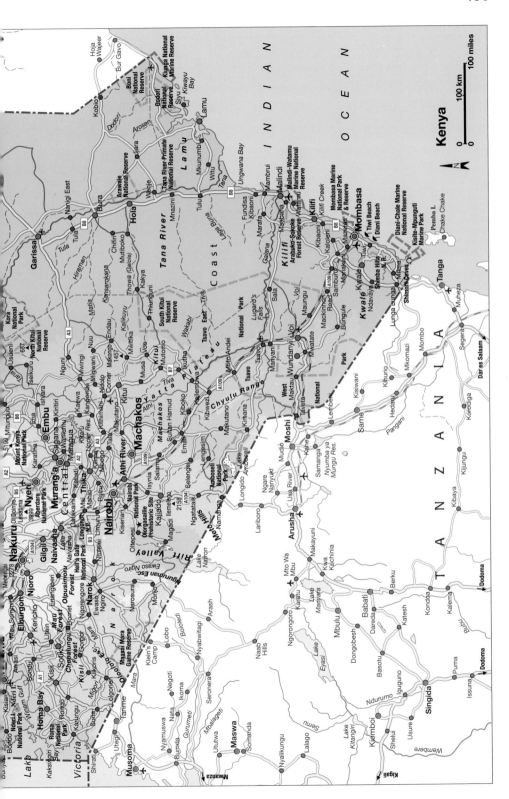

Kenyatta Avenue.

NAIROBI

A sprawling modern city barely 100 years old, the capital of Kenya is a vigorous tumult of cultures, drawn together and driven by fierce commercial instincts.

The most populous city in East Africa, Nairobi is also the region's main economic, financial and transportation hub, and the site of its largest concentration of high-rise buildings, oldest and largest stock exchange, and busiest international and domestic airports. Despite its logistical significance, however, Kenya's traffic-clogged and unabashedly modern capital cannot really be billed as a tourist destination in its own right, but rather as a convenient port of exit and entry, and most leisure travellers spend no longer than a night there at the start and/or end of a safari.

Few visitors would make a point of dwelling longer in Nairobi than travel logistics dictate, but equally those who do set time aside to explore the city will find it has a wealth of worthwhile diversions. Foremost among these are the underrated Nairobi National Park, which offers some great wildlife viewing within sight of the city's skyscrapers, and the informative National Museum and charming Karen Blixen Museum. There is also the vibrant city centre, which – despite a longstanding reputation as a crime hotspot – has cleaned up its act considerably, and is now reasonably safe to explore during office hours, provided you do not venture northeast of Moi Avenue into the more notorious River Road area.

Stallholder at the City Market.

If nothing else, Nairobi has an enviable climate. Set at a breezy elevation of 1,700 metres (5,600ft) little more than 100km (60 miles) south of the equator, it is seldom uncomfortably hot or cold, and the combination of high precipitation and fertile soil ensures that the city's parks and its less densely populated suburbs retain an unexpectedly wonderful lush and leafy feel. Indeed, greater Nairobi is now studded with a growing selection of small suburban hotels whose verdant gardens, interspersed with

Main Attractions

Nairobi National Museum
Nairobi Safari Boardwalk
AFEW Giraffe Centre
Karen Blixen Museum
Nairobi National Park

FACT

Nairobi's population has grown tenfold over the five decades since independence, from around 300,000 in the early 1960s to more than 3.3 million today.

patches of indigenous forest, make it difficult to believe you are actually in one of Africa's largest cities.

Humble origins

Kenya's capital started life in 1899 as an inauspicious railway depot situated at what was then the temporary terminus of the Uganda Railway from Mombasa. It was set in Maasai grazing grounds that bordered on the higher agricultural land of the Kikuyu, and named after a swampy watering hole called Nkare Nairobi *(Place of Cool Water)*. The site was chosen partly for its pleasant climate and partly for its location midway between the coast and Kampala (the Uganda capital), and though the early years were characterised by regular outbreaks of

malaria, exacerbated by a plague epidemic that forced the original town to be burnt and rebuilt, Nairobi officially replaced Mombasa as the colonial capital in 1905.

Commercial enterprise followed the colonial administration along the railway line to Nairobi. Within a short time, the sprawling shanty town had displaced Mombasa as the country's centre of business. Indians – some of them ex-railway workers – helped establish Nairobi's economic preeminence, providing financial services to the fledgling East African governments and railway authorities. The city also attracted wealthy international sportsmen from all over the Western world to hunt in the much-vaunted game lands of upcountry Kenya.

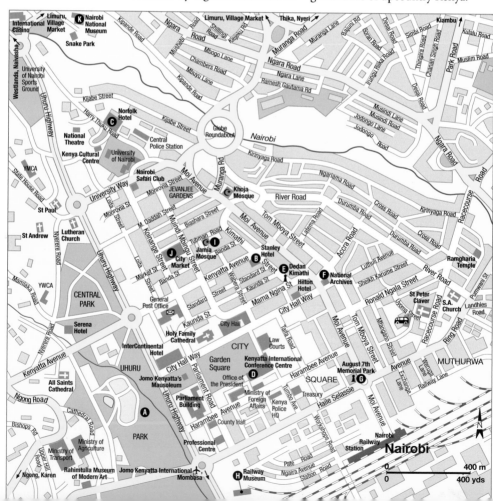

The essential nature of Nairobi has remained cosmopolitan. Today, as ever, settlers from all over Africa, Asia, Europe and North America cohabit here with indigenous Kenyans. By far the most numerous population group is the Kikuyu, which is hardly surprising since Nairobi stands on the fringe of their traditional homelands. Convoys of trucks and pick-ups stream in nightly from the rich farmlands in Kikuyu country, providing the bulk of the fresh produce that sustains the city.

Nairobi's population has grown at a phenomenal rate in the century since the tented labour lines of the founding railway. The city is now crowded with more than 3.3 million people. This rocketing population growth is obviously a major concern to the Government, with its tide of people leaving the land and pouring into the city in the hope of finding the streets paved with gold. For most of them, there is nothing but poverty, since neither employment opportunities nor accommodation could possibly grow fast enough.

Today, Nairobi's trees and gardens are as distinctive a feature as its towering skyline. Yet when the railway arrived, the land that now comprises the city centre had very few trees – as is clearly shown in early photographs. The transformation was thanks to Administrator John Ainsworth, who immediately set about making shaded avenues out of Nairobi's dusty tracks, often planting trees that were not native to Kenya. And some indigenous forest also stands within the city limits, preserved within the **City Park**, bounded by the Limuru and Forest roads just north of the centre. The **Nairobi Arboretum**, just off State House Road, is another significant forest within the close bounds of the city that is being preserved for future generations. The vast recreational **Uhuru Park** Ⓐ is adjacent to the city centre – a distinction for Nairobi in an era of sprawling concrete jungles.

Hard cash from tourism

Visitors are well looked after in Nairobi. The city has had long experience of hospitality, way back to the first station café and the original incarnations of the Stanley and Norfolk Hotels, which opened their doors in 1902 and 1904 respectively. It has long been recognised that Kenya's wildlife attracts tourists and their hard currency. It was from this early concept of tourism that Kenya – and Nairobi in particular – developed a special style in catering for visitors. First this was exclusive, with professional 'white hunters' providing luxury (as well as sport) in the bush. In due course, the hunters were succeeded by today's motorised game-viewing safaris around the country's parks. This long evolution in Kenyan tourism has made Nairobi one of the most traveller-oriented cities in Africa.

Accommodation in the city covers a near-complete range of prices and standards, from do-it-yourself hostels and camping grounds to multinational (and some local) 5-star hotels. For years, the outdoor Thorn Tree Café at the high-rise **Stanley Hotel** Ⓑ

The luxurious Norfolk Hotel.

– now part of the Sarova chain – has been the epicentre of safari-base Nairobi. (The original acacia tree that gave the café its name was cut down when it grew too big, but its replacement is thriving.) The hotel itself has been built and rebuilt since its origins above a shop on the shanty town main street.

The other old-timer of the industry, the **Norfolk Hotel** , now part of the prestigious international Fairmont Group, has also undergone numerous extensions and renovations over the years, but it retains a strong colonial ambience with its green lawns, Tudor-style black beams, tiled rooms, wide balcony and white stucco.

Other international-class hotels in the city centre include the **Serena**, **Hilton** and **InterContinental**, though the latter two now cater primarily to a business clientele rather than to leisure tourists. In part, this is due to a boom in the number of smaller and more characterful hotels that dot the suburbs. These range from swanky Edwardian gems such as **Giraffe Manor** (www.giraffemanor.

com) and **Ngong House** (www.ngonghouse.com) in the southern suburbs, to more low-key under-canvas gems such as **Wildebeest Camp** (www.wildebeestecocamp.com) in Langata and **Nairobi Tented Camp** (www.nairobitentedcamp.com) bordering the national park, to the stylishly funky ethnic-influenced **Tribe Hotel** (www.tribe-hotel.com) opposite the Village Market Mall.

City centre sights

Probably the best-known landmark in the city centre is the **Kenyatta International Convention Centre** (KICC; tel: 020 326 1000; www.kicc.co.ke), a 27-storey round tower whose sober 1960s architectural style has been 'Africanised' with a tumbling riot of flowers and shrubs, and an amphitheatre supposedly designed in the shape of a traditional hut. Standing 105 metres (340ft) tall, the KICC was the highest building in Nairobi when it opened in 1973, and it remained so until the turn-of-the-millennium construction of the 140-metre (455ft) 38-storey Times Tower, which houses the Kenyan Revenue Authority and is

The Great Hall of mammals, Nairobi National Museum.

closed to the general public. In 2015, the latter was outrun by a 93-storey office high-rise, UAP Tower, which is now the tallest structure in Kenya and third in the whole of Africa. Tickets to the top floor of the KICC, which is reached by a speedy lift and offers sensational views over the city centre and beyond, can be bought in the foyer.

In front of the KICC, **Garden Square** (though less green than its name implies) is one of the few open spaces within the city centre proper. Sometimes host to open-air trade shows, the square is overlooked by a handsome sculpture of Jomo Kenyatta, the first president of Kenya. Two blocks away, on Mama Ngina Road, in front of the Nairobi Hilton, a bronze statue dedicated to the freedom fighter **Dedan Kimathi** ⓔ was unveiled on 18 February 2007, to mark the 50th anniversary of his execution as a terrorist by the colonial government. Also overlooked by the Nairobi Hilton, the **National Archives** ⓕ (tel: 020 222 8959; www.archives.go.ke; Mon–Fri 8.30am–4pm, Sat 8.30–1pm; free) on the northeast side of Moi Avenue houses a collection of paintings, books and other historic artefacts in probably the city's most impressive early colonial relics, the former Bank of India building constructed in 1906.

On the corner of Moi and Haile Selassie Avenue, the city's most poignant landmark, the **August 7th Memorial Park** ⓖ (tel: 020 341 062; www.memorialparkkenya.org), marks the site of the former US Embassy destroyed by al-Qaeda suicide bombers on 7 August 1998. At least 218 people died in the bombing, and another 4,000 were injured. The park's centrepiece is a granite memorial wall inscribed with the names of the victims of the bombing. Other features included are a fountain made in the shape of the Yin-Yang sign, a symbol of life, and a sculpture made with debris from the blast.

On the south side of Haile Selassie Avenue, the central **Railway Station** around which Nairobi mushroomed

is still where overnight trains to Mombasa leave. Five minutes' walk to the west, the **Railway Museum** ⓗ (tel: 020 340 049; http://krc.co.ke; daily 8am–5pm) has an interesting display of old steam engines and memorabilia from the East African Railways and Harbours Corporation. These include the coach from where the engineer Charles Lyall was dragged to a grisly death by Tsavo's man-eating lions in 1900, another coach used as a set in the movie *Out of Africa*, and a wonderful collection of beautifully reproduced monochrome photos of places like Voi, Nakuru, Nairobi and Kisumu during the construction of the Uganda railway.

There are many places of worship in the city, of all religions. Perhaps the most beautiful is **Jamia Mosque** ⓘ, designed in the Indian style in 1925. Nearby is the **City Market** ⓙ, between Muindi Mbingu and Koinange streets. The main building contains a colourful jumble of fruit and vegetables, while outside stalls sell a huge range of curios and craftwork from all over Kenya and beyond. It's a great place to go craft shopping thanks to the

TIP

For those with a day to spare in Nairobi, a rewarding excursion runs south along a 100km (60-mile) asphalt road to the fascinating Olorgesailie Prehistoric Site and brooding Lake Magadi, both set in a stretch of the Rift Valley rich in wildlife (see page 157).

Pots and paintings for sale in the City Market.

TIP

Visitors of a literary persuasion might be tempted to drive the 45km (25 miles) from Nairobi to the once rustic town immortalised in Elspeth Huxley's novelistic account of her childhood *The Flame Trees of Thika*. Be warned, however, that Thika today is more aptly summarised in its twin mottos: 'Your Industrial Town' and 'The Birmingham of Kenya'.

hassle-free atmosphere, and there are often some genuine bargains to be had, assuming you are prepared to haggle.

Nairobi National Museum

Museum Hill, on the northern outskirts of the city central, is the site of the **Nairobi National Museum** (tel: 020 374 2131; www.museums.or.ke; daily 8.30am–5.30pm), which reopened in 2008 following a long period of closure for renovations. Founded in 1910, it is one of the oldest museums in East Africa, and it houses some truly fascinating artefacts, notably a pair of ivory ceremonial Siwa Horns crafted on Pate Island in 1688, several of Joy Adamson's famous ethnographic paintings and a collection of 700 hominid fossils, only a few of which are actually on display. An extensive zoological collection includes a life-size replica of the famous elephant Ahmed – the largest tusker in Kenya at the time of independence, and accorded special protection by President Jomo Kenyatta – along with a collection of stuffed oddities that are seldom seen in the flesh, for instance

The Nairobi Railway Museum.

aardvark, giant forest hog and okapi (a relative of the giraffe endemic to the Congo). If stuffed animals aren't your thing, be warned that the adjacent **Snake Park** (daily 8.30am–5.30pm) is also likely to feel somewhat dispiriting to anybody who enjoys seeing animals alive and unfettered.

Outside the centre

Spectator sports in Nairobi include polo, showjumping, rugby, football (soccer), hockey, athletics, boxing and cricket. Horse racing at the **Ngong Road Racecourse** ❶ is meticulously organised by the Jockey Club of Kenya (meetings most Sundays of the year; www.jockeyclubofkenya.com) and even if you are down with the bookies, the superb garden setting of the course more than compensates. As for participant sports, there are numerous swimming pools, facilities to play tennis or squash, and nine 18-hole golf courses in and around the city. Special interests are also catered for, from skindiving, go-carting, water sliding and sailing to tenpin bowling and Scottish country dancing.

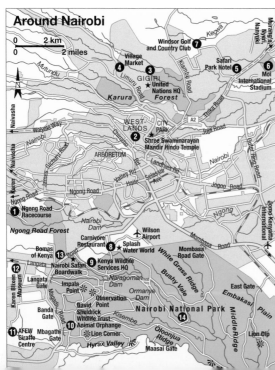

Heading five to twenty minutes (depending on the traffic) northwest of the city centre you reach the suburb of **Westlands ❷**, which includes three main shopping malls (one of which was attacked in 2013 by Al-Shabaab militants) and a large assortment of shops and restaurants run by people of many different nationalities. On Forest Road (just off Limuru Road) is Africa's first traditional Hindu Temple, **Shree Swaminarayan Mandir**, with its incredibly carved wooden and stone domes, ceilings, pillars, walls and windows, the result of over 1 million man-hours of craftsmanship. On the Limuru Road, beyond Muthaiga, is **Gigiri ❸**, the US$30-million complex that houses the United Nations Environmental Programme and other UN organisations (tel: 20 762 2034; http://visitors.unon.org; guided tours Mon–Thu 9am–2pm, Fri 9am–noon) – the first world headquarters of the United Nations to be established in a developing country.

Further north is the **Village Market ❹** (www.villagemarket-kenya.com), approximately 15 minutes from the city. It contains attractions such as water slides, mini golf, tenpin bowling and four cinemas, as well as a great variety of food stalls in an atmospheric open-air food court, restaurants, a nightclub and, of course, shops and a supermarket. Every Friday, the very popular open-air **Maasai Market** is held in one of the parking areas near the children's playground.

Heading north out of Nairobi on the Thika Road, at Kasarani, is the **Safari Park Hotel ❺** (www.safaripark -hotel.com), about a 15-minute drive from the city centre. It offers diverse bars and restaurants, houses a casino and is located in beautiful grounds. Across from this hotel, the **Moi International Stadium ❻**, built in 1987 for the All Africa Games (but since renovated) it can accommodate up to 60,000 people and is the venue for many international sporting events, including most home matches played by the national football team. Between the Thika Road and the Kiambu Road, about 20 minutes' drive from the centre, is the **Windsor Golf and Country Club ❼** (www.windsorgolfresort.com), a peaceful resort built in beautifully

A guided tour of the historic Parliament Building (any day of the week) can be arranged by telephoning the office of the Chief Sergeant-at-Arms, on 020 221 291.

AFEW Giraffe Centre.

laid-out grounds, with one of the finest golf courses in East Africa.

Going south of the city, just outside town on the Langata Road past the domestic Wilson Airport, is the famous **Carnivore Restaurant** ❽ and, next door, the **Splash Water World** (tel: 020 240 5799; www.splash.co.ke; Wed–Sun 10am–5.30pm) with its great water slides and vast swimming pools. Around the corner a **go-cart track** provides more thrills and spills.

The **Kenya Wildlife Services** (**KWS**) **Headquarters** ❾ (tel: 020 600 2345; www.kws.go.ke) is five minutes further up Langata Road, at the main entrance to Nairobi National Park (see page 149). Just inside the park entrance, the uninspiring **Nairobi Animal Orphanage** (daily 9am–6pm) is the oldest such institution in Kenya, and over the years it has evidently morphed into something more like a zoo, one whose inhabitants mostly live in rather cramped conditions. Altogether more worthwhile, and situated immediately outside the national park entrance, is the **Nairobi Safari Boardwalk** (daily 9am–6pm), which consists of a long footpath, in parts elevated to be a wooden boardwalk, between large enclosures whose inhabitants include lion, cheetah, leopard, white rhino, buffalo and bongo antelope. Part of the walk also runs through an unfenced area of natural forest where you may well encounter some very habituated monkeys and baboons, as well as duiker and other small forest inhabitants.

Also well worth a visit is the world-renowned **David Sheldrick Wildlife Trust Animal Orphanage** ❿ (tel: 020 230 1396; www.sheldrickwildlifetrust.org; daily 11am–noon) situated in a compound in the west corner of the park, just inside the Mbagathi Gate on Magadi Road. Sheldrick was the founder-warden of the Tsavo National Park, and here his widow Daphne cares for orphaned elephants and rhinoceroses.

Further out, on the Gogo Falls Road about 30 minutes southwest of town, the **AFEW Giraffe Centre** ⓫, or African Fund for Endangered Wildlife, (tel: 020 807 0804; www.giraffecenter.org; daily 9am–5pm) was founded in 1979 by Jock and Betty Leslie-Melville as a private sanctuary to breed Rothschild's giraffe, a five-horned race that had become – and still is – endangered in the wild. The breeding program here has allowed populations of Rothschild's giraffe to be established similar to that of Lake Nakuru National Park and the Soysambu, and a breeding group of around a dozen individuals is held on site. It's popular with children, who can feed specially formulated pellets to these serene giants from a raised observation platform. Other activities include a self-guided bird walk in an adjoining patch of natural forest, and wildlife videos and lectures in the auditorium.

Returning to Langata South Road, turn left and continue for another five minutes or so, until you get to Karen Road, where you turn left and go past **Karen Country Club** (www.karencountryclub.org) for about 3km (1.5 miles) to the **Karen Blixen Museum** ⓬ (tel: 020 800 2139, 0736 919 321; www.museums.or.ke; Mon–Sat 7.30am–5.30pm). This

Karen Blixen's house.

comprises Karen Blixen's old house, complete with period furnishings and memorabilia both of her time in Kenya and of the shooting of the film *Out of Africa*, and it is set within a charming garden that commands a lovely view of the Ngong Hills. The museum staff take visitors on guided tours of the house and grounds, and explain how Blixen managed the coffee plantation.

Opposite Magadi Road, near the entrance to the Nairobi National Park, the **Bomas of Kenya** ⓭ (tel: 020 806 8400; www.bomasofkenya.co.ke; performances Mon–Fri at 2.30pm and Sat–Sun at 3.30pm) is a permanent exhibition of traditional homesteads (or *bomas*) representing various Kenyan cultures. The main event of the day, held over about 1.5 hours every afternoon, is a multicultural drumming, dancing and acrobatic display that represents a cross section of traditional Kenyan cultures, performed by a troupe of professional dancers that change costumes for each different dance. Though a little contrived, it is a dynamic and exciting performance, marred only by the warehouse acoustics of the tall roofed auditorium.

Nairobi National Park

The capital's most-visited tourist attraction is the 117-sq-km (45-sq-mile) **Nairobi National Park** ⓮ (tel: 020 600 2345; www.kws.go.ke; daily 6am–6pm), which borders the southeastern suburbs of the city. This remarkable tract of open grassland and acacia savannah is fenced on the city side, in order to protect residents of the capital from regular visitors by lions and other potentially dangerous beasts, but it remains unfenced to the south, allowing the wildlife to move freely between the national park and the bordering Athi Plains.

The park exists because Nairobi stands in an area that once supported prodigious herds of wildlife, comparable in number to the legendary Mara-Serengeti to the southwest. Animals were so prolific in the early days that nightwatchmen along Nairobi's main thoroughfare (then Station Road, now Moi Avenue) used to be protected within lock-up sentry boxes. A soldier of the time, Col. Richard Meinertzhagen, recalled at least two race meetings being disrupted by rhinos.

KAREN BLIXEN IN KENYA

The leafy Nairobi suburb of Karen is named after its most famous former resident, the Danish author Karen Blixen (1885–1962), subject of the Oscar-winning movie *Out Of Africa*, starring Meryl Streep. Born Karen Dinesen, she married her second cousin Baron Bror von Blixen-Finecke in 1913 and a year later the couple moved to Kenya, where they established a coffee plantation in the forested southern outskirts of Nairobi (whose population was then a mere 15,000).

The couple separated in 1921 due to the Baron's infidelities, and divorced in 1925, with Karen holding onto the plantation and its farmhouse. It was at around this time that Karen became involved with the British hunter Denys Finch Hatton (played by Robert Redford in the movie), who used her farm as his base until 1931, when he fatally crashed his *Gypsy Moth* shortly after take-off at Voi, near present-day Tsavo East.

It's uncertain to what extent the death of her long-term lover influenced Blixen's near-simultaneous decision to sell her struggling plantation to a residential developer. But sell it she did, returning to Denmark to embark on a literary career under the pen name Isak Dinesen. Her most famous work, published in 1937, is *Out Of Africa*, the account of her time in Kenya on which the film was based. Blixen's old farmhouse now houses the Karen Blixen Museum, a popular tourist attraction.

TIP

Nairobi National Park is at its best between July and August, when its permanent water is the target of a seasonal migration of wildebeest, zebra and gazelle from the dry Athi Plains.

The populace may not have wholly welcomed the presence of wild animals in the centre of town, but they seem to have recognised the cachet of having the wildlife around. Most of the Athi Plains were sold and settled, but a large area to the southwest of town was reserved as Nairobi Commonage. A few Somali herdsmen and their families were allowed to live there (as a reward for military service rendered to the Crown), but otherwise the land was left wild. During both world wars the Commonage was taken over as a weapons range, and the wildlife accordingly took a hammering. But in 1945 the land was gazetted a national park – the first in Kenya.

Since then, buffalo and rhino have been reintroduced, so that the full range of the area's original fauna has been reassembled, with the notable exception of elephant. Today, Nairobi National Park is one of the best places in Kenya to see white rhino, and lion and cheetah are also likely to be encountered stalking the plains. Other wildlife includes eland, impala, Coke's hartebeest, gazelle, zebra, giraffe and more than 400 species of birds, ranging from colourful weavers and rollers to bulky vultures and prim secretary birds, and it is a good place to seek the localised northern pied babbler. In order to see a good range of wildlife, however, you usually need to dedicate a few hours to the park, ideally starting at 6am, when the entrance gates open and animals are most active, rather than waiting for the more normal post-breakfast departure.

A near constant feature of Nairobi National Park is the distinctive skyline of the city centre, and more so perhaps the burgeoning string of high-rises that line the main road between Wilson and Jomo Kenyatta Airports. Depending on how you look at it, these prominent urban landmarks form a disturbing and unsightly reminder of 21st century human pre-eminence, or pay reassuring testament to the tenacity of large wildlife within roaring distance of one of sub-Saharan Africa's largest cities. Either way, Nairobi is unique among African capitals in being fringed by a partially unfenced national park that offers truly world-class game viewing.

Coke's Hartebeest or Kongoni, Nairobi National Park.

Kikuyu

Kenya's most populous ethnic group accounts for about 22 percent of the national population, and includes such renowned international figures as the late environmentalist Wangari Maathai.

About 40 percent of the population of Nairobi are Kikuyu (or Gikuyu), a Bantu-speaking people who number some 10 million in total, making them the largest of all Kenya's ethnic groups. The ancestors of the Kikuyu migrated to their present homeland in Kenya's Central Province from Meru and Tharaka some 400 years ago. The Kikuyu burned and cleared the dense forests of their new home by purchase, blood-brotherhood and intermarriage.

Tribal organisation is based on the family, with several families living together to form a homestead. A Kikuyu community is traditionally governed by a council of elders *(kiama)*, a select few of whom are members of the secret council known as *njama*.

Cattle, formerly a symbol of social status and wealth, also provided hides for bedding, sandals and carrying straps. Sheep and goats are still used for religious sacrifices. Permanent crops such as bananas, sugar cane, cassava and yams, together with beans, millet, maize, sweet potatoes, a variety of vegetables and black beans form the staple diet.

Kikuyu crafts include making pots for cooking, carrying and storage. Pots were also a major item of barter in pre-colonial days. The Kikuyu weave baskets *(kiondo)* from a variety of fibres, originally obtained from the bark of shrubs, now of sisal or synthetic thread. Arrowheads, spears, swords, cowbells and rattles were made by blacksmiths, who were believed to have magical abilities. The Kikuyu traded livestock, agricultural produce and iron implements, tobacco, salt and ochre at local markets, and maintained trading contacts with the Maasai, Kamba and Okiek.

A confrontation occurred in the late 1920s between Kikuyu tribal leaders and the European missionaries over the socio-religious rite of clitoridectomy of girls. (Male youths are also circumcised when they join the ranks of the warriors.) Disaffection with the missionaries led to the establishment of the Kikuyu Independent Schools Association and the Kikuyu Karing'a (Pure) Educational Association, out of which evolved the African Pentecostal Church and African Orthodox Church – both based on the Old Testament, which nowhere condemns female circumcision.

The Kikuyu Association

The Kikuyu adapted to the challenge of Western culture, perhaps better than any other ethnic group in East Africa. They displayed a political awareness that resulted, in 1920, in the formation of the Kikuyu Association. Forced labour, land expropriation and the lack of public services and educational opportunities were to remain the main unresolved grievances until the end of the colonial era.

Since independence, progressive Kikuyu farmers have bought most of the former 'White Highlands' farmlands and adopted modern agricultural practices, benefiting from the upgrading of their livestock, the accessible markets of Nairobi and a growing export trade. They have emerged as Kenya's major farming community, and are also very active in business and commerce throughout the country.

Among the most influential Kenyans in recent Kenyan history are the former President Jomo Kenyatta and his son and incumbent Uhuru Kenyatta. The outspoken Kikuyu environmentalist Wangari Maathai, who died in September 2011, became the first African woman to receive the Nobel Peace Prize in 2004. Other famous Kenyans of Kikuyu descent include the marathon runners Douglas Wakiihuri and the late Samuel Wanjiru, and the novelist Ngugi wa Thiongo.

Kikuyu warrior.

Defassa waterbuck, Crescent Island Game Sanctuary on Lake Naivasha.

Lesser Flamingos on Lake Bogoria.

THE RIFT VALLEY LAKES

The largest split in the earth's crust runs through Kenya, hemmed in by a kilometre-high escarpment and studded with dormant volcanoes and freshwater and soda lakes.

Nairobi

The **Great Rift Valley**, the world's largest terrestrial geographic feature, measures around 6,000km (3,728 miles) from north to south, equivalent to roughly one-seventh of the earth's circumference. The valley started to form some 20 million years ago, when tectonic activity split Africa into two separate incipient landmasses, referred to by geologists as the Somali and Nubian plates.

The main eastern Rift Valley runs from the Jordan Valley in the north, takes in the whole of the Red Sea, sheers through Eritrea, Ethiopia, Kenya, Tanzania and Malawi, and finally reaches the sea near the Zambezi Delta. A separate western arm starts in the Sudanese Nile Valley, then runs southward along the Congolese border of Uganda, Rwanda, Burundi and Tanzania to join the main Rift close to the northern tip of Lake Nyasa-Malawi.

In places, the walls of the Rift rise little more than 30 metres (100ft) above the valley floor. Elsewhere, steep cliffs rise sharply to 1,200 metres (4,000ft) above the floor, but nowhere is the Rift more sharply defined than where it cuts through the highlands of Kenya. In addition to the towering walls that contain it, the base of the Kenyan Rift Valley is studded with steaming geysers and dormant volcanoes, relics of the violent tectonic activity that is also responsible for such montane giants as Kilimanjaro, Mount Kenya and Elgon.

Also scattered along the length of the Kenyan Rift is a chain of seven lakes. These are unusual in that not a single one of them has an obvious outflow. Water pours in from the rainfall on the surrounding land and more or less stays there in the shallow pans. While a high rate of evaporation keeps the levels fairly constant, it also causes an accumulation of salts and minerals in

Main Attractions
Lake Naivasha
Hell's Gate National Park
Soysambu Conservancy
Lake Nakuru National Park
Lake Bogoria National
    Reserve
Lake Baringo

Great White Pelicans, Lake Nakuru National Park.

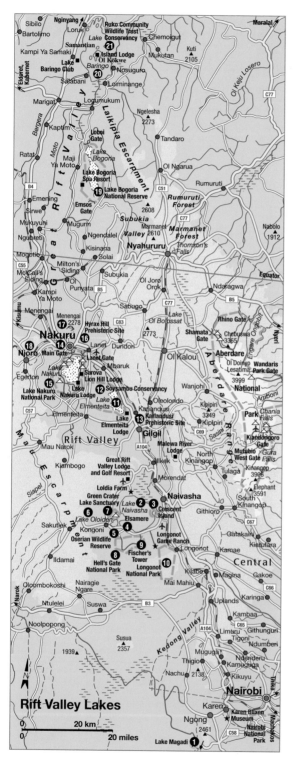

Rift Valley Lakes

0 ___ 20 km
0 ___ 20 miles

the waters of the lake. As a result, all but two of the Rift Valley lakes are so saline that they are virtually undrinkable.

Magadi

The most alkaline of all these lakes is **Magadi ❶**, in the extreme south of the country, but easily accessible from Nairobi. The drive, on a good 110km (68 miles) road that climbs up to the southern shoulder of the Ngong Hills before dropping precipitously into the Rift, takes little over an hour.

The descent to the valley close to Magadi occurs in stages, down scarp after steep scarp, through a harsh, stark landscape that is increasingly dry and hot as the altitude falls. At the end of the road, shimmering in temperatures above 38°C (100°F) in the shade, is Lake Magadi itself. At first glance, the term 'lake' seems a misnomer since there is little water evident. The lake-bed appears white; in fact, it's an enormous pan of trona – an agglomeration of mixed salts – over 100 sq km (40 sq miles) in extent.

Around the periphery is a series of hot springs, highly charged with salts and bubbling out of the ground at temperatures of about 45°C (113°F). They flow into the huge evaporation pan, where the sun and searing winds leave nothing but the thick white deposits of sludge. But in this is an almost endless source of potash, salt and related chemicals which have been exploited by the Magadi Soda Company since before World War I – Kenya's oldest mining venture, with a company township built up on a peninsula into the lake.

At the far southern end of Lake Magadi, where the largest springs occur, is an area of open water. Although undrinkable, it produces a wealth of microscopic aquatic life, which in turn, attracts many water birds and birdwatchers. Many African species are permanently on show, including flamingos, and the lake also hosts waders and many others escaping the winter in Europe.

En route to Magadi, it is well worth stopping at **Olorgesailie Prehistoric Site** (www.museums.or.ke; daily 8am–6pm), which lies 65km (40 miles) south of Nairobi, in an arid but scenic stretch of Maasailand where giraffe, gerenuk and a plethora of colourful dry-country birds are still common. The site museum displays fossils of extinct species of giant elephant and hippo, which lived here 500,000 years ago, when the site overlooked a large shallow lake, along with a stash of Acheulean stone-age tools used by *Homo erectus* hunter-gatherers that once roamed the area.

Lake Naivasha

The next lake along the Rift is **Naivasha ❷**, which lies about 100km (62 miles) north of Magadi as the crow flies, but is almost twice that distance by road, returning to Nairobi then travelling for about 80km (50 miles) northwest along the main road towards Kisumu. This road snakes down the eastern Rift Valley wall, following an ancient elephant trail, and offering a magnificent view of the lake and the extinct volcanoes Suswa and Longonot as you descend to the valley floor, which stands at about 1,890 metres (6,200ft) above sea level.

Naivasha's water level has fluctuated a great deal over the years, reaching its lowest recorded points in the 1890s, mid-1940s and late 1980s, with its average depth decreasing to an all-time low of 60cm (2ft) in 1945. Normally, however, it has an average depth of around 6 metres (20ft), and a surface area of around 140 sq km (53 sq miles).

An oddity characterises Lake Naivasha: although it has no visible outlet, it is one of the two freshwater lakes in the Rift (Baringo is the other). Many theories have been put forward to explain the phenomenon, but none are entirely satisfactory. The most obvious is that there must be massive underground seepage through the lake flow – a diffused outflow that takes the place of a conventional discharging river. Whatever the reason, Naivasha water is indeed fresh, drinkable, abundant and excellent for irrigating the surrounding fertile volcanic soils. Not surprisingly, the lake is ringed by agricultural land, from which spring many tons of vegetables and flowers harvested for both the Nairobi and overseas markets.

Although it is not formally protected, and has suffered negatively from pesticides associated with the flower industry as well as the introduction of invasive fish (mostly carp) and plant species, Naivasha still supports a fair amount of wildlife, notably large numbers of giraffe and zebra, and much of it is concentrated in private sanctuaries, though the likes of hippo might be seen anywhere on the lakeshore, and the birdlife is astounding. Accessible by boat from the southern shore, **Crescent Island ❸** (tel: 050 202 1030; www.crescent island.co; daily 8am–6pm), the partial rim of a collapsed volcanic caldera whose submerged floor forms the deepest part of the lake, is home to

Family of hippos in Lake Naivasha.

FACT

In the 1940s, Lake Naivasha Country Club was Kenya's international air terminal: British Overseas Airways flying boats landed on the lake on their way from Cairo to Cape Town.

small numbers of giraffe, buffalo and waterbuck, and can be explored freely on foot. Among the resident birds here are African fish eagle, osprey, African jacana, and a variety of waders and herons. Except when the lake is very high, the easiest access is along a causeway connecting the island to Sanctuary Farm, but boat trips can also be arranged through any lakeshore hotel.

Another popular site on the southern lakeshore, **Elsamere** (tel: 050 202 1055; www.elsamere.com; daily 9am–6pm) was the home of lion aficionado Joy Adamson from 1966 until her death in 1980, and is named after her most famous felid companion Elsa (of *Born Free* fame). Now a Field Study Centre, Elsamere is also maintained as a museum dedicated to the writings and paintings of its former inhabitant, as well as a low-key guesthouse famed for its expansive afternoon teas. The lakeshore lawn, shaded by tall fever trees, attracts a multitude of colourful birds and is regularly visited by a troop of black-and-white colobus monkeys.

Immediately west of the lake, the most focussed wildlife experience in the vicinity of Naivasha is offered at the private 100-sq-km (38-sq-mile) **Oserian Wildlife Reserve** , where two exclusive lodges (www.chuisafari collection.com) offer package stays including guided game drives in an area frequented by leopard, cheetah, buffalo and introduced white rhinoceros, along with the very localised grey-crested helmet-shrike.

Lake Olioden

Continuing past the entrance to Oserian, the asphalt road terminates at the small village of Kongoni, a junction village from where a left fork leads along a rough and little-used back route to Narok and the Maasai Mara, while a curve to the right takes you around the western side of Lake Naivasha. A bare 500 metres/yds along the latter road, it passes **Lake Olioden** , a small circular soda lake separated from Naivasha by a narrow spit of wooded land. Despite its small size, Olioden is home to an estimated 300 hippos, while giraffe and various antelope are regularly seen along the shore. The most alluring feature of the so-called little lake, however, are spectacular seasonal concentrations of lesser flamingo, with more than 10,000 birds sometimes in attendance, their pink coloration contrasting with yellow bark and green leaves of the surrounding fever trees. There's no charge to visit the lake, and you can get pretty close to the birds on foot, but a community project also now offers boat trips for close up views of the birdlife and hippos.

About 5km (3 miles) drive further north, the private **Green Crater Lake Sanctuary** (http://craterlakecamp. com) is centred upon an attractive tented camp overlooking the scenic but ultra-alkaline Songasoi Crater Lake, which attracts large flocks of lesser flamingo over June to August, and also supports a varied selection of mammals, ranging from the

Mount Longonot.

conspicuous black-and-white colobus monkey to the more secretive leopard and buffalo. Guided walks, horseback excursions and night drives are all on offer here.

Flamingo facts and fancy

Kenya's most alluring avian attraction is the flamingos associated with the soda lakes of the Great Rift Valley, where they sometimes amass in their millions. Two species are recognised, the scarcer greater flamingo *Phoenicopterus ruber* and the pinker lesser flamingo *Phoenicopterus minor*, and they are often seen together, sifting the algae that forms their main diet through filters in their downturned bills. These proverbial odd birds have exerted a fascination over humans for thousand of years: flamingo paintings thought to be 7,000 years old adorn a cave in Mediterranean Europe, and the ancient Egyptians used them as a hieroglyph for the colour red. Indeed, it has been suggested that the folkloric phoenix is based on confused reports of flamingos breeding in the ash-strewn volcanic Natron area of Tanzania.

Hell's Gate and Longonot

Two scenic national parks whose landscapes were shaped by the violent volcanic activity associated with the formation of the Rift Valley lie within easy day tripping distance of Lake Naivasha. The more popular of these is the 68-sq-km (27-sq-mile) **Hell's Gate National Park** ❽ (tel: 050 50407, 0770 070 405; www.kws.go.ke; daily 6am–7pm), which was gazetted in 1984 and whose main entrance gate lies only 5km (3 miles) south of the lake shore.

The park's centrepiece is the impressive Hell's Gate Gorge, a riverine gorge hemmed in by spectacular burnished cliffs that stand about 120 metres (400ft) tall. Close to the entrance is **Fischer's Tower** ❾, a lone 25-metre (82ft) -high rock outcrop. Powerful geysers, which gave the park its name, have been harnessed with foreign aid

to generate electricity. The geothermal electricity project has been carefully executed so that it does not affect the beauty of the park.

Hell's Gate supports a wide variety of cliff-nesting raptors, including Verreaux's eagle, Egyptian vulture, Rüppell's vulture and augur buzzard. Sadly, however, the resident lammergeiers that once bred here vanished some time in the 1970s, and two post-millennial attempts to reintroduce these magnificent birds have not met with long-term success. Other cliff dwelling wildlife includes the klipspringer and rock hyrax.

The main reason for Hell's Gate's popularity with active travellers is that it is one of the few savannah reserves in East Africa where it is permitted to walk or cycle unguided, despite the potential presence of dangerous wildlife. This can be a thrilling experience, and while most of the wildlife here is relatively placed – common species include Thomson's gazelle, Grant's gazelle, eland, wildebeest, giraffe and zebra – there is also a chance of encountering cheetah or

TIP

Since Hell's Gate is one of the few national parks in Kenya where it is permitted to explore on foot, it is a favourite with picnickers, hikers and rock climbers.

Burchell's zebra, Hell's Gate National Park.

buffalo, and lion and elephant pass through upon occasion.

To the southeast of Hell's Gate is the **Longonot National Park** ❿ (tel: 050 50255; www.kws.go.ke; daily 6am–6pm), access to which is from the 'Old Naivasha Road' towards Nairobi. The young volcano rises to 2,776 meters (9,105ft) above sea level, and last erupted in the 1860s. Mount Longonot offers a wide range of attractions for those who are keen on activity holidays, including hiking, rock climbing and birdwatching. The ascent to the spectacular crater rim usually takes up to two hours, and there is no shade along the way, so leave early to avoid exposure to the midday sun. It is possible to walk around the crater rim in three to four hours. There is also a path to the crater floor, though this is reputedly unsafe.

Highland lakes

From Naivasha, you need only drive a further 80km (50 miles) up the Kisumu Highway to view two more lakes situated at about the same altitude in the highland part of the Rift. Both are highly saline, and – like

Defassa waterbuck, Soysambu Conservancy.

Naivasha – they vary enormously in depth and extent, sometimes disappearing altogether, during which time they are reduced to white salt flats, swirling with dust devils.

The first, **Lake Elmenteita** ⓫, about 40km (25 miles) from Naivasha, is one of the stop-off points for millions of flamingos en route to Magadi, Nakuru or Lake Natron in Tanzania. Elmenteita is also now the centrepiece of the **Soysambu Conservancy** ⓬ (tel: 071 123 5039; www.soysambuconservancy.org; no day visitors), a scenic 250-sq-km (90-sq-mile) private reserve set on private land whose western border is shared with Lake Nakuru National Park. Though rather sparsely populated with wildlife by Kenyan wildlife, the conservancy hosts plenty of buffalo and antelope, and it provides an important refuge to the endangered Rothschild's giraffe. The lake itself is often frequented by large aggregations of flamingo, along with large numbers of pink-backed and great white pelican, and a plethora of other water birds. Wildlife numbers are likely to be boosted if plans to break down the fence with Lake Nakuru ever come to fruition.

Not far from Elmenteita, bordering the small town of Gilgil, the **Kariandusi Prehistoric Site** ⓭ (www.museums.or.ke; daily 9.30am–6pm) was excavated by Louis Leakey between 1928 and 1931, and has yielded so many Stone Age tools – some made from glassy obsidian sourced at nearby Mount Eburu – that it is believed to have been a kind of factory for tool production around 700,000 years ago.

Another 40km (25 miles) to the northwest, **Nakuru** ⓮ is an important agricultural and administrative centre whose workaday appearance belies its status as the fourth-largest town in Kenya, supporting a population estimated at 300,000. The town is at its best in November, when the jacarandas that line its streets come into purple bloom, but its only real point of interest is the large daily market in front of the railway station.

Far more alluring than Nakuru town is the bordering **Lake Nakuru National Park** ⓯ (tel: 020 267 1686; www.kws.go.ke; daily 6am–6pm), which was created in 1961 as a bird sanctuary centred upon the eponymous lake, an alkaline body of variable proportions that dried up completely in the mid-1950s, when strong daily winds swept up the dust into a dense white soda smog which blew 65km (40 miles) up the Rift Valley.

The main attraction of Lake Nakuru is the immense flocks of greater and lesser flamingo that thrive on the blue-green algae and diatoms nurtured by its alkaline water. Indeed, the water here is so algae-rich that the birds assemble in flocks of up to 2 million, creating a roseate mass of immense beauty along the shorelines. In addition to flamingos, another 400 bird species have been recorded here altogether, including great numbers of pelican along the southern and eastern shores.

The original national park comprised only the lake and its immediate surroundings, including the escarpment at its western side known as **Baboon Cliffs**, but it was later extended to include an extensive area of savannah to the south. The entire area – about 200 sq km (80 sq miles) – has now been fenced in to protect the introduced endangered animals, and also to prevent dangerous wildlife from roaming into the adjacent town. Today, Lake Nakuru is the only public reserve in Kenya where rhinos – both black and white – are readily seen, and it also supports a herd of the rare Rothschild's giraffe, which was introduced in 1977. Other mammals include buffalo, lion, leopard and hyena, and it is the best place in Kenya to see Bohor reedbuck and Defassa waterbuck. Also set within the park, on the cliffs to the east of the lake, is Kenya's finest euphorbia forest, a vast stand of these odd looking, tree-sized, cactus-like succulents.

Two other sites of interest lie close to Nakuru. **Hyrax Hill Prehistoric Site** ⓰ (tel: 051 221 7175; www.museums.

View from baboon cliff, Lake Nakuru National Park.

or.ke; daily 9.30am–6pm), 4km out of town, has yielded some of the oldest Iron Age artefacts known from East Africa, and several of the surrounding rocks are adorned with hand-carved Bao games of unknown antiquity. Slightly further afield, the 2,278-metre (7,474ft) **Mount Menengai** is a dormant volcano whose name translates from Maasai to mean 'Place of Demons'. The mountain encloses one of the world's largest nested calderas, with an average diameter of 8km (5 miles), and steam still hisses through cracks in the solidified lava.

Njoro

Only 18km (11 miles) southwest of Nakuru, tiny **Njoro** ⑱ comes across as rather undistinguished on first inspection, but it is actually the older of the two towns, though its bizarrely wide roads are the only obvious clue that it was founded in the late 19th century as a potential capital of the East African Protectorate. Njoro is also where the original Lord Delamere first settled in Kenya in 1904, prior to establishing his extant estate around Elmenteita.

Relics of its early days include the Njoro Golf Club (day members welcome, and equipment can be rented), an 18-hole course that was founded by railway workers alongside the Njoro River in 1903, and whose clubhouse is adorned with old monochrome photographs of the British Royal family and early settlers. Further out of town lies the 52-room Egerton Castle, built by Lord Egerton, a keen hunter and photographer who first came to Kenya in the 1920s and established the highly regarded Egerton Agricultural College about 5km (3 miles) from Njoro. Although the soon-to-be-renovated property is now just a shadow of its former glory, its well-manicured lawn is great for relaxation. A good base for exploring this forgotten corner of Kenya is Kembu Cottages (http://kembu cottages.com), a family run operation set on a hilly working farm about 10 minutes' drive away.

Bogoria and Baringo

To the north of Nakuru, the land falls away from the highlands. At this point, the Kisumu Highway veers to the west

Lesser Flamingos, Lake Bogoria National Reserve.

to break out of the Rift, but the way to the next valley lake, **Bogoria**, is straight on to the north. Formerly known as Lake Hannington (after a missionary bishop murdered in Uganda in the 19th century). Bogoria is a slender stretch of blue water under towering cliffs, like a splinter sticking into the northern foot of the highlands.

This shallow soda lake is protected within the 110-sq-km (44-sq-mile) **Lake Bogoria National Reserve ⑲** (daily 6am–7pm), gazetted in 1973 as a sanctuary for its resident greater kudu, an antelope that has been rare in most parts of Kenya since the rinderpest epidemic of the 1890s. Kudus are seldom seen here by visitors, since they live mainly on the western slopes of the Laikipia Escarpment, which towers over the near-inaccessible eastern shore. However, Bogoria does boast two other compelling attractions. The first are the large flocks of flamingo that tend to congregate here most profusely when conditions at Lake Nakuru are unsuited to them. The second are the spectacular sulphuric geysers that erupt steaming from the bowels of the earth at Loburu, feeding a network of scalding multihued channels that drain into the lake.

No one who travels a few more kilometres north from here misses **Lake Baringo ⑳**, the second freshwater body in the Rift, with a setting below the Laikipia Escarpment reminiscent of Bogoria. Baringo is larger than Naivasha at 150 sq km (58 sq miles), and it poses the same question: how, with no outlet, does the water stay fresh? Baringo is home to great numbers of birds, crocodiles and hippos, which can be seen in the evenings grazing on the lawns of the lakeshore hotels, or by arranging a boat trip to Ol Kokwe Island, a dormant volcanic peak in the heart of the lake.

Although there isn't a lot of terrestrial wildlife to be seen around Baringo, the lake and its environs are renowned among ornithologists for supporting in excess of 500 species of birds. A wide variety of water-associated species can be taken for granted, but the grounds of the lakeshore hotels also support a profusion of woodland birds. For rarity hunters, the place to head for is the low basaltic escarpment 2km (1.2 miles) west of the lakeshore, where northern specials such as Hemprich's hornbill, white-crested turaco and bristle-crowned starling are regular.

The latest significant development at Baringo is the setting aside of a 100-sq-km (38-sq-mile) conservancy by **the Ruko Wildlife Trust ㉑** (http://rukokenya.org), a community project involving the local Pokot and Njemps people. The centrepiece of this new reserve is Longichoro Island and the abutting wetlands, which are home to a profusion of birds including a breeding colony of various herons and cormorants. Restocking of the reserve started in earnest in 2011, when eight Rothschild's giraffes – also known as Baringo Giraffe, though they have been extinct in the vicinity of the lake for 70 years –were transported to Longichoro from Soysambu by boat. Now they roam the conservancy freely.

African darter, Lake Baringo.

THE MAASAI MARA

The Mara is a natural continuation of the famous Serengeti Plain: undulating grassland, dramatic escarpments, beautiful acacia forests – and the greatest wildlife show on earth.

Extending over 1,510 sq km (580 sq miles) abutting the Tanzania border, the Maasai Mara National Reserve is one of the most famous protected areas in Africa, and it indisputably ranks among the continent's Top Five wildlife viewing destinations. Used as a backdrop to some of the most memorable scenes in the movie *Out of Africa*, the reserve has more recently been beamed across television screens globally as the setting for the acclaimed BBC series *Big Cat Diaries*, whose felid stars – including the famous lions of the Marsh Pride – are often encountered in person in the central plains between the rivers Mara and Talek. Indeed, few reserves anywhere in Africa offer such reliable cat sightings as the Mara: its trademark handsome blond-maned lions are encountered on most game drives, and most people spending three days or longer in the reserve will see leopard and cheetah.

But there is more to the Mara than big cats. Indeed, few places in Africa support such a profusion of wildlife. Elephant herds march across the savannah in purposeful processions, tusks glowing white in the tropical sun. Panicked warthogs scurry away, tails comically erect, at the approach of a vehicle. Topis, with their long mournful faces, stand sentinel on termite mounds, or sunbathe with

their chins resting lazily on the ground. Regally horned impalas mill between herds of gazelle, while groups of eland, the world's largest antelope, cling skittishly to the horizon. Towering giraffe glide between the acacias, fluttering their eyelids at passing 4x4s, while buffalo stare down all comers with an unfathomable mix of inquisitiveness and machismo. Above all, there is the endless drama of the wildebeest migration, which crosses over from Tanzania to take up residence in the

Main Attractions
Keekorok Lodge
Rekero Camp

Lion cubs.

Mara for a few months every year, usually between July and October.

Also known as the Maasai Mara (or once you feel sufficiently familiar, just the Mara), this unfenced national reserve in southwest Kenya is effectively a northern extension of Tanzania's equally famous and much larger Serengeti National Park, with which it shares its southern boundary. The Mara is bounded by the Loita Hills in the east, the splendid Oloololo Escarpment to the west, and the Itong Hills, below the Mau Escarpment, in the north. But the reserve itself is relatively flat, comprising open plains of red oat grass, and gently rolling hills mottled with groves of whistling thorns and other species of spiky *Acacia* tree.

Mara and Talek rivers

It is often claimed that the name Mara (a Maa word meaning spotted) alludes to the patchwork nature of the reserve's habitats, or the speckled inundation of ungulates that inhabit them. More likely, however, that it is simply borrowed from the **Mara River**, one of two major waterways to flow through the reserve, the other being the tributary **Talek River**. Certainly, this muddy brown waterway, fringed as it is by a ribbon of lush riparian forest of tall fever trees and seasonally fruiting wild figs, is the site of the most famous wildlife spectacle associated with the Maasai Mara: the river crossings that form a thrilling highlight of the annual wildebeest migration.

The Maasai Mara has enjoyed a reputation for superb wildlife game viewing since the early colonial era, when it was a popular destination for hunting safaris out of Nairobi. Although the Maasai who traditionally inhabit the area are natural conservationists, who seldom hunt for the pot, the first formal conservation efforts date to 1948, when the 520 sq km (190 sq mile) Mara Wildlife Sanctuary was gazetted to protect the westerly part of the modern reserve known as the Mara Triangle. In 1961, the reserve was extended to cover 1,820 sq km (655 sq miles) and management was ceded to Narok County Council

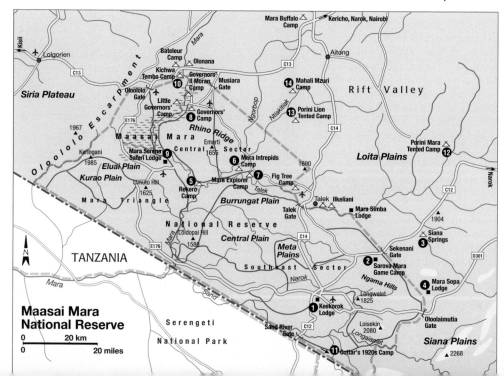

Maasai Mara National Reserve

(NCC), which handed back parts of the reserve to local communities in the mid-1970s, leaving it at its present size. In 1995, following a national reorganisation of counties, control was split between the NCC and the newly formed TransMara County Council (TMCC), with the southwesterly Mara Triangle falling under the latter authority. As a result, separate park fees must now be paid to visit the part of the reserves east and west of the Mara River, a circumstance that generally discourages visitors staying on one side of the river to cross to the other on game drives.

The Great Migration

In terms of statistics, Barnum & Bailey were never close to the show provided by the Serengeti-Mara's wildebeest migration: a company of over 2 million animals, an arena 3,200km (2,000 miles) round, and a non-stop year-long spectacle that has followed a similar pattern for hundreds of thousands of years. At the last count, there were 1.7 million wildebeests in the main cavalcade, accompanied by

hundreds of thousands of gazelles, zebras, hartebeest and 64,000 other grazers and browsers.

Dominating this extraordinary natural circus is the blue wildebeest (or white-bearded gnu), whose ungainly appearance and legendarily sheep-like intellect belie its extraordinary ecological success. True, its elongated head may look too big for a creature with such a spindly torso and legs, while its small horns and wispy white beard add to its faintly preposterous visage, but zoologists will point out that few large mammals survive in such numbers anywhere in the world as the wildebeest of the Serengeti-Mara. They are also surprisingly playful, arching their backs as they buck up and down in a manner reminiscent of the Maasai *ipid* dance, then spinning and falling, or charging about like a pack of excited puppies. Furthermore, the sight – and baaing sound – of tens of thousands of wildebeest trekking across the plains of the Serengeti-Mara is truly inspirational.

Given the option, the wildebeest would probably never come up to the

Wildebeest skull on the bank of the Mara River.

Burchell's zebra at a watering hole.

Adult topi with calf.

Blue wildebeest.

Mara. They would stay down south, on the vast alluvial short-grass plains of the Serengeti, which they prefer because there is virtually no cover for predators. The wildebeest usually disperse into the southern Serengeti during November, and calve there in January, but they soon mow the grass to stubble, and as the land dries up, they are forced to move northwest, following the bearing of the 'long rains'.

The great journey generally has a disorderly start. None of the animals seems to know what's happening, except for a few individuals in the 1.7 million who must sniff the air, decide it's time and amble off through the Serengeti's **Western Corridor** towards Lake Victoria. The others follow – straggling individuals and small groups – but eventually they bunch into broad lines marching, which look like columns of safari ants. They wheel before the lake, moving due north to cross the Mara, Sand and Talek rivers at exactly the same places each year.

This brings them into Kenya, where there will be good grazing in the best-watered section of the ring from the Mara and the dozen other rivers that flow off the western wall of the Rift. The wildebeest are highly vulnerable to predators launching out of the thickets, so whenever they smell the October 'short rains' moving up from the south, the hordes reform and restart the migration south. This time, for some unknown reason, the lines are narrower and more dispersed for the southeastern arc, as they head back to where it all started.

Resident game

The Mara is undoubtedly at its most impressive during the three months that it hosts the wildebeest migration, but this is also when it attracts the highest tourist numbers, so it should be emphasised that game viewing is superb throughout the year. It hosts an extraordinarily dense lion population, estimated at 250 to 300 lions, and pride sizes are unusually large, in some cases comprising 20 to 30 individuals (rather than the more normal up to 10). It's also

a good place to see cheetah pacing the plains, though numbers of these sleek spotted cats have dropped in recent years, possibly as a result of competition with lions and spotted hyenas. Leopards are also surprisingly commonly seen, especially in the plains between the Mara and Talek Rivers, where the highly habituated members of the matriarchy featured in *Big Cat Diaries* is resident.

Other predators include spotted hyenas, black-backed jackals and the more secretive serval and caracal. There are many buffalo in the Mara, some impressively tusked elephants, and even a few surviving black rhino. Also common are giraffe, zebra, warthog, Thomson's and Grant's gazelles, Coke's hartebeest, eland, topi and impala. And even when the main migration is south of the border, resident wildebeest are plentiful, their numbers supplemented by a relatively small migratory population from the Loita Hills during the second half of the year.

There are over 500 recorded species of birds in this reserve. Birds of prey likely to be seen include Verreaux's eagle-owl, martial eagle, bateleur, tawny eagle, pallid harrier and six species of vulture. Conspicuous ground birds include ostrich, kori bustard, Denham's bustard, crowned crane, marabou stork, southern ground hornbill and secretary bird. The wooded plains usually support good numbers of perching birds including such safari favourites as lilac-breasted roller, superb starling and various hornbills and bee-eaters. A notable niche habitat is the riparian forest along the Mara River, home to the likes of Ross's turaco, Schalow's turaco and grey kestrel, while the Musaria Swamp near the eponymous entrance gate is the best place in Kenya to look for the localised and rufous-bellied heron.

Not long ago, the Maasai Mara was an archetypal modern African arena of conflict between man and nature. Wheat schemes and livestock programmes to the north threatened to restrict the movement of the world's greatest remaining wildlife migration, while conservationists

Wildebeest crossing the Mara River during their migration across the Serengeti.

RIVER CROSSINGS

The most dramatic aspect of the migration is the multiple crossings of the Mara River that usually take place between July/August and September/October. Contrary to popular impressions, these crossings are not one-off directional events that occur as the migration enters and leaves the Mara. Throughout the season, herds of a few hundred or thousand wildebeest regularly cross back and forth, using a total of eight favoured crossing points most regularly along the 5km (3-mile) stretch upriver of the Mara's confluence with the Talek. Often preceded by several false starts, these crossings are breathless, adrenalin-charged spectacles whose drama is heightened by the crocodiles that weave gape-mouthed through the crossing herd, ready to snatch any individual that makes a false move.

and ecologists strived to reconcile their needs with the aspirations of the Maasai landowners. However, burgeoning upmarket tourism since the 1990s has injected plentiful cash into the region, with encouraging results, as local landowners and communities bordering the reserve have recognised that wildlife can be a resource worth husbanding, and have set aside their own land for tourism-based enterprises such as tented camps, meaning that the Maasai Mara now lies at the centre of a much larger mosaic of private conservancies and reserves.

Getting there

Most visitors to the Mara fly there. Several carriers offer daily flights from Nairobi to the Mara, stopping at any of a dozen or so airstrips, depending on which is closest to your lodge or camp. Connecting flights from Nairobi, ideally booked through the same carrier, allow one to travel on to or from the likes of Lamu, Mombasa, Malindi or Laikipia in one day. There are also

occasional direct fights between the Mara and destinations such as Amboseli, Naivasha and Nakuru.

There are two ways to drive to the Maasai Mara from Nairobi: either the high or the low road west towards Nakuru. Either way, the route leads to the northern end of the **Kedong Valley** about 50km (30 miles) from Nairobi. At the bottom of the escarpment, in the village of May Mahia, a left turn is signposted to **Narok**, the town that administers the northern half of Maasailand, its streets full of strolling *moran* (warriors) buying very little from shanty *dukas* (stores).

Sixteen kilometres (10 miles) out of Narok, on a good tarmac road, is a Game Department barrier at **Ewaso Ngiro** ('brown river' in Maa). At this point, take the left turn to **Sekenani Gate**, then straight ahead to **Aitong**, for Governor's Camp and the western end of the Mara road. After the river, the road – or rather confusion of tracks – deteriorates quite badly, and some sections are spine-jarringly rutted and uncomfortable.

African elephant.

The Eastern Mara

The Maasai Mara can be divided into four main geographic and touristic regions: the largest and busiest part of the reserve to the southeast of the Talek and Mara rivers, the smaller central triangle of land that divides the same two rivers north of their confluence, the so-called Mara Triangle to the west of the Mara River, and the patchwork of private conservancies that lie outside the reserve's boundary. Each of these four areas has its own character, and since most camps and lodges stick to their own sector when it comes to game drives, it is worth looking at a map to determine the location of any accommodation you plan on booking before you commit.

Most developed in touristic terms is the **southeast sector**, which is the closest part of the reserve to Nairobi coming by road, and was traditionally where safaris to Tanzania's Serengeti National Park passed through en route from the Kenyan capital prior to the closure of the international border between the Serengeti and Mara in the early 1980s. The main point of entry here is the Sekenani Gate, set below the impressive Ngama Hills, whose distinctive outline forms a useful landmark for those driving themselves. The game viewing in this part of the Mara is excellent, with buffalo, giraffe and other ungulates being particularly numerous, and plenty of lion, cheetah and spotted hyena around (though leopard sightings are infrequent).

Lodges in this part of the reserve tend to be relatively large and impersonal, and closer in feel to a conventional hotel than a genuine bush camp. An established landmark of this sort is **Keekorok Lodge** ❶ (http://sunafricahotels.com), which has a prime location next to its own airstrip midway between Sekenani Gate and the Mara River, and is where the original balloon safaris above the Mara were pioneered. Other well-known lodges that lie within this sector, or just outside its borders, include **Sarova Mara Game Camp** ❷ (www.sarovahotels.

Rüppell's Vulture in the Maasai Mara National Reserve

Ostrich.

com/maracamp), about 5km (3 miles) into the reserve from Sekenani Gate; the lovely **Siana Springs Tented Camp** ❸ (www.siana-springs.co.ke), set in a fever tree forest about 20km (12 miles) outside Sekenani Gate; and **Mara Sopa Lodge** ❹ (www.sopa lodges.com) in the Oloolaimutia Valley just outside the reserve's eastern boundary.

For cost-conscious visitors, the eastern part of the Mara is the focal point for almost all group camping safaris to the Mara, and its lodges generally cater to lower budget safaris. But it also has several drawbacks: driving off the (rather rutted) roads is strictly forbidden, most of the accommodation is some distance from the main river crossing points, and the density of lodges – boosted by camps based immediately outside the boundaries – generates a high volume of tourist traffic, particularly during peak season. Also, because most camping and other road safaris from Nairobi focus on this sector, a high proportion of safari drivers are relatively bush-illiterate city dwellers, at least

by comparison to the more knowledgeable and sensitive guides who typically work within the Mara.

Central sector

In pure game viewing terms, the **central sector**, which extends northward from the confluence of the rivers Talek and Mara, and includes the Musiara Swamp, takes some beating. It is here that much of the footage for *Big Cat Diaries* was shot, and close-up encounters with lion, leopard and cheetah are all quite commonplace. There's excellent hyena viewing here too, plenty of buffalo, elephant and other ungulates, and it is superbly sited for catching river crossings during the migration. Tourist traffic can be high, but congestion levels seldom approach those in the eastern sector (except sometimes at leopard sightings), and off-road driving for good sightings is tolerated.

There are few large lodges in the central part of the reserve, indeed most of the accommodation is in the form of luxury tented camps,

African elephant mother and calf.

typically with between 10 and 20 accommodation units. These include the superb **Rekero Camp** ❺ (http://rekero.asiliaafrica.com), set near a crossing site on the north bank of the Talek River, and the nearby **Mara Intrepids Camp** ❻ and **Mara Explorer Camp** ❼ (www.heritage-eastafrica.com). The central sector is also the site of the reserve's oldest lodging, the rustic **Governors' Camp** ❽ (www.governorscamp.com), situated on a forested stretch of the Mara River where old colonial governors used to pitch their tents; it is now a very upmarket retreat. The same family-run company also owns the luxurious **Little Governors** and **Governors Il Moran**.

Mara Triangle

The least-developed part of the reserve proper is the so-called **Mara Triangle**, which has a spectacular location hemmed in by the Mara River to the east and the Oloololo Escarpment to the west. Only one lodge lies within this sector: the large but stylish **Mara Serena Safari Lodge** ❾ (www.serenahotels.com), set high on a saddle overlooking rolling grasslands and one of the busiest crossing points on the Mara River. The Oloololo Gate is the only road entry to this untrammelled sector, and a few of the private lodges that lie immediately outside it – most notably the superb **Kichwa Tembo Camp** ❿ and its luxurious young nine-tent sibling **Bateleur Camp**, both operated by &Beyond (www.andbeyond.com) – base all their game drives there.

The main attraction of the Mara Triangle is its wilderness feel, and if game viewing is not quite as spectacular as it is further east, this is amply compensated for by the low volume of tourist traffic – indeed this is the only part of the national reserve where you might frequently drive for an hour without seeing another vehicle. It is the best part of the reserve for elephants, herds of which are frequently seen crossing through the tall grass, and black rhino, rare elsewhere in the Mara, are regularly sighted in the swampy

Cheetah on a kill.

Spotted hyena pup.

area near to Oloololo Gate. Cheetah and lion are both common, along with large ungulate herds, and the stretch of river below around the Serena Lodge is a very popular wildebeest crossing point.

Private concessions

Budget permitting, the best way to see the Maasai Mara is to stay at one of several established private **Maasai concessions** bordering the reserve proper. As a rule, these offer the best of both worlds: within the concession, there is almost no other tourist traffic, and also no restriction on off-road driving or night drives, but if things are quiet animal-wise (which they seldom are) you can always pop across into the reserve proper to look for wildlife there. To the southeast of the Mara, for instance, a private concession bordering on the Serengeti is the site of the classic **Cottar's 1920s Camp** ⓫ (www.cottars.com), an old-style tented camp run by the great-grandson of one of the hunters who led the very first photographic safari in East Africa in 1919.

One of the finest concession camps, set in the eastern part of the ecosystem, is the six-unit **Porini Mara Tented Camp** ⓬ (www.porini. com), which operates only three vehicles that collectively have exclusive traversing rights over the 150-sq-km (55-sq-mile) **Ol Kinyei Conservancy**, home to one of the largest lion prides in Kenya (more than 30 individuals at last count). Further west, the affiliated **Porini Lion Tented Camp** ⓭ is one of just three camps in the 300-sq-km (110-sq-mile) **Olare Orok Conservancy**, which borders the superb central sector of the reserve and also offers wonderful game viewing in its own right. A relatively recent addition, north of the conservancy, is Virgin Group founder Richard Branson's stylish 12-tent luxury camp called **Mahali Mzuri** ⓮ (www.virginlimitededition. com/en/mahali-mzuri). Guests here have fromt row seats to see the annual Great Migration and to abundant game all year round, including lions, wildebeast, zebra, elephants, cheetah, giraffe and impala.

A room at a luxury safari camp.

Up, Up and Away

Almost every visitor to Kenya dreams of floating above the magical Mara plains in a hot-air balloon, as wildebeest, buffalo or elephant traipse ant-like through the greenery below.

Jules Verne's novel *Five Weeks in a Balloon*, published in 1862, was the first to mention ballooning in Africa and was the inspiration for English gas balloonist Anthony Smith's visit 100 years later. Using a hydrogen-filled balloon, he successfully crossed from Zanzibar to Tanzania, and also completed flights over the Serengeti and the Great Rift Valley.

Accompanying Smith as cameraman during these early flights was Alan Root, now a renowned wildlife film-maker. He realised that, if problems of expense and manoeuvrability could be overcome, a balloon basket was the perfect place from which to appreciate the majesty of the African landscape.

Root had a hot-air balloon delivered to Kenya and, with the aid of a trained pilot, set about learning to fly it. Early flights were hazardous until European flying techniques were adapted to African conditions. The result of Root's efforts was one of his most popular films, *Safari by Balloon*.

While on location, Root was several times asked by passing travellers for rides over the savannah. It was these visitors to Kenya, wanting to see the game from a different perspective, who prompted him to set up Kenya's first balloon company, Balloon Safaris, at Keekorok Lodge in the Maasai Mara Game Reserve. Since the inaugural flight in 1976 hundreds of thousands of passengers have soared above the Mara Plains in a hot-air balloon. However, the original five-passenger balloons with their cramped baskets have now been superseded by balloons three times bigger, with baskets containing seats for up to 16 passengers. For more information on Root's Balloon Safaris see www.balloonsafaris.co.ke.

Booking a flight

Since those first flights, balloon safaris have now become a major (albeit somewhat pricey) attraction for many visitors in Kenya – on morning game drives, you might easily count half-a-dozen balloons in the air at one time. There are now several launch sites, and you will be close to one or the other wherever you stay in the reserve. A balloon trip can be booked through practically any lodge or camp, usually at short notice

if you are staying a few nights. In peak season, however, it might be worth making an advance booking through your lodge or tour operator.

Although flights operate all year round, the optimum time to balloon in the Mara is from July to mid-September during the annual wildebeest migration, when over 2 million animals cross the plains. Be warned, however, the wind and animal movements are unpredictable, so even at this time of year, there is no guarantee of what wildlife you will see from the air.

The daily flights always follow the same pattern: passengers are picked up from their camp or lodge at around 5.30am and driven to the launch site. The balloon lifts off with the rising sun for a 60 to 90-minute journey over an average distance of about 12km (8 miles). Being highly manoeuvrable, the balloon can skim treetops or rise to over 300 metres (1,000ft) for panoramic views of the rolling Mara plains. All balloon companies serve a bush breakfast wherever they land in the park, cooked either on wood fires or over the balloon's gas burners, and invariably accompanied by a glass of champagne.

Because balloons are transported by the prevailing winds they cannot fly back to their take-off point. After breakfast, passengers are driven slowly back to the camp by retriever vehicles. All companies return passengers to their camp or lodge by mid-morning.

Hot air balloon ride at dawn.

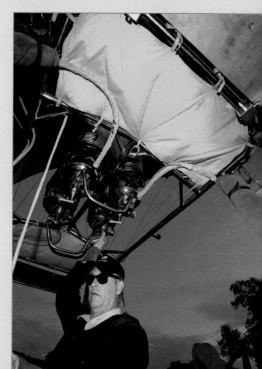

MAASAI: NOMADS OF THE PLAINS

East Africa's most famous and dramatically attired tribe has a long history of nomadic pastoralism. But today its unique lifestyle is under threat.

The Maasai probably arrived in Kenya about 500 years ago, migrating southward from the lower Nile region of the Sudanese/Ethiopia border region via Lake Turkana to the fertile part of the Rift Valley bordering Tanzania. By the 19th century, they had established a reputation as powerful and ferocious warriors who frequently formed raiding parties that went deep into neighbouring territories to steal cattle and demand tribute from the coastal trade caravans.

During the colonial era, the British moved the Maasai out of their northern grazing lands into the less fertile savannah region in the south. Nevertheless, they have largely maintained their traditional nomadic way of life, grazing their cattle over vast areas, and living in temporary villages (*manyattas*) of huts ringed by a thorn fence as defence against wild animals. Their diet consists mainly of milk and blood drawn from their cattle. Maasai wealth is measured in cattle, which are rarely slaughtered, and then only for ceremonial purposes. The flesh of wild beasts is forbidden, except for eland and buffalo. Beadwork is an important facet of Maasai body decoration, and often used to indicate social status.

In their teens, Maasai males are initiated as a new age-set of *moran* (young warriors), their duty to tend livestock and defend against enemies. Strict taboos apply to them, including a prohibition on marriage and alcohol until they graduate to become *eunoto* (elders) at around age 30. The Maasai traditionally practice Female Genital Mutilation (FGM), which was made illegal in 2011. Rites of passage that do not involve any physical harm have been promoted throughout the country.

Maasai women sit at the entrance of a traditional homestead, which has smooth adobe (mud) walls built on a framework of wooden poles.

Maasai beadwork uses nine main colours. The meanings for each colour vary regionally, but in general black symbolizes rain, orange the rainbow, light blue water, red blood or bravery, dark blue god, white peace, gold groundwater, yellow the sun, and green life.

Maasai women still mostly wear a traditional dress of draped cloth, but can be distinguished from most other women in Kenya by their extensive use of beaded jewelry.

The traditional dance performed by Maasai men, usually to an entrancing accompaniement of humming and singing, is reminiscent of pogoing, as the men take turns to jump high in the air. The best dancer is considered to be the one who jumps highest.

THE MAASAI AND TOURISM

Maasai are excluded from the national parks and reserves, though they may have seasonally grazed their cattle in these areas for many generations. The government claims that conservation areas attract lucrative tourism, which in turn benefits local people. But the Maasai are rarely the beneficiaries of tourist revenue. In effect, they have been denied access to vital grazing grounds in the name of tourism. The results have been dramatic. To raise money, some Maasai now charge tourists an admission fee to visit their villages and to take photographs. They also sell Maasai handicrafts such as beadwork jewellery and other souvenirs. Even on the coast, far from their traditional homelands, Maasai are seen selling trinkets to tourists. Elsewhere they have created permanent group ranches, where they herd their cattle and grow food. But the land on these ranches is often unsuitable for intensive grazing or agriculture. Whatever their future, a radical change to the traditional nomadic lifestyle of the Maasai seems inevitable.

A popular game with the Maasai is enkeshui, a local variation on the ancient board game of bao, which is played with stones or beads throughout sub-Saharan Africa.

...aasai warriors (Ilmoran) are initiated in age-sets every ...–15 years. The central ritual of the initiation ceremony is ...norata (circumcision, performed without anaesthetic). Once ...itiated, the ilmoran can wear the traditional male attire of a ...ga-like red or purple shuka.

Tea plantation, Kericho.

WESTERN KENYA: A SCENIC CIRCUIT

A circular tour of the west takes in rolling tea plantations, lush swamps and equatorial forests, along with Kenya's second-highest mountain and the largest lake in Africa.

West of Nakuru, the Uganda Highway climbs the western wall of the Rift Valley by a less spectacular route than its descent on the eastern side. It is a steep climb nonetheless since **Nakuru ❶**, Kenya's fourth largest town, lying on the valley floor, is around 1,800 metres (6,000ft) above sea level, while the highest point the road reaches above the western wall is well over 2,700 metres (9,000ft).

At that point, 8km (5 miles) off the main trunk route, the small farming town of **Molo ❷** is set in open high-altitude downs reminiscent of Scotland – more so with the chill and mists of the morning. It's not surprising that the area attracted the early white settlers, who saw it as prime sheep country. The result is the superb 'Molo' lamb, a staple on many Kenyan dinner tables.

Close by Molo, near **Mau Summit**, the trunk route splits. The Trans-Africa Highway heads northwest across the highland plateau west of the Rift to Eldoret, eventually reaching the Uganda border at Malaba. The other road heads southwest as the main route to Lake Victoria.

Eldoret

Not far from the fork, the highway crosses the equator and the wide level plain of the Uasin Gishu Plateau to the town of **Eldoret ❸** – or '64' as it's

sometimes called, since it was set up by milepost 64 of an ox-wagon route from Londiani forged by *voortrekkers* – Dutch-speaking farmers – from South Africa.

When these settlers arrived, prior to World War I, the plateau was teeming with wildlife, rather like the Athi Plains around Nairobi or the Mara-Serengeti. The game soon disappeared, however, since the farmers turned the Uasin Gishu into Kenya's main granary. Maize and wheat fields stretched from horizon to horizon, and still

Soapstone carvings, Kisumu.

Until recently the Molo Hunt – hounds, horns, hunting pinks, the works – used to roam the farmlands of Nakuru.

do in parts. Founded to service this agricultural wealth, Eldoret may be somewhat lacking in character, but it is now the fifth largest town in Kenya, and the fastest growing, boasting a mushrooming industrial belt, and an airport of international standards. To the northeast of Eldoret, the breathtaking but little visited **Kerio Valley/Kamnarok National Reserve** ❹ is bisected by a nippy asphalt road that descends into the Rift Valley near Lake Baringo.

Mount Elgon

Northwest of Eldoret, **Mount Elgon** ❺ dominates the horizon, at least on the rare occasions when it is not shrouded in cloud. At 4,321 metres (14,178ft), Elgon is around 880 metres (3,000ft)

short of Mount Kenya in terms of altitude, but the circumference of its base makes it a bigger massif. The upper slopes of this extinct volcano support a cover of lush montane forest giving way to moorland at higher altitudes, and are protected within **Mount Elgon National Park** (www.kws.go.ke; daily 6am–6pm), one of the country's least-developed sanctuaries.

The dense tall forest and a lack of roads inhibit game viewing on the mountain, but it is possible to hike up to the summit, across moorlands of giant heather. **Mount Elgon Lodge**, a converted farmhouse with wonderful views, midway between Kitale and the peak, makes a serviceable base, though the recently refurbished self-catering **Kapkuro Bandas** at the park

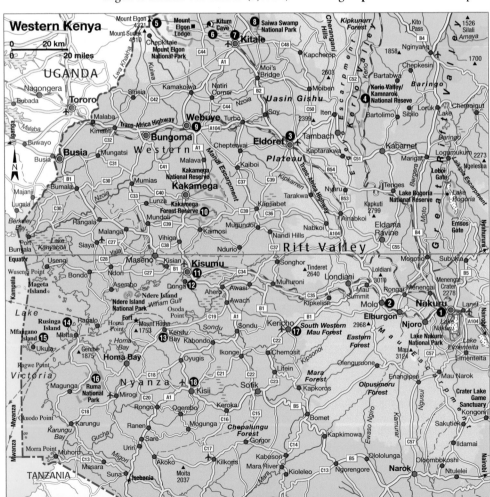

entrance are much better value. There is also a campsite.

While the volcanic soils of Kenya's mountain ranges are fertile, they don't seem to yield the minerals the elephants crave – except at rare salt-licks, one of them in the distinctive **Kitum Cave ❻**, which has attracted the big mammals for centuries. Quite literally, the elephant mine the cave, gouging out the walls and extending the shafts hundreds of feet into the mountain.

At the foot of Elgon stands **Kitale ❼**, the northernmost of the agricultural towns built by the settlers in the colonial era. With Elgon's slopes to the west and the high Cherangani Hills to the east, the agriculture about Kitale is as diverse as it can get in Kenya. Beef and dairy farms, coffee estates, wheat and maize fields surround the town, and on the higher slopes are orchards of temperate European fruits, like apples. It is a more subdued and greener town than Eldoret, though sightseeing is limited to the **Kitale Museum** (tel: 054 30996; www.museums.or.ke; Mon–Fri 9am–6pm), whose indoor ethnographic and natural history displays are supplemented by a snake pit housing two massive crocodiles, and a pleasant walking trail through a patch of riverine where a variety of monkeys and birds might be seen. Recent years have also seen the opening of the privately run **Treasures of Africa Museum** (tel: 054 30867), which showcases the personal collection of African artefacts of the owner-cum-curator John G. Wilson, and the **Kitale Nature Conservancy** (www.kitalenature.or.ke), located on the road to Lodwar.

Swamps and forests

About 30km (18 miles) northeast of Kitale, **Saiwa Swamp National Park ❽** (tel: 0789 312 901; www.kws.go.ke; daily) is Kenya's smallest, at only 300 hectares (740 acres). It was opened in 1974 to protect the semi-aquatic sitatunga antelope, notable for its wide-splayed hooves, which allow it to walk on the soggy surface of the swamp. Though it is not teeming with big game, Saiwa is also home to several other forest and swamp dwellers. These include the De Brazza's monkey, which (like the sitatunga) has a very limited distribution in East Africa, along with the African clawless otter, giant forest squirrel, black-and-white colobus, bushbuck and grey duiker.

Unusually for a national park, Saiwa can be explored only on foot. A nature trail runs through the heart of the park, incorporating a long footbridge across the swamp, and several elevated viewing platforms overlooking it. The most productive spot for wildlife viewing is Platform Four, where you are almost certain to see sitatunga if you arrive before 8am, and might also glimpse African clawless otters and De Brazza's monkeys. The birdlife here, generally most active between 8am and 10am, is amazing: Saiwa is the best place in Kenya to look for the spectacular Ross's turaco, the secretive grey-winged robin-chat (sometimes seen on the footpath close to Platform Four) and the yellow-billed barbet, while other specials include the double-toothed

TIP

It is possible to climb Mount Elgon at any time of year, though December to March are the best months. For more information, contact the Mountain Club of Kenya (www.mck.or.ke).

Misty morning on the footslopes of Mount Elgon.

barbet, blue-headed coucal, crowned crane and black sparrowhawk.

From Elgon, the country to the south falls away fairly gently towards Lake Victoria and the Nile Valley. The highway passes **Webuye** ❾, which has heavy-chemical and sugar manufacturers, and until recently was home to the largest paper factory in the region. The area features dense settlement, principally of the Luhya peoples. Their headquarters are in the township of **Kakamega**, which is 42km (26 miles) to the south of the highway.

Not far from the town is the **Kakamega Forest** ❿, a jungle-like centre of significant ecological interest since it is a relic of the equatorial rainforest that once spread from West Africa to the East African coast. Though it lies somewhat off the main tourist trail, Kakamega is an increasingly popular destination for butterfly lovers, birdwatchers and other specialists looking for species more normally associated with central and west Africa. Sykes monkey and black-and-white colobus are both very common, and overnight visitors with a spotlight stand a good chance of picking out the nocturnal potto, a sloth-like primate distantly related to the better-known bushbabies. In addition, around 10 percent of the reserve's 300 bird species occur nowhere else in Kenya, most alluringly perhaps the great blue turaco, flocks of which fly clumsily between the trees like psychedelic turkeys.

Around 200 sq km (72 sq miles) of undisturbed forest remains, divided into the two main sectors. These are the **Kakamega National Reserve** (tel: 020 241 8419; www.kws.go.ke), which is managed by Kenya Wildlife Service and lies to the north of Kakamega on the east side of the Webuye Road, and the **Kakamega Forest Reserve** (tel: 0726 951 764; www.kakamegarainforest.com; daily), which falls under the Department of Forestry and lies to the east of town along a dirt road through Isecheno. The forest reserve is generally regarded to offer the best birding, and it is also where the bulk of the accommodation lies, including the upmarket Rondo Retreat (www.rondoretreat.com) and very affordable KEEP Bandas (http://kakamegarainforest.com/bandas). However, dedicated birders will also want to check out the national reserve, which protects a slightly different selection of bird species, and has a small *banda* and camping site.

Kisumu

Kenya's third-largest city, with a population of over 400,000, **Kisumu** ⓫ stands on the shores of Lake Victoria about 48km (30 miles) south of Kakamega, where it forms the main centre of economic activity for the region's four million Luo people. Founded in 1901 as the lakeshore terminus for the Uganda Railway, the town was originally known as Port Florence (after Florence Preston, the wife of a railway engineer), but later reverted to its original Luo name, which means 'Place of Barter'. The town was developed not only as the major administrative centre for most of western Kenya, but also

Stallholder, Kisumu municipal market.

as an important regional port with shipbuilding and repair facilities.

Following the dissolution of the original East African Community – a political and economic arrangement whereby Kenya, Uganda and Tanzania shared steamer and general communications services – in 1977, Kisumu fell into economic decline. For much of the rest of the 20th century, the once bustling town centre, all potholed roads and flaking walls, exuded an atmosphere of economic stagnation, and even today the port and associated railway station, though still functional, are barely more than that. However, Kisumu itself has undergone a major post-millennial revival, thanks to its diversification into light industry and communications, to the extent that it now comes across as a real city, with a genuine buzz of energy about its streets.

As with so many Kenyan towns, Kisumu is not exactly over-endowed when it comes to scintillating sightseeing opportunities. Despite its location on Africa's largest lake, it has no waterfront worth talking about, and the architectural highlights amount to a pretty **Jamia Mosque** and **Hindu Temple** in the city centre. There is also an excellent **central market**, at the junction of Kenyatta Avenue and the main road to Nairobi, while the nearby **Kisumu Museum** (tel: 057 202 0332; daily 9am–6pm) incorporates an aquarium housing several cichlid and other fish species associated with Lake Victoria. About 2km (1.2 mile) south of the city centre, the **Kisumu Antelope Sanctuary** (tel: 0774 305 916; www.kws.go.ke; daily) is home to a small herd of the eponymous antelope (which you are certain to see in larger numbers and less-contrived circumstances in almost any of the country's savannah reserves or national parks) and a thoroughly depressing small zoo.

An attractive alternative base to Kisumu, only 5km (3.1 miles) south of the city centre, is the small village of **Dunga** ⑫, where the pleasant Kiboko Bay Hotel offers tented accommodation in a lakeshore location that attracts plenty of waterbirds and occasional hippo visits. The

Fisherman fixing nets, Dunga Bay, Lake Victoria.

Arab slave traders from the Swahili Coast introduced the dhow to Lake Victoria, and the style was copied by Luo shipwrights.

Kakamega Forest Reserve.

centre of activity is here is the Dunga Beach fisheries compound, where you can watch traditional dhows glide serenely onto the water at dusk, usually to return at around 11am with the day's catch – attracting hordes of very habituated egrets, storks and hamerkops. It is also a good place to arrange boat trips to look for hippos and to see the abundant water birds in a protected breeding colony in the nearby marshes.

Arab sails on Lake Victoria

Lake Victoria is not only the largest lake in Africa, but also the second-largest freshwater body anywhere in the world, extending over some 68,500 sq km (26,500 sq miles), an area comparable to that of the Republic of Ireland. Shared between Kenya, Tanzania and Uganda, the lake supports several million people, including the Luo of Kenya, many of whom are still fishermen. Dunga is one of many places on the lake where you can see their fleets of traditional fishing dhows, whose white lateen sails, set against a deep blue background, appear to

be out of the romantic myths of the Sinbad coast. And there is, in fact, a connection to the coast, dating back to the time when the Arab slavers were marauding around Victoria, building boats for the lake in the same style as their dhows on the ocean.

A good place to watch the fishing dhows in action is the small town of **Kendu Bay** ⑬, about an hour's drive south of Kisumu. Try to be at the out-of-town jetty at noon, when dozens of dhows land there, complete with the day's catch. Kendu Bay boasts two other diverting attractions. The first is a handsome and surprisingly large Tawakal Mosque, set along the road between the town centre and the jetty. The other, about 2km (1 mile) south of town, is **Simbi Nyaima**, a pretty green crater lake whose shallows occasionally support large numbers of flamingo. Simbi Nyaima means 'Village That Sank', an allusion to the Luo legend that the lake was created when a fearful storm engulfed what was formerly a village, to punish its inhabitants for refusing to help an old woman who

PRESIDENT OBAMA'S KENYAN ROOTS

US President Barack Hussein Obama II is the son of Barack Hussein Obama Sr, a Luo economist born in 1936 to a mixed Islamic-Christian family near Kendu Bay, and raised in the village of Kogelo to the west of Kisumu. In 1959, Obama Sr became the first foreign African student to enrol at the University of Hawaii, on a scholarship organised by the renowned Luo politician Tom Mboya. It was here that Obama Sr met President Obama's mother Ann Dunham, who he married bigamously, claiming untruthfully to be divorced from his Kenyan wife Kezia, with whom he had already had two children.

Obama Sr returned to Kenya in 1964, three years after the birth of the future president. There, he worked for several years as a senior government economist, an initially promising career derailed by the combination of a severe drinking problem and the unspoken anti-Luo policy pursued by President Kenyatta in the aftermath of Tom Mboya's assassination in 1969.

Direct contact between Barack Obama Sr and Jr was limited to the father's one-month visit to the US in 1971, an encounter to which the US president attributes his lifelong enthusiasm for basketball and jazz. In 1982, Obama Sr died in a car accident at the age of 46. However, several members of the president's extended family live in Kenya, among them his step-grandmother Sarah Onyango Obama.

had arrived there looking for food and shelter.

If you want the (somewhat limited) challenge of tackling one of Lake Victoria's giant Nile perches, the place to stay is **Rusinga Island** , where there is a comfortable lodge for fishermen in idyllic surroundings, or **Mfangano Island** ⓯, where there is a tented camp. The introduction of these huge fish into the lake in the 1950s has been controversial. In the 1980s there was an explosion in their numbers and, as a result, many indigenous species of fish have since disappeared, particularly the small cichlids: Nile perch now account for about 80 percent of the fish in the lake. In commercial terms, this has been a great success, generating a multi-million dollar processing and export industry. However, scientists maintain that it has had a disastrous impact on the lake's ecosystem.

Kenya's main sugar-growing area lies close to Kisumu, in the **Nyando Valley** at the head of the Winam Gulf. Production is from both large estates as well as from smallholders in a policy unusual in Africa for its tolerant flexibility.

On the north side of the gulf, about 30km (19 miles) from Kisumu, is one of Kenya's smaller national parks, the 4-sq-km (1.5-sq-mile) **Ndere Island**, which has been a sanctuary since 1986.

On the far side of the gulf from Kisumu, in the lee of **Homa Bay** town, lies the **Ruma National Park** ⓰ (tel: 020 352 91129 or 0717 176 709; www.kws.go.ke; daily). This is mostly uninhabited because of tsetse fly and the sleeping sickness it carries, which is no worry to in-and-out tourists but a major concern to local inhabitants. Although it is the refuge for Kenya's remaining roan antelope, the park is rarely on tourist itineraries.

Tea plantations at Kericho

Back to the fork at Mau Summit, the southern highway runs some 50km (30 miles) through forest reserve and plantations before reaching the 'tea capital' of **Kericho** ⓱. High ground, temperate climate and high rainfall off Lake Victoria make the district ideal for the production of tea.

When the Europeans first arrived, much of the area was under tall montane forest. With a massive import of capital, the land was cleared and planted so that ridge after ridge is now patterned a bright, almost apple-green as one of the most productive tea areas on earth. A relict of the original forest can be seen at the **Chagaik Arboretum**, which lies on a tea estate a few kilometres out of town along the Nakuru Road, and supports an impressive range of natural (and introduced) trees inhabited by a conspicuous troop of black-and-white colobus monkey and plentiful forest birds.

From Kericho a major road descends to Kisumu, while another holds to the high ground through Sotik, **Kisii** ⓲ and eventually to the Tanzanian border. The Kisii Highlands, the home of the Gusii people, are exceptionally rich, although very little of their land is now left fallow. As in other areas

Ruma National Park was created as a sanctuary for the roan antelope, which is found nowhere else in Kenya.

Luo fishing boats off the eastern lakeshore of Lake Victoria.

Soapstone carvings made by the Gusii people around Tabaka, south of Kisii, are sold in curio shops all over the country.

Tawakal Mosque, Kendu Bay.

of the Western Highlands, the population growth is exceptionally high and causes a constant migration of people to other parts of the country in search of employment or new land to cultivate.

Hidden away in Southwest Kenya, the agricultural contribution that the Gusii people make to the country's economy is often overlooked. Yet they produce tea, coffee and pyrethrum – major foreign exchange earners – in considerable quantity. Unlike in Kericho, where the tea plantations are owned and run by large commercial concerns backed by international capital, production by the Gusii and their neighbours is mainly from smallholdings. For a century or more, conventional wisdom held that tea could only be efficiently grown on large plantations. This was challenged by Leslie Brown, famous as an authority on birds of prey, but also Kenya's senior agriculturalist at the close of the colonial era.

He was right: Kenya is now the world's third-largest tea producer after China and India, and more than half the output is being collected from thousands of individual African planters on small plots of tea-growing land. As a result, the local tea economy is particularly robust and the same policy is now being applied to the country's sugar production.

Because Kisii and the southwest of Kenya generally are so densely populated, it's not wildlife country and thus off the main tourist circuits. The visitor is unlikely to have any contact with the Gusii or their culture, except through their soapstone carvings, attractive if somewhat stereotyped artefacts, mostly animal figurines dyed black, red or blue, or left in the natural pinks, whites and greys of the soft stone.

From Kisii, it is possible to travel south to the Tanzanian border, which is 98km (61 miles) away at Isebania. However, most visitors turn off east on the way – at **Suna**, 77km (48 miles) from Kisii – and then head through **Lolgorien** (the scene of a minor gold rush in the interwar years), down the Siria escarpment and into the Maasai Mara.

The Luo

Kenya's second most numerous ethnic group, the Nilotic-speaking Luo are traditionally fishermen and farmers, as well as being the main rivals to the politically dominant Kikuyu.

The most populous of the non-Bantu-speaking ethnic groups in Kenya, the 6 million-strong Luo of the Central and South Nyanza districts, around the Winam Gulf of Lake Victoria, represent the most vigorous of several southward drives of Nilotic-speakers from the Sudan.

The first wave of Luo immigrants probably arrived in Nyanza about five centuries ago. The arrival of the last of the Luo groups in the 18th century coincided with the thrust into South Nyanza, which caused the Gusii, Kuria and Suba to retreat and also brought the Luo people into contact with the Maasai and the Kipsigis.

Cattle and constant migrations in search of pastures for their herds dominated the life of the first Luo immigrants. But they adjusted to growing population pressures by adopting a sedentary way of life in relatively isolated homesteads. Although cattle continued to dominate ritual and economic activities, agriculture and fishing became increasingly important for subsistence. These people still maintain their migratory instincts – tens of thousands seeking employment have flooded the major towns, especially Nairobi and Mombasa.

Foremost among Kenya's people in their fishing skills, the Luo today mainly use gill nets and long-line fishing to catch tilapia and other fish. Extensive use is still made of basket traps, either on their own or in conjunction with the *osageru* fish maze and the *kek* river fence at the mouths of rivers. The Luo formerly used crude log and bundle rafts of papyrus or saplings on Lake Victoria. In deeper water, hollowed-out log canoes or plank-built craft of considerable complexity and size are employed.

The dhow-type fishing boats used in offshore fishing were first constructed on the Winam Gulf by Arabs and later adapted and built by the Luo people themselves. They have also adopted the more advanced *Ssese* canoe of the Baganda, and many are now moulded in glass-fibre and often powered by outboard motors.

The head of a homestead has his own hut (*duol*) built near the cattle enclosure. Here, important matters relating to the household and community are discussed among the clan elders. Wives have their individual huts and may not sleep in the *duol*. Traditionally, a young woman whose suitor had given her parents enough cattle would be carried off by force by the bridegroom and his friends. Today, bride prices are often paid in cash in lieu of cattle and marriages are formalised by Christian rite.

Political activity

The Luo are an articulate, community-conscious people, and were prominent in Kenya's struggle for independence, providing many leading trade unionists and politicians, including the late Tom Mboya and the former Vice-President of Kenya, Oginga Odinga. This political activity has extended into the modern era, with rivalry between the Kikuyu supporters of Mwai Kibaki and followers of his Luo rival Raila Odinga having been the major cause of the outbreak of lethal violence that followed the 2007 elections. The son of the former Vice-President, Odinga took office as Prime Minister of Kenya in April 2008.

Luo folklore has been imaginatively captured in the modern fiction of Tom Okoya and Grace Ogot, whose 1966 novel *The Promised Land* was the first published by a Kenyan woman.

Luo woman near Kit Makayi.

PALMS, BAOBABS AND OTHER TREES

Kenya's varied landscape is adorned by a great variety of trees – some dramatic, some beautiful, and some are downright eccentric.

As well as harbouring hundreds of indigenous trees, Kenya had been adopted by a remarkable number of exotics – trees introduced by man, usually from tropical zones elsewhere in the world. There are several palm trees, for instance, but only one species is truly indigenous to Kenya – the doum palm, the only member of its family to grow branches. The long, slender stems repeatedly divide into two, giving the doum its distinctive appearance.

The wild date palm, on the other hand, was introduced to these parts by Arab traders, presumably so that its fruit could be cultivated, but it has spread wild along rivers and around swamps. Some authorities believe the coconut palm originally came from Polynesia, others from South America. But seaborne coconuts were washed up on African shores so long ago that this versatile tree has provided food and manufacturing materials here for centuries.

There are more than 40 species of indigenous acacia in Kenya – plus several that have been introduced, such as the golden wattle, brought by Europeans from Australia. There are Australian eucalypts, too, including the fast growing blue gum and the red-flowering gum, both first brought to Nairobi to beautify the streets of the scruffy little frontier town.

Australian flame trees grow alongside the native Nandi flame tree – both with spectacular fiery blooms. And there are imports from Asia, the South Seas and Central and South America. The countryside, especially after the rains, is a colourful riot of botanical glories.

The umbrella thorn (Acacia tortillis) is a distinctive feature of the savannah. Giraffes browse its leaves, and its fallen seedpods are a favourite of impalas.

When jacaranda blooms (Sept–Nov), its petals form a thick carpet in Nairobi and other towns.

The beautiful frangipani, originally from Central America, is named after an Italian nobleman who made perfume from it.

The baobab tree, a favourite with elephants.

THE TREE WHERE MAN WAS BORN

The baobab *(Adansonia digitata)* is central to many African legends, and it is not hard to see why. It is a bizarre tree.

Its trunk can grow up to 9 metres (30ft) in diameter, yet its thick branches do not grow in proportion and, being bare of leaves for most of the year, they look more like roots. The Kamba tribe says that God planted the baobab upside-down as punishment for its not growing where he wanted.

Then there is the tree's remarkable longevity. There are baobabs growing today that were young trees at the time of Christ. The creation myths of several tribes tell of the first humans descending from a baobab – the tree where man was born.

Ancient baobabs have survived centuries of ravages by elephants, which tear off the bark, possibly to get at the calcium it stores.

The trees' trunks are riddled with hollows and crevices, which become reservoirs of rainwater for wildlife and which serve as a home for nocturnal creatures such as bushbabies, owls and bats – and, according to many tribes, for nocturnal spirits as well.

e 'candelabra tree' is a cactus-like euphorbia. Its candlestick
anches reach up to 15 metres (50ft).

ythrina abyssinica is one of many flowering trees that depend
birds to distribute their seed: hence the colourful flower.

The coconut palm provides food, drink, cooking oil, fibre for rope and matting, and leaves for thatching.

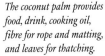

Chania Falls, on the moorlands of
the Aberdare Mountains.

MOUNT KENYA, THE ABERDARES AND LAIKIPIA

Kenya's highest region climbs from savannah through rainforest and bamboo jungle to moorland heath and finally snow-capped peaks. It's a unique part of the country.

Mount Kenya and the Aberdare Mountains, protected in a pair of national parks whose closest borders lie about 60km (30 miles) apart, comprise the highest reaches of the central highlands north of Nairobi, peaking at altitudes of 5,199 metres (17,058ft) and 3,999 metres (13,120ft) respectively. Connected by a grassy saddle, these massive mountains are also the country's most important watersheds, and their upper reaches support a unique and largely pristine highland habitat noted for its wealth of hardy endemic plants and small animals. Below this lies a forest zone, which is shared between the national parks and various surrounding forest reserves, and supports a varied selection of wildlife.

The two national parks of the central highlands were set aside mainly for their significance as the country's most important sources of freshwater. And in touristic terms, their majestic upper reaches – a starkly beautiful Afro-alpine moorland studded with clear freshwater tarns and, in the case of Mount Kenya, giving way to sheer rocky crags and glaciers – are accessible only to dedicated hikers prepared for high altitude conditions, subzero temperatures, and the possibility of blinding blizzards. Of greater interest to more sedentary tourists are a trio of hide-like 'tree hotels' that stud the

mountains' lower slopes, offering a superb opportunity to watch big game from the comfort of your room.

A popular stopover for safaris heading further north and an increasingly important wildlife-viewing destination in its own right, the Laikipia Plateau extends northward from the central highlands to form an ecological stepping stone to the barren badlands of Samburu. Unlike Kenya's other safari destinations, Laikipia has no official protected area at its core (unless you count an

Main Attractions

Mount Kenya National Park
Serena Mountain Lodge
Mount Kenya Safari Club
Ol Pejeta Conservancy
Lewa Wildlife Conservancy
Aberdare National Park
Solio Ranch

A Malachite Sunbird on a protea flower.

*Snowcovered giant
groundsels on the upper
slopes of Mount Kenya*

as yet undeveloped 70-sq-km/25-sq-mile national park proclaimed in 2011; for more information on the area visit Laikipia Wildlife Forum on www.laikipia.org), but is instead composed of a patchwork of small reserves of which the best known are Lewa Downs, Ol Pejeta and Solio Ranch. The region collectively hosts Kenya's most important populations of black rhino, white rhino, cheetah, Grevy's zebra and greater kudu, alongside most other typical safari favourites.

Kenya's highest mountain

The highest mountain in Kenya and second highest in Africa (after Kilimanjaro), Mount Kenya is an extinct volcano that formed within the last five million years and has two main peaks: **Batian** ❶ (5,199 metres/17,057ft) and Nelion (5,188 metres/17,022ft). The entire area above the 3,470-metre (11,375ft) contour line, together with two areas on the western slopes, are protected within **Mount Kenya National Park** ❷ (tel: 020 356 8763; www.kws.

Blue monkey.

go.ke; daily), which covers an area of roughly 715 sq km (275 sq miles), and is encircled by a 2,100-sq-km (810-sq-mile) forest reserve. Gazetted in 1949, the national park and forest reserve were jointly inscribed as a Unesco World Heritage Site in 1997. To keep wild animals from straying onto farmland, a 450km (280-mile)-long electric fence is currently being built to encircle much of the country's highest peak. The project should be completed in 2017.

The western areas excepted, Mount Kenya National Park begins where the upper forest merges with the heath zones of mostly *Erica arborea*, a weirdly shaped bush often as large as a tree and covered with moss and lichen. From above 3,300 metres (11,000ft), this giant heather is replaced by open moorland covered in tussock grass and studded with many species of giant lobelia and groundsel growing to a height of about 4 metres (15ft). The ground is a rich profusion of everlasting *helichrysums* and *alchemillas*, interspersed with gladioli, delphiniums and red-hot pokers.

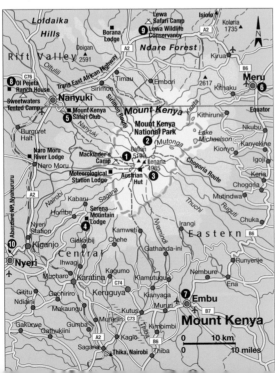

The many mountain ridges resemble the spokes of a wheel meeting at a central hub formed by the gigantic spikes of Batian and Nelion. These are surrounded by many other smaller peaks, snowfields and glaciers, tarns, lakes, waterfalls and imposing scree slopes. The peaks are the remnants of a central core of an ancient volcanic crater, the rim of which has long since eroded away. Below these jagged summits are intersecting glacier routes up 4,985 metres (16,355ft) to **Point Lenana** ❸, the highest peak attainable to visitors without specialised climbing equipment or experience. The mountain's wide variety of birds ranges from the mighty Verreaux's eagle and lammergeyer (bearded vulture) to the delicate multicoloured sunbirds. Other distinctive species include crowned eagle, mountain buzzard, Mackinder's eagle-owl, Jackson's francolin, golden-winged sunbird, scarlet-tufted malachite sunbirds and moorland chat.

The forests below the moorlands contain a rich abundance of wildlife including elephant, buffalo, lion, leopard, bushbuck, giant forest hog, bushpig, several species of duiker, black-and-white colobus, and Sykes' monkeys. The remains of an elephant and several buffaloes have been found in the peak region above 4,300 metres (14,000ft) but no one knows why they ventured into these high zones. Tracks of leopards and wild dogs have occasionally been recorded in the snow at around 4,600 metres (15,000ft) above sea level.

The attractive features of the mountain are 32 small lakes and colourful tarns. **Hall Tarn** is superbly situated, overlooking a valley and **Lake Michaelson**, well over 300 metres (1,000ft) below. At the **Curling Pond**, beneath the **Lewis Glacier**, it's possible to skate and the game of curling has been played there.

Dense rainforests cover the lower slopes of the mountain and the main tree species are the cedar, olive and podo *(podocarpus)*. Above this lies a bamboo zone at approximately 2,400 metres (7,800ft), which in turn gives way to a belt of glorious rosewood *(hagenia)* trees and giant St John's

TIP

To enjoy the beauty of Mount Kenya without the arduous trials of climbing, contact Tropic Air Kenya at Nanyuki airfield (www.tropicair kenya.com) for a breathtaking one-hour flight around the peaks.

Mount Kenya and the Lewis Glacier.

Climbing Mount Kenya

The highest peaks of Mount Kenya are not accessible to hikers, but can be conquered only by those with climbing skills and good specialist equipment.

The prime attraction for rock climbers and mountaineers in Kenya is the challenge of Mount Kenya, with its twin peaks of Batian and Nelion, both over 5,000 metres (16,400ft). Below these, jutting upwards abruptly from fields of scree and ice, is a complex of ridges, walls and couloirs, which offers high-standard technical rock and ice routes of about 650 to 1,200 metres/yards in length, at an altitude of more than 4,400 metres (14,500ft).

Climbs here are graded – though definitive grading is impossible because of variable seasonal and meteorological conditions. About half of the climbs are alpine Grade V, and the remainder are equally Grades IV and VI. Under prime conditions, some routes may be easier while under bad conditions a route may be a grade or more harder.

Climbing is generally attempted only during the two dry seasons: late December to early March, and July

Ascending Mount Kenya.

to early October. It is still possible during the off-seasons, but the accumulations of ice and snow make approach conditions very difficult: the climbs are usually at least one grade harder and take several hours longer.

Mount Kenya is on the Equator, which means seasonal variations in climbing routes. In January and February, when the sun is in the southern hemisphere, the south faces of the mountain receive direct sunlight, making them suitable for rock climbing, while the north faces remain iced-up and inaccessible. From July to September, the situation is reversed.

Equipment

Steep rock and technical ice routes are usually climbed on two 9mm ropes for greater security and a smoother descent, while easier rock and snow may be negotiated on a single 11mm rope. Most rock routes can be climbed with a selection of nuts and slings, although a few blade and angle pitons are usually carried for safety on unfamiliar routes. Tabular screws, wart-hogs, front-point unhinged crampons and ice hammers or axes with a good drooping pick are necessary for ice routes.

A tent is not normally required, as all routes can be approached from established huts, but bivouac equipment should be carried on all climbs, particularly on the longer, harder routes. Tourist lodges around the mountain provide everything you will need: guides, porters, cooks, tentage, climbing and camping equipment, food and transport to roadheads.

Altitude problems remain the most serious limitation to good performance. Conditioning is important, and acclimatisation at high altitude for a few days before the ascent is required to prevent pulmonary oedema and other altitude illnesses.

Technical climbing on the main peaks is not for everyone. **Point Lenana**, the third peak at 4,985 metres (16,355ft), offers spectacular ridge walks, and some of the outlying peaks are accessible to non-technical climbers. The mountain can be traversed over several days by keen walkers or climbers wishing to acclimatise gently before attempting a summit ascent.

Mountain Club of Kenya

For more information, as well as details of organised climbing excursions in and around Mount Kenya, see the Mountain Club of Kenya website at www.mck.or.ke. This website also includes some very useful details about less remote and lower altitude climbing sites, such as Hell's Gate National Park and Lukenya, which is the most popular crag in Kenya, largely because it lies a mere 45 minutes' drive from Nairobi.

wort *(hypericum)* before dying out at the heath zone at 3,200 metres (10,400ft).

Exploring Mount Kenya

Little more than a century ago, Mount Kenya was barely known to the outside world. Indeed, when the German missionary Johann Krapf first reported the snow-capped mountain's existence to European geographers in 1849, he was generally disbelieved. In 1887, Count Samuel Teleki von Szek and his Austrian companion, Ludwig von Höhnel, climbed to within 900 metres (3,000ft) of the summit of Mount Kenya. Twelve years later, an Englishman, Sir Halford Mackinder, finally made it to the top. Another 30 years elapsed before the distinguished mountaineer Eric Shipton made the second recorded ascent. Thereafter, the climb became popular, and there are now many well-established main routes to the summit and scores of minor ascents for the experienced alpine mountaineer.

Several vehicle tracks on both sides of the mountain wind their way up the forested ridges to the edge of the national park. Once at the park boundary, all visitors must sign in at the relevant park entrance gate. You are not permitted through the gates unaccompanied – except on a day trip, which must end at 4pm. For longer stays on the mountain, there must be at least two people, plus guides and porters. Full scale hikes to Point Lenana require at least four days, ideally longer, and should only be undertaken with an experienced operator – otherwise there is a very real risk of getting lost, especially if a blizzard rises, or succumbing to altitude sickness without experienced assistance to hand.

There are several routes to the peaks. The quickest and easiest is the Naro Moru Route, which is motorable to an altitude of 3,020 metres (9,900ft), along a track that passes through extensive forest and stops immediately below the moorlands. A popular starting point for this hike, and good place to make arrangements and rent equipment, is the **Naro Moru River Lodge** (www.naromoruriverlodge.com),

Shipton's Cave Campground, Mount Kenya.

Birdwatchers on Safari, Mount Kenya National Park.

a delightful spot set in beautiful gardens bisected by the Naro Moru River. There is higher altitude accommodation at the **Met Station Lodge** (3,000 metres/10,000ft) and at **Mackinder's Camp** (4,330 metres/14,200ft).

Several other hiking routes ascend from the footslopes to Point Lenana. The toughest and most demanding, but also the most beautiful as it goes through thick forest, **Chogoria Route** was opened up in 1929 when Edward Carr drove a Model-T Ford up the mountain, somewhat incredibly taking it to an altitude of 4,260 metres (13,980ft). Another recommended option is the very gradual **Sirimon Route**, which is particularly good for large mammals and Afro-alpine moorland flora, but requires at least five days to ascend.

Views of Mount Kenya

You don't need to camp at altitude to enjoy the spectacle of Mount Kenya's snow-capped peaks gleaming in the sun. Several small towns and lodges accessible from the surfaced circular road that rings the mountain offer

great views of the peaks, weather permitting. Particularly recommended to wildlife enthusiasts is **Serena Mountain Lodge** ❹ (www.serenahotels.com), on the forested southwestern slopes, which overlooks a small waterhole encircled by tall gallery forest alive with colourful forest birds. The wildlife viewing here, though unpredictable, can be truly exceptional, with four of the so-called Big Five – elephant, buffalo, leopard and lion – making an appearance on a good night. This is the best place in Kenya to see the nocturnal bushpig, and the most reliable spot anywhere in Africa for the seldom-seen giant forest hog. Other conspicuous forest wildlife includes Sykes' monkey, black-and-white colobus and Harvey's red duiker, the latter often seen from the walkway between the lodge and car park towards dusk.

The largest town on the western side of the ring road is **Nanyuki**, which is also the administrative capital of Laikipia District and main gateway to the reserves of the Laikipia Plateau. Founded by British

Newborn bongo antelope baby and its mother at the Mount Kenya Game Ranch.

settlers in 1907, Nanyuki is known within Kenya for its military associations – it hosts a large air force base, as well as a British army training centre – but it has little to detain tourists other than the moderately interesting colonial architecture along the main road.

Outside Nanyuki, the **Mount Kenya Safari Club** ❺ (www.fairmont.com/mount-kenya-safari), established by a Texan oil baron, a Swiss millionaire and film star William Holden, offers superb views of the mountain from its beautifully manicured gardens, and it also has a private golf course and a heated swimming pool. Surrounding the club is the **Mount Kenya Game Ranch**, an important breeding centre for the endangered mountain bongo.

Two substantial but little visited towns lie along the ring road running east of Mount Kenya. **Meru** ❻, the country's seventh-largest town, is best known perhaps as a gateway to Meru National Park (see page 207), but it is also an important agricultural centre, and Kenya's main centre of production

for the leafy stimulant known as *khat* or *miraa*. The former District Commissioner's office, built in 1916, now houses the **Meru National Museum** (tel: 064 32482, 0786 559 427; daily 9am–6pm), which is dedicated to the culture of the Meru people. Further southwest, **Embu** ❼ is at its prettiest in November, when its jacaranda-lined avenues come into purple bloom, and has only one major landmark in the form of an African-themed Catholic Cathedral built in 1986.

Ol Pejeta Ranch

Day visitors are also welcome at **Ol Pejeta Conservancy** ❽ (tel: 020 203 3244; www.olpejetaconservancy.org), which is the busiest conservancy in Laikipia thanks to the presence of a 40-room tented camp, and the closest to Nanyuki Airport. Ol Pejeta incorporates the original **Sweetwaters Game Reserve**, which was set aside in 1988 as a rhino sanctuary, but it now incorporates the entire 365-sq-km (140-sq-mile) ranch following its acquisition by the UK-based conservation organisation Fauna and Flora International.

Vervet monkey, Ol Pejeta Wildlife Conservancy.

A family group of black-and-white Guereza Colobus monkeys in the forests of the Aberdare Mountains.

Jackson's Hartebeest, Ol Pejeta Wildlife Conservancy.

The Karuru Falls.

Game viewing here is excellent, with a good chance of encountering lion, elephant, buffalo, and white and black rhinos (the population of the latter numbers more than 100) over the course of an overnight stay. Also present are reticulated giraffe, Beisa oryx, Thomson's and Grant's gazelle (the latter an unusually dark form), Jackson's hartebeest and Beisa oryx. Both Kenyan species of zebra are present and it is one place where they regularly hybridise.

Two smaller and more specialised sanctuaries lie within Ol Pejeta. The better known is the **Sweetwaters Chimpanzee Sanctuary** (9–10.30am, 3–4.30pm), which was founded in 1993 to protect orphaned chimps, housed at the Jane Goodall Institute in Burundi prior to the outbreak of civil war there. This is Kenya's only population of chimpanzees (which do not occur in the country naturally) and it can be viewed from the footpath forming part of the sanctuary's boundary that follows the opposite bank of the Ewaso Nyiro River.

Rather more esoteric is the **White Rhino Sanctuary** (daily 6am-7pm; separate charge for entry into this part of Ol Pejeta Ranch), where as of 2015, two (both females) of the world's last four remaining northern white rhino live. They are the only surviving animals out of six there were transported there from a European zoo in 2008. Easily distinguished from their southern counterparts by their hairier ears, the sanctuary's northern rhinos were all dehorned, a move that made them less vulnerable to poachers (and, it must be said, less attractive to photograph).

Lewa Wildlife Conservancy

Back on the main road from Nanyuki to Isiolo, about 3km (2 miles) past the junction for Meru, is the entrance to the **Lewa Wildlife Conservancy** ❾ (tel: 064 313 1405; www.lewa.org; no day visits), a Unesco World Heritage Site since 2013. The home of the Craig family since 1924, the 265-sq-km (93-sq-mile) area operated solely as a cattle ranch until 1983 when part of it was set

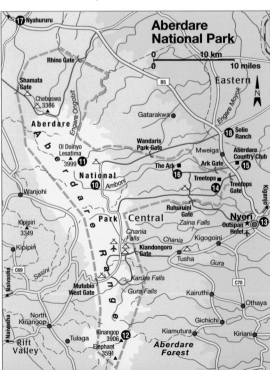

aside as a wildlife sanctuary, and was followed by the rest of the property a few years later. The adjacent family ranch house (www.lewahouse.com) and Lewa Safari Camp (http://lewa safaricamp.com) offer accommodation and a choice of guided game walks, horseback rides, daytime game drives and night drives through an area of craggy hills inhabited by plentiful wildlife. Lewa is a vital stronghold for Grevy's zebra (an estimated population of 400 individuals represents 15 percent of the global total), and it also harbours more than 120 rhino, with both black and white species likely to be seen over the course of a two-night stay. Also likely to be seen are lion, cheetah, elephant, buffalo, reticulated giraffe and a wide variety of antelope including the localised sitatunga antelope, which was translocated to Lewa from Saiwa Swamp National Park in the 1980s. The sanctuary is run as a non-profit-making organisation, with proceeds being pumped back into conservation, or diverted to local community projects and economic development.

Aberdare National Park

Where Mount Kenya is a geological infant, the nearby **Aberdare National Park** ❿ (tel: 020 204 6271; www.kws.go.ke; daily 6am–6pm) protects one of the most ancient mountain ranges in East Africa, comprising bedrock thought to be at least 100 million years old. Known as Nyandarua (Drying Hide) to the Kikuyu, due to its faint resemblance to a pegged-out cattle skin, the range's existence was first documented in 1885 by the explorer Joseph Thomson, who named it after Lord Aberdare of the Royal Geographic Society. The national park, which extends across the upper slopes for 767 sq km (296 sq miles), was gazetted in 1950, and since 2009 has been enclosed entirely by a 400km (249-mile) -long electric fence to protect its rhinos – a process implemented with the financial backing of the charity Rhino Ark (www.rhinoark.org).

The mountains rise in the north to the highest moorland peak of **Ol Doinyo Lesatima** ⓫ at 3,999 metres (13,120ft), and some 40km

Vegetation on the slopes of Mount Kenya.

Chimpanzee, Sweetwaters Chimpanzee Sanctuary, Ol Pejeta Wildlife Conservancy.

(25 miles) to the south stands the well-known summit of **Kinangop** ⑫ at 3,906 metres (12,816ft). Between these two peaks is a plateau of moorland – gently undulating country covered in tussock grass and large areas of mixed giant heath. Ice-cold streams, well stocked with trout, thread their way across the moorlands and cascade as a series of waterfalls to form the headwaters of several of the major rivers. The Park is criss-crossed with tracks, many made by British troops during the Mau Mau rebellion in the 1950s. The most important of these is the road that climbs the eastern slopes from Nyeri, running across the moorlands, to a height of 3,170 metres (10,400ft), then descending the western slopes to cross the Kinangop farmlands to terminate at Naivasha.

The Aberdares are well endowed with a great variety and quantity of wild animals despite the occurrence of periodic cold and mist. The western slopes of the range are principally part of the Rift wall, and are therefore relatively steep and generally not as attractive to game as are the more gentle slopes of the eastern side. Elephant, buffalo, eland, waterbuck, bushbuck, reedbuck, several species of duikers, suni, bushpig, warthog, serval, lion, Sykes' monkey and hyena occur in varying numbers and most of them are easily seen. Rhino are sparse here, as everywhere else in the country, but they can be seen on the moors and particularly on the **Treetops Salient**. Herds of elephant and buffalo migrate with the rain, occupying the bamboo and rainforest zones during the dry seasons. When the rain begins, the game migrates to the plateau moorlands and the lower areas of the Treetops Salient, where the forest is not so dense and the ridges are less steep.

Nyeri

The urban gateway to the Aberdares, **Nyeri** ⑬ is the administrative capital of Central Province and birthplace of such prominent Kenyans as President Mwai Kibaki,

Grevy's zebra, Lewa Wildlife Conservancy.

Nobel Peace Prize winner Wangari Maathai, and the runner Catherine Ndereba. Here, the Outspan Hotel is an attractive colonial relic set in large gardens that offer distant views of Mount Kenya and access to the forested Chania River and a Kikuyu cultural village. Lord Baden Powell, the founder of the Scout movement, spent the last three years of his life here – his old cottage at the Outspan is now a museum – and is buried alongside his wife in the cemetery at St Peter's Anglican Church.

The Outspan is also the congregation point for overnight guests to be transported to **Treetops** ⓮ the famous lodge where the future Queen Elizabeth II learned of her accession to the British throne in February 1952. Overlooking a waterhole on protected land within Aberdare National Park, this the most historically poignant of the 'tree hotels' of the central highlands, with a lounge rich in royal memorabilia, and it attracts elephant and buffalo most nights, as well as a variety of smaller game.

On the road northwest from Nyeri, the **Aberdare Country Club** ⓯ (www.aberdarecountryclub.com), set on the side of Mweiga hill, affords great views of Mount Kenya and the Laikipia plains, and attractive grounds with a golf course and horse riding among other outdoor activities. It is mainly of interest, however as the place where visitors to **The Ark** ⓰ (www.thearkkenya.com) assemble before being transported there for an overnight stay. Similar in conception to Treetops and Serena Mountain Lodge, The Ark is situated over a natural water hole, which is illuminated at night when it reliably attracts the likes of elephant, buffalo, bushbuck, genet and spotted hyena, but is also quite often visited by lion, leopard and rhino.

To the north of the Aberdares, along a back route to Nakuru, **Nyahururu** ⓱ is Kenya's highest and possibly chilliest town, with an altitude of 2,360 metres (7,741ft). It is best known as the site of the pretty 75-metre (243ft) Thomson's Falls, which lies on the Ewaso Nyiro

The Outspan Safari Lodge, Nyeri town.

Smallholders' tea gardens beside the Mathioya River.

River as it makes its way from the Aberdares to the arid lowlands around Samburu-Buffalo Springs. Overlooked by the underutilised colonial-era Thomson's Falls Lodge, a path leads from the top of the falls to the river below, where a ribbon of riverine harbours plenty of birds and monkeys.

The Laikipia Plateau

Running northwest from the moist highland saddle that divides Mount Kenya and the Aberdares, the 9,500-sq-km (23,670-sq-mile) **Laikipia Plateau**, with an average elevation of around 2,000 metres (6,600ft), is ecologically intermediate between Kenya's central highlands and northern badlands. Incised by the Ewaso Nyiro and Ewaso Narok Rivers, which run through spectacular gorges in the north, the plateau extends westward to the dramatic Rift Valley escarpment overlooking Lakes Bogoria and Baringo, sloping away gently to become lower-lying and more arid in its far north.

In the colonial era, Laikipia was widely settled by European farmers,

Black rhinoceros with calf, Solio Game Ranch.

whose vast ranches were interspersed with community land, and the area's wildlife was often persecuted. Today, by contrast, the plateau comprises a few dozen privately and communally owned sanctuaries, overseen by the Laikipia Forum (www.laikipia.org), and it is the only part of Kenya in which wildlife numbers have significantly increased since independence. Collectively, it is the country's second-largest protected ecosystem (after Tsavo), with a strong wilderness character complemented by about 7,000 elephant, the country's most significant populations of black rhino, greater kudu, Jackson's hartebeest, Grevy's zebra and African wild dog, as well as plenty of lion, leopard and other predators. The scenery is also impressive, particularly on the southern reaches of the plateau, where the rocky snow-capped peaks of Mount Kenya and more modest outline of the Aberdares form a dramatic backdrop, weather permitting.

Compared to Amboseli or the Maasai Mara, Laikipia remains

somewhat off-the-beaten-track, but as the site of some of Africa's most luxurious and exclusive safari camps, it is slowly emerging as an upmarket touristic hotspot. However, unlike most other conservation areas in Kenya, it is essentially a mosaic of small exclusive conservancies, many of which are fully or partially fenced, each functioning as a self-contained destination running its own game drives in open 4x4s using skilled guides that know the property backwards. In addition, because the conservancies are private as opposed to public property, guided walks and spotlighted night drives are also on the activities menu at most camps.

The main gateway to the region, **Nanyuki** lies on the northwest slope of Mount Kenya some 200km (120 miles) along a good surfaced road from Nairobi. The most usual point of entry, however, is nearby Nanyuki Airport, which is connected to the capital and other tourist centres by regular flights. Access roads from Nanyuki to the scattered individual conservancies in Laikipia vary in quality, but some are very rough, so most people visit one specific property within the ecosystem, transferring there either by 4x4 or by charter flight. Some Laikipia conservancies are more-or-less directly accessible from surfaced roads. Lewa, for instance, lies alongside the road between Nanyuki and Isiolo, while Solio Ranch is immediately east of the main road between Nyeri and Nyahururu, and Ol Pejeta is only 10km (6 miles) on dirt west of Nanyuki.

The most southerly conservancy in Laikipia, the family-run **Solio Ranch** ⑱ (www.thesafaricollection.com), is also one of the oldest, founded in 1970 as a breeding centre for introduced founder populations of 23 black and 16 white rhino. Such is the success of the breeding programme that the ranch now supports around 150 rhino in total, and more than 100 individuals have been translocated to other private reserves in Laikipia as well as Lake Nakuru, Tsavo West and Aberdare National Park. There is genuinely no better place in Africa to

The famous Treetops Hotel.

see both rhino species – it is perfectly normal to see a few dozen white rhino and more than five black in one game drive – and the open plains that cover most of the reserve also harbour large numbers of buffalo, zebra, giraffe, eland and Beisa oryx. The riparian forest of yellow fever trees that follows a marshy waterway through the reserve is a good place to look for lion, leopard, waterbuck and impala. Unlike most other reserves in Laikipia, Solio actively encourages private day visits in 4x4s – indeed it was only in 2010 that the first lodge opened on the property.

Camps and lodges

In the more arid hills to the north-west of Lewa Downs, the **Il Ngwesi** group ranch is home to Il Ngwesi Lodge www.ilngwesi.com), which has won awards for ecotourism. It is constructed out of local driftwood and clay, and has no windows. The furnishings are in keeping with the theme of the lodge – simple but elegant. On Lekueeuki Community Group Ranch there's another eco-lodge, **Tassia** (www.tassiasafaris. com), with breathtaking views towards Samburu and Shaba. Just north of Wamba is **Sarara Camp** (www.sararacamp.com), located in the Namunyak Wildlife Conservation Trust, which is also promoted and supported by the Lewa Wildlife Conservancy. You can either go self-catering or pay for a fully catered stay. To reach this wilderness area, drive northwards from Nanyuki on a rather rough tarmac road; Mount Kenya lies on your right, with vast stretches of open bush country ahead of you. Not far from Timau is the turning to Borana Ranch, which takes you (after about an hour's drive) through the wildlife area to **Borana Lodge** (www.borana.co.ke). This offers first-class accommodation in six unique cottages built of cedar and glass, with fine views of Mount Kenya. This retreat (where the writers of *The Lion King* supposedly got their inspiration) sits on a private game ranch in a valley running from the Laikipia Plateau to the Samburu plains.

A shady spot under an acacia tree at Il Ngwesi safari lodge.

Picture This

The parks and reserves of Kenya offer some wonderful opportunities for wildlife photography, but for decent results, you'll need to bring along the right equipment.

East Africa attracts photographers the way a zebra carcass attracts vultures. Nowhere else in the world is it possible to find such diversity and concentrations of photogenic creatures, not to mention such a variety of dramatic scenery.

Early cameras were too big to carry in the field. A picture taken circa 1900 shows an earnest photographer pursuing a rhino with a camera the size of a microwave oven. It weighed 7kg (16lbs). Exposure took minutes – too long to capture an unrestrained creature on film. Since then, cameras and wildlife photography have changed dramatically. Fast digital imaging systems, telephoto lenses and motor drives give photographers additional flexibility.

The best times to take pictures in the Kenyan bush are before 9am and after 4pm, when the sun is low and not too fierce. In the middle of the day, unless it is overcast, the light is simply too bright, 'bleaching out' colours, and shadows are impenetrably black.

Most safari pictures are taken from the roof-hatch of a vehicle, but shooting everything from above can create stereotyped images and often results in odd angles when the subject is very close to the car (like photographing a person from above rather than square on). Shooting from a lower angle out of a side window frequently results in more striking and dramatic pictures, though this is less the case when you are dealing with a tall subject such as a giraffe or elephant at a distance.

Equipment

The most suitable camera for wildlife is an SLR with interchangeable lenses. Where possible, professional wildlife photographers like to work with fixed telephoto lenses, with a 500mm or 600mm lens being the practical upper size limit for work in the field. But zoom lenses are more versatile and much cheaper, with 80 to 200mm or better still 80 to 400mm being ideal ranges. A 1.4x or 2x converter will increase your magnification capacity, but at the sacrifice of some quality.

Telephoto lenses are prone to camera shake since they magnify image movement. Shoulder supports help to reduce camera shake. When photographing out of vehicles, sand or bean bags are the best option, and while they can be bought from camera shops, it also easy enough to make one yourself and fill it with something suitable (rice, beans, any grain) when you arrive in Kenya. Lay the bag on the roof of your open safari vehicle and mould the lens on to it. Tripods provide better stability but are very cumbersome when used in vehicles. A monopod is a practical compromise.

An ultraviolet or polarising filter can help to diffuse the worst of the sun's rays; a 'warm' amber filter is useful, too, to correct the 'bleaching out' of colour. With a good quality SLR, it is probably best shooting in RAW mode, to give maximum flexibility at the processing stage.

During dry times of the year, dust can be a serious hazard to your photographic equipment. It is particularly important to protect the camera from wind-blown dust if you load film. Keep all your cameras and lenses in sealed polythene bags when not in use.

Digital photography is greedy for batteries. Be sure to bring plenty of spares or, better still, rechargeable batteries and a charger. These days, almost all camps and lodges provide a facility for recharging batteries overnight, but if you are heading to very remote areas, it's best to always check in advance.

Flamingo watching at Lake Bogoria

Leopard in the long grass, Meru National Park.

NORTHERN GAME CIRCUIT

The vast desert and semi-desert region stretching north and northwest of Mount Kenya to the borders with Sudan, Ethiopia and Somalia is a magnificent and largely unexplored wilderness.

Nairobi

Kenya's northern safari circuit is very different in character from its more popular southern counterpart. It is centred upon the contiguous Samburu and Buffalo Springs national reserves, tracts of arid, thorny bush that flank the perennial Ewaso Ngiro River, but also include the nearby and climatically similar Shaba National Reserve and the underutilised Meru National Park. Not only do these reserves possess a wilder and relatively untrammelled mood than the ones to their south, but they also host a collection of unique dry-country endemics – the outsized Grevy's zebra, the striking reticulated giraffe, and the oddball gerenuk for instance – whose global range is more-or-less focussed upon the north of Kenya.

Meru National Park

Extending over 870 sq km (335 sq miles) to the west of Mount Kenya, **Meru National Park** ❶ (tel: 061 230 3094, 0786 348 875; www.kws. go.ke; daily 6am–7pm) is in many respects transitional between the moist central highlands and semi-arid north. Straddling the equator, it lies in the rain shadow of the Nyambeni Hills, and spans altitudes of 1,000 metres (3,300ft) in the foothills that form the northern boundary to less than 300 metres (990ft)

on the Tana River as it runs along the southern boundary. In addition to the Tana, which is Kenya's longest river, the park is run through by another 15 perennial tributaries, of which the Rojewero River, lined by a belt of riparian forest and tall doum palms, is the most voluminous.

Geologically, Meru is an extremely interesting park. Most of the land surface is comprised of olivine basalt, which was deposited by lava flows from the Nyambeni, and is overlaid with rich brown and grey volcanic or

Main Attractions
Meru National Park
Samburu-Buffalo Springs National Reserve
Shaba National Reserve

Bathing hippopotamus.

TIP

If you plan to drive into remote parts of Meru, especially in the rainy seasons, it is wise to check with the Park HQ (south of Leopard Rock Lodge) on the condition of tracks, especially along the rivers.

black cotton soils strewn with small pumice boulders. The basement rock occasionally forms lows inselbergs or kopjes (rocky outcrops), while numerous swamps and springs occur where the lava is spread thin on the basement system, particularly along the fault line that runs southwest from Kinna to Kilimakieru. The largest of these are Kithima ya Mugumu (Fig Tree Springs), Murera Springs and the Bisanadi, Buguma and Mulika Swamps.

Meru has enjoyed mixed fortunes over the past few decades. Game was reputedly very scarce back in 1959, at which point the local Meru people seized the initiative from the colonial government and designated the area for conservation and rehabilitation. It attained global renown in the 1960s as the location where Joy Adamson released the hand-reared lioness Elsa into the wild, as documented in the book and movie *Born Free*. As a result of this publicity, and a rapid increase in wildlife numbers, Meru soon became one the recognised highlights of Kenya's safari

A baobab tree near Elsa's Kopje.

circuit, attracting around 40,000 visitors annually into the mid-1980s. At that point, the park supported an abundance of elephant and black rhinoceros, and it even hosted a small, protected herd of white rhinoceros, introduced from South Africa.

That changed almost overnight in the late 1980s when the park was targeted by commercial poachers who killed its famous rhinos, and the guards assigned to protect them, attacked several tourist vehicles and mowed down the majority of its once prolific wildlife. The park remained in poor shape throughout the 1990s, but in 2000 it became the subject of a five-year restoration programme, funded largely by a US$1.25 million donation from the International Fund for Animal Welfare (IFAW), and wildlife numbers are now approaching their 1970s peaks.

Getting to Meru

Two routes lead from Nairobi to Meru National Park: one around Mount Kenya, through **Nanyuki**, and the other one through Embu.

Meru National Park and Kora National Park

Theera
Murera Gate
Kinna
Kiengu
Bisanadi Gate
Rhino River Camp
Meru Rhino Sanctuary
Leopard Rock Swamp
Leopard Rock Lodge
20 km
20 miles
Nyambeni Forest
Park Headquarters
Skot
Elsa's Kopje
Meru National Park
Bisanadi National Reserve
Rojewero Plains
Rojewero
Murera
Kiolu Sand
Equator
Ura Gate
Ura
Tana
Kathithine
Adamson's Falls
Kanjora
Kora National Park
Kalangachini
Meru
E a s t e r n
C o a s t
Tana
Usueni
North Kitui National Reserve
Tharaka
Tseikuru
Mwitamisyi
Mwingi, Thika, Machakos

Both roads go to Meru town, from where it is 78km (48 miles) to the park. If you go via Nanyuki, you can enter the park from the west using the **Murera Gate**. Some visitors prefer to fly in to avoid the slow and winding road. Within the park, the main tourist roads are in the west, with only a few roads in the remote east, where the park is bordered by a quartet of national reserves – Bisanadi, North Kitui, Kora and Rahole – that encompasses 4,670 sq km (1,868 sq miles) of largely inaccessible wilderness.

Meru highlights

Vegetation is mainly wooded savannah, with *Combretum* bush prevailing in the north and *Commiphora* in the south. The northeast is dominated by grassland with *borassus* palms and acacia woodland. There is plenty of water thanks to the many rivers that rise in the Nyambeni Hills and flow into the Tana. Most of these rivers are bordered by riverine forest. Some valleys are partially flooded during the rainy season, providing a swampy grassland habitat favoured by waterbuck as well as large herds of elephant and buffalo.

Meru also supports a range of species more usually found in northern areas, including Grevy's zebra and Beisa oryx. The reticulated giraffe – rust-red coloured with distinctive thin white lines creating a 'crazy paving' effect – flourishes here. Dik-dik, gerenuk and the big cats are abundant, though the latter are sometimes difficult to see because of the tall grass cover and thick bush. Eland and kongoni prefer the wetter grassland areas. Lesser kudu, either alone or in pairs, can be found in thickets or in valley bottoms in the evening.

Set in the northwest corner of the park, close to the main Murera Entrance Gate, the fenced 4x4-only **Meru Rhino Sanctuary** ❷ (http://merurhinosanctuary.com) was created in 2005 as part of an initiative to draw tourists back to this oft-neglected park. Around 50 rhinos, both black and white species, from Lake Nakuru National Park and the Laikipia Plateau were introduced to the

Grevy's zebra, Meru National Park.

White rhinoceros, Meru Rhino Sanctuary.

Reticulated giraffe.

The beast that gave Buffalo Springs its name.

sanctuary over the subsequent two years, and the area now hosts a population estimated at more than 80. Despite the population within this small area being among the world's densest, the rhino can be difficult to spot in the bushy vegetation. The Mururi Swamp, set within the sanctuary, is a good place to look, especially in the late afternoon, and it is also a favoured haunt of elephant – whose population has now reached 700 here – and buffalo. Ironically, the game viewing roads running immediately to the southeast of the sanctuary are among the park's best, as wildlife regularly gathers there to follow animal paths blocked by the electric fence – but rather disconcertingly, most of this wildlife will be on the opposite side of the fence to human observers.

Birdwatchers should look out for the relatively uncommon palm-nut vulture, which feeds on a mixture of palm nuts and carrion. In addition, the palm swift can be seen building its nest on the underside of palm fronds. Pel's fishing owl nest quietly in riverine woodland, while the secretive African finfoot – which resembles a slender long-necked duck or small cormorant – is sometimes seen swimming close to the riverbank under overhanging trees. Also worth looking out for is the half-collared kingfisher, a handsome but unobtrusive bird that seems to be unusually conspicuous in the park's riverine vegetation. The striking vulturine guinea-fowl and yellow-throated francolin are common along the roadsides.

The backdrops at Meru are picturesque, sometimes abstract. On clear mornings, the snowy peaks of Mount Kenya appear in the southwest, but perhaps the definitive Meru skyscape is when the sun stands directly behind the bordering Nyambeni Hills, scattering light shafts through the summits. At **Adamson's Falls** ❸ on the Tana River, blocks of granite have been weathered and watered into weird shapes, like modern sculptures. Nearby, set in a quiet forest clearing, is Elsa's Grave, where the subject of *Born Free* was buried after contracting

a fatal malaria-borne disease aged only five.

Bordering Meru on the middle reaches of the Tana River, the 1,790-sq-km (700-sq-mile) **Kora National Park** ❹ (tel: 020 2321 696, 0720 765 445; www.kws.go.ke; daily) was made famous by the late George Adamson (www.georgeadamson.org), who for years engaged in the dangerous business of reintroducing captive lions and leopards to the wild. This remote region, composed of riverine woodland along the Tana River and miles of bush in the interior, is studded with rocky outcrops with their own unique habitats and fauna. Wildlife is generally sparse, however, and access is difficult unless you mount a full-scale 4x4 expedition.

Meru lodges and camps

Accommodation options were almost non-existent in Meru in the 1990s, and its development today is limited to a handful of small upmarket lodges, which is good news for those who do visit, as the park retains an aura of wilderness and exclusivity. The most upmarket camp is the stunning **Elsa's Kopje** ❺ (http://elsaskopje.com), situated on Mughwango Hill, with breathtaking views over the plains. Near the Mulika Swamp, on the banks of the Murera River, is **Leopard Rock Lodge** ❻ (www.leopardmico.com). Set on private land just outside the park, close to the fenced rhino sanctuary, is the new **Rhino River Camp** (http://rhinorivercamp.com).

Samburu and Buffalo Springs

The descent from the Mount Kenya ring road via the frontier town of Isiolo to tiny **Archer's Post** ❼ marks the transition from the green meadows of the central highlands into the region once known as the Northern Frontier District – a stark, rugged landscape where nomads still drive their herds across arid plains covered in acacia scrub and meagre seasonal crops of grass. It is a wild and empty landscape, one epitomised by two contiguous national reserves, **Samburu** ❽ and **Buffalo Springs** ❾

FACT

The Tana River is the habitat boundary between two races of giraffe. The reticulated giraffe lives north of the Tana; its cousin, the Maasai giraffe, to the south.

Ewaso Ngiro River.

Freedom Fighters

Joy and George Adamson achieved renown in the 1960s for their success in rehabilitating hand-reared lions and leopards, and their work continues through the Born Free Foundation.

Joy-Friederike Gessner was born in 1910 in Troppau, then part of Austria-Hungary, now in the Czech Republic. After an education in Vienna followed by two divorces, she came to Kenya in 1939.

George Adamson was born in India in 1906, and at the age of 18 travelled to Kenya to seek his fortune. After working as a gold prospector, goat trader and big-game hunter, he landed work as an assistant game warden in 1938.

The couple met at Christmas 1942, and married in 1944. It was the beginning of a partnership that became world-famous for hand-rearing orphaned big cats and reintroducing them to the wild.

The story began in 1956, when George was forced to shoot a lioness that was attacking him. She left three cubs, which the Adamsons 'adopted' and raised. One of them, Elsa, became internationally

Joy Adamson and Elsa.

famous through Joy's trilogy of bestselling books – most famously *Born Free* – that were also adapted into successful films, starting in 1966.

By then, Joy Adamson had founded the Elsa Wild Animal Appeal and George had left his job as a game warden to devote his energies to the task of rearing and releasing lions – not only Elsa and her family, but many other orphaned cubs that were brought to the Adamsons as their fame spread. Joy also trained a young cheetah, Pippa, back to her wild ways, and even found time to write an illuminating book, *The Peoples of Kenya*, in 1967.

In 1970 the couple separated. George moved to Kora and established Kampi ya Simba (Lion Camp) to continue his work. By 1978 he had released more than 23 orphaned or captive lions into the wild. Meanwhile Joy moved to Shaba, where she began to concern herself with leopards. In 1980, she was murdered in her Shaba camp by a disgruntled employee.

Although they had lived apart for nine years, the death of his wife deeply affected George Adamson. He withdrew from all public activity and rarely left Kora, which like neighbouring Meru National Park, was then suffering from severe poaching. Despite this, Adamson and his associate, Tony Fitzjohn, worked there devotedly with their beloved lions and a small team of dedicated workers.

In August 1989 poachers ambushed some of George Adamson's camp staff. He drove out to help, and was shot dead. He was 83. He is buried at Kampi ya Simba, beside his favourite lion, Elsa's son 'Boy'.

Born Free Foundation

The Adamsons did much to change public attitudes to wild animals and their most important legacy today is the Born Free Foundation, founded in 1984 by Virginia McKenna and Bill Travers, the real-life husband and wife who played Joy and George in *Born Free*. The foundation, whose logo is a lioness representing Elsa, is concerned not only with direct conservation issues, but also with public awareness campaigns and with the welfare of animals in zoos and other captive situations.

Within Kenya, the Born Free Foundation (www. bornfree.org.uk), which celebrated its 25th anniversary in 2009, is an important supporter of the Amboseli Elephant Research Project, the Mount Elgon Elephant Monitoring Project and the Bill Woodley Mount Kenya Trust. It is also involved in eight other African countries – one of its most famous projects is South Africa's Shamwari Big Cat Rescue Centre, which provides sanctuary to mistreated lions and leopards rescued from captivity.

(www.samburucouncil.com; daily 6am–7pm), whose main entrance gates lie close to Archers Post, about 50km (30 miles) along what is now a paved road from Isiolo, though they can also be entered via the **Ngare Mara Gate**, only 20km (12 miles) north of Isiolo.

Samburu and Buffalo Springs, which flank the Ewaso Ngiro (Brown Water) River to the north and south respectively, are usually treated as one unit by safari operators – as well as by the local wildlife. However, the only land connections between the two reserves are the bridge across the river on the main road between Isiolo and Archer's Post, and another bridge near the administrative headquarters about 20km (12 miles) further west.

Ololokwe

Physically dramatic, with a great table mountain called **Ololokwe** in the background, the 100-sq-km (40-sq-mile) Samburu National Reserve is baked red-brown for most of the year. A permanent relief is in the broad green ribbon of trees along the Ewaso Ngiro, which originates on the Laikipia Plateau, fed by the runoff from the Aberdares and Mount Kenya, and eventually drains into the recesses of the Lorian Swamp in the east towards Somalia. The central part of both reserves is dry, open, thorn-bush country that becomes green only during the rains, but the river, lined by acacias, tamarind and doum palms, is a permanent source of water for animals.

A variety of animals can be found. Crocodiles sun themselves on the banks of the river, while elephant, buffalo and waterbuck feed on the associated vegetation and adjoining swamps. Lion, cheetah and leopard are also fairly easy to see, thanks to the sparse grass cover. Grevy's zebra, beisa oryx, reticulated giraffe, lesser kudu and gerenuk are all found only in this sort of dry, semi-arid country. Dik-dik are far more common and particularly like the rocky hills and dry acacia woodland here. Smaller mammals include ground squirrels, which are common around the lodges, and dwarf mongooses,

FACT

Leopard baiting was once practised by lodges in Samburu-Buffalo Springs, to attract these elusive cats to spotlighted viewing points. The practise has been discontinued, but the descendants of the baited leopards remain among the most habituated in Africa.

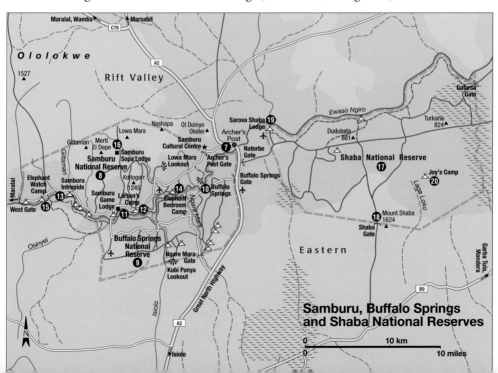

Samburu, Buffalo Springs and Shaba National Reserves

FACT

An unverified local legend has it that the pools at Buffalo Springs are not natural, but were created in World War II when an Italian bomber plane from occupied Somalia missed its target of Isiolo by 50km (30 miles).

Samburu tribe performing a welcome dance for tourists.

frequently seen scampering across the open ground.

Birds are abundant, with more than 365 species recorded, including the localised Somali ostrich, whose blue (as opposed to pink) legs are particularly conspicuous during the breeding season. Birds of prey, such as the Egyptian vulture, martial eagle, bateleur and pygmy falcon, are also commonly seen. The rare Narina trogon, a bird with a bright green and red breast, is often seen in the riverine woodland. Of particular interest are a number of dry country species difficult to see elsewhere in Kenya, among them vulturine guineafowl, Somali bee-eater, white-headed mousebird and black-capped social weaver.

The three clear pools of **Buffalo Springs ❿**, for which the more southerly of the two reserves is named, lie a short distance from its eastern gate immediately south of the Ewaso Nyiro. The only one of the three springs left open is an important dry-season magnet for thirsty wildlife, with Beisa oryx

and reticulated giraffe being especially common visitors. Of the other two springs, the larger is protected within a tall concrete wall, while the other feeds a disused and rather slimy looking swimming pool associated with the defunct Buffalo Springs Lodge.

Cultural villages

Another attraction of Samburu-Buffalo Springs is the opportunity to visit one of several semi-formal cultural villages inhabited by the Samburu people, close affiliates of the Maasai. Several such villages are dotted around Archer's Post, which – despite its rather dusty and scruffy appearance – is an important trade centre for the local Samburu. Arranged through any of the reserve's lodges, Samburu village visits can feel a touch voyeuristic, but it does ensure some of the money from tourists filter down to local communities, and the photogenic Samburu dances – a gleeful display of wild ululation and pogo-style bouncing – are genuinely thrilling.

Samburu-Buffalo Springs accommodation

Samburu-Buffalo Springs is serviced by almost a dozen camps and lodges, most of which are quite large and lie on the north bank of the Ewaso Ngiro River in Samburu National Reserve. Among these are the stalwart and rather impersonal **Samburu Game Lodge ⑪** (www.wilder nesslodges.co.ke), which has an ideal location near the western boundary; the small but elegant **Larsens Camp ⑫** (www.wildernesslodges.co.ke); the medium capacity **Samburu Intrepids ⑬** (www.heritage-eastafrica. com); the luxurious **Elephant Bedroom Camp ⑭** (www.atua-enkop. com);and the eco-friendly **Elephant Watch Camp ⑮** (http://elephant watchportfolio.com). The latter lies 10 minutes from an elephant research centre established by Iain Douglas-Hamilton, who founded the Save the Elephants charity and, together with his wife Oria, wrote the books *Among the Elephants* and *Battle for the Elephants*. The only lodge away from the river is **Samburu Sopa Lodge ⑯** (www.sopalodges.com) which has a hillside location suited to seeking out dry-country birds.

Shaba National Reserve

The largest and least developed of the three reserves centred upon Archer's Post is **Shaba National Reserve ⑰**, which lies about 8km (5 miles) to the east of Samburu-Buffalo Springs, on the opposite side of the road between Isiolo and Archer's Post. Set on the south bank of the Ewaso Ngiro River, this 240-sq-km (93-sq-mile) reserve, though somewhat obscure compared to its westerly neighbours, is known as where Joy Adamson of *Born Free* fame was murdered in 1980. More recently, it served as the setting for the 2001 reality show *Survivor Africa* and attracted global attention a year later when a resident lioness, nicknamed Kamuniak (Blessed One),

attempted to rear half-a-dozen oryx calves in close succession.

The reserve's central attraction is again the wide, sauntering Ewaso Ngiro on its way to the Lorian Swamp, as well as the tall trees of the stark riverine forest that provide a sharp contrast to the rugged and pitted tracts which make up much of the sanctuary. Many small hills diversify Shaba and, with four springs, the reserve is better watered than its neighbours. Heavy downpours often render the already rough tracks accessible only by 4x4 vehicles. All this serves only to enhance the traveller's sense of the reserve's isolation, which is the essence of Shaba – a place for the connoisseur, where an authentic African experience is the objective.

Mount Shaba

Shaba National Reserve takes its name from the 1,624-metre (5,324ft) **Mount Shaba ⑱**, a copper-coloured sandstone hill which lies partially in the reserve and is famous for the lava flows that oozed down from the

The Ewaso Nyiru River flows through a spectacular gorge in Shaba National Reserve.

Nyambeni Hills only 5,000 years ago. The western side of the reserve is bushed grassland savannah, dotted with thorn bushes, gradually becoming acacia woodland nearer Mount Shaba. Beyond the mountain the vegetation becomes grassland plains.

Shaba protects a similar range of creatures to Samburu-Buffalo Springs, including elephant, lion, cheetah, leopard, waterbuck and dry-country specials such as Beisa oryx, gerenuk, Grevy's zebra, reticulated giraffe and Somali ostrich. Wildlife densities are lower, however, and animals tend to be rather shy. As some compensation, the overall feel of the reserve is wilder, and it is often possible to drive long periods without seeing another safari vehicle.

Shaba lodges and camps

The only large lodge in the reserve is the **Sarova Shaba Lodge** ⓳ (www.sarovahotels.com), which lies in the west, close to the main entrance gate. Both the lodge and the associated western game-viewing loop offer some wonderful views over the palm-fringed Ewaso Ngiro River to the basaltic cliffs of the 1,880-metre (6,168ft) Ol Doinyo Sabache, which supports a breeding colony of Rüppell's vulture. The open plains – strewn with old lava flows – support a good variety of dry-country birds, including rosy-patched shrike, golden-breasted starling and masked lark.

Even more remote in feel is the eastern part of the reserve, where a series of springs bubble up in the river. The main landmark in this part of the reserve is the campsite formerly used by Joy Adamson, which is now the site of an exclusive tented lodge called **Joy's Camp** ⓴ (http://joyscamp.com), and overlooks a waterhole where a wide range of wildlife – including elephant, buffalo and lion – comes to drink. The black lava fields of eastern Shaba are home to Williams lark, a very localised Kenyan endemic. Another important landmark, situated along the Ewaso Ngiro 20 miles (32km) beyond the reserve's eastern boundary, is the remote Chanler's Falls.

Shaba National Reserve.

The Samburu

The Samburu are nomadic warriors whose strong pastoral tradition still lives on in the vicinity of the national reserve that bears their name.

A nomadic Maa-speaking people, the Samburu, who comprise less than 1 percent of the national population, live mainly in northern Kenya between Lake Turkana and the Ewaso Ngiro river. Known long ago as the *Loibor Kineji* (people of the white goats), the Samburu sometimes refer to themselves as *il-Oikop*, which is said to mean 'Owners of the Land'. The main centres of Samburu administration are Maralal, Baragoi and Wamba.

Pastoralist way of life

As with other pastoralists of the north, the Samburu lifestyle has in some respects changed little over the last hundred years. They live in low huts carefully crafted with interwoven sticks and plastered with mud and cattle dung. Samburu homes are windowless and dark so as to keep out flies. They also keep in smoke, which probably accounts for the existence of chronic chest infections and trachoma, which can eventually result in blindness.

An extended family of brothers, wives and parents live in a circular formation of huts surrounded by a high thorn branch fence called a *boma*. Livestock is herded inside at night where the thorn forms an effective barrier against marauding predators. The smallest animals are brought into the huts.

The Samburu live on the livestock – more specifically, on a thick curdled milk that tastes like smoke-flavoured yoghurt. Sometimes this is mixed with cattle blood and, on special occasions only, they eat meat. Their entire lifestyle is centred on cows, camels and goats, which they refer to as their wealth and only sometimes slaughter for ritual events. Money means little to them and the little they have is carried by the warriors in socks, knotted and hung from their belts.

Clan divisions

The tribe is divided into eight clans: four belong to the 'white cows' and four to the 'black cows', with these further divided into series of sub-clans. Greetings between strangers always include a who's-who breakdown of clan, sub-clan and age group, which usually results in the satisfying discovery of a distant relationship of some sort.

Cattle keeping is a male preserve among the Samburu. As a child, a boy tends his father's herds. Then, when he reaches puberty, he is circumcised and becomes a warrior, known as a *murrani* or a *moran*. The warrior years are halcyon for the young men, but they must also undertake tough and sometimes dangerous assignments to ensure the safety and well-being of their community. On the ochre plains of El Barta, you may encounter caravans of cattle herded by these warriors carrying twin spears. During droughts, they may drive their herds hundreds of kilometres from one patch of sparse grazing to another.

In addition to tending children and cooking, Samburu women are in charge of building and maintaining the rather meagre shelters that these hardy nomads call home. Their role also involves gathering vegetables and roots, and collecting water.

Unlike the warlike Maasai, whose language and cultural heritage they share, the Samburu do not adopt an aggressive and dominant cultural stance towards other tribes. Instead they place a high social value on a mature sense of respect. Today, group and individual ranching schemes and improved educational facilities are bringing about long-resisted change. Numerous Samburu *il-murran* enlisted in the British Forces during World War II, and many still serve in the Kenyan armed forces and police.

Samburu guide.

Fisherman on Lake Turkana.

NORTH TO LAKE TURKANA

The journey to Kenya's northernmost regions by road is a gruelling trek across rugged but fascinating terrain. And the journey's end, the 'Jade Sea', is a place of spellbinding beauty.

The term 'Northern Kenya' in the safari lexicon encompasses almost half of the country: thousands of square kilometres of arid and thinly inhabited plains, relieved by daunting volcanic formations and whimsical dry rivers known as *luggas* – lazy avenues of sand that occasional flash floods transform into torrents of rushing water. The general area – known as the 'Northern Frontier District' (NFD) in colonial times – extends north and west from Lake Baringo and Lake Turkana to Sudan. On the eastern side, it spreads from the Lorogi Plateau up to Ethiopia and east to Somalia. Like much of Kenya, the access routes into the region are delineated by the few main roads leading to district centres such as Lodwar, Maralal, Marsabit and Isiolo.

Northern ethnic groups

The people of northern Kenya – the Samburu, Turkana, Rendille and Boran among others – are nomadic pastoralists born of a warrior tradition, and even in the 21st century, their lifestyle makes few concessions to modernity. Central government maintains a sparse presence, and its authority is, in practice, often subservient to tradition customs: intertribal cattle raiding is a regular occurrence, and disputes are more likely to be settled by the gun or the spear, or

by negotiation between clan elders, than they are through formal legal channels. In certain areas – particularly the long rutted road north from Archer's Post via Marsabit to the Ethiopian border – travel in convoy is advised during occasional outbreaks of *shifta* banditry.

In colonial days, the British closed this lawless area to all but civil-service officials and professional hunting parties. Today, travel is unrestricted, but not necessarily easy. Apart from the physical challenges described below, travellers should be aware that armed hold-ups

Main Attractions
Lake Turkana
Sibiloi National Park
Chalbi Desert
Marsabit National Park

Nabuyatom crater at the southern end of Lake Turkana.

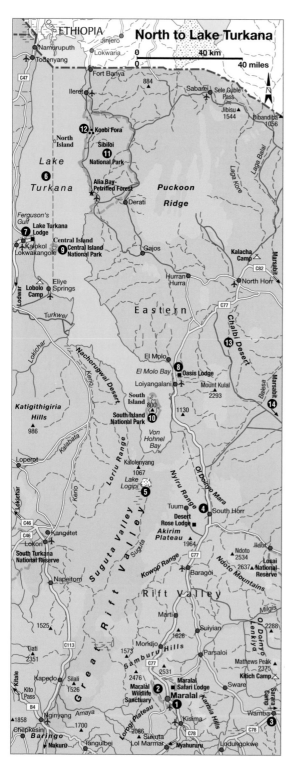

along the route are not unknown. There are bone-shaking stretches of corrugated track, which make a safari an endurance test. But it is worth it for the stunning scenery, colourful people and herds of wild animals. So long as you stick to the more conventional routes, you will be able to find accommodation at camps and lodges.

The roads – beyond the realm of comparison with standard thoroughfares – pose a challenge to both man and machine. In the dry season, it's a bit like driving on an old-fashioned washboard and, after rain, on a river of mud. Always take a high-rise jack with you, plus a shovel, and two planks for getting out of a bog or soft sand drifts.

Disregard distances given on maps and seek local advice instead. Depending on weather and road conditions, it may take a whole day to drive 80km (50 miles). In fact, schedules should be discarded entirely, so far as this can be reconciled with bookings at lodges. Part of the allure of the north is to succumb to its gentle pace.

Maralal

Perched on the edge of forested hills is **Maralal ❶**, the administrative centre for Samburu District. The town's name – Samburu for 'glittering' – was reputedly inspired by the first building, erected in 1934: a shack with a corrugated iron roof that gleamed in the sun. Since then the place has grown to support a population of roughly 20,000, but it still has all the aspects of a frontier town. Pepper trees and flaking *dukas* (stores) line the dusty main street. So too do the red-robed Samburu people, who comprise the majority of its population, and provide a colourful preview of what lies ahead on this route.

An important landmark in Maralal, **Jomo Kenyatta House**, the simple tin-roofed bungalow where its namesake, the future first president of Kenya, was detained by the British in 1961, is now a national monument. The town is also famous for its

Camel Derby, a fun event that's held annually in August, and attracts a lively crowd of Kenyan residents and foreign visitors. For travellers heading north, however, Maralal's most precious amenities are arguably its filling stations, almost the last between there and the Ethiopian border.

Just out of town, left at the main roundabout and a mile or so down the road, **Maralal Wildlife Sanctuary** ❷ is the site of an eponymous safari lodge (http://maralalsafarilodge.com), the most upmarket accommodation in the area. Overlooking a waterhole where zebra, impala and other antelope gather, it also attracts occasional visits from semi-habituated leopards, though these have declined in frequency since the practice of baiting it with goat meat was discontinued some years back.

Also ask at the lodge for a guide to take you to a lookout point further north along the road where the **Lorogi Plateau** drops steeply to the rugged country below. The best time to visit is during the hazy hours of early morning, when layer upon layer of volcanic ranges can be seen stretching northwards to the southern shore of Lake Turkana. Not for nothing is this spot known as World's End.

East of Maralal lies the small outpost of **Wamba** ❸, with its mission hospital and a few *dukas* to serve the nomadic tribesmen. Just to the north of Wamba is, the luxurious **Sarara Camp** (www.sararacamp.com), located in the community reserve overseen by the Namunyak Wildlife Conservation Trust, offers game viewing on foot or in a vehicle, and is well known for sightings of leopard and, more infrequently, the endangered African wild dog.

Located at the southern end of the Mathews Range is **Kitich Camp** (http://kitichcamp.com), nestling in a grove of indigenous fig trees on the banks of the seasonal Ngeng River, specialising in walking safaris in the remote and beautiful surrounds.

Samburu lifestyle

Centred upon Maralal, the Samburu inhabit an area of roughly 28,500 sq km (11,000 sq miles). This includes the higher Lorogi Plateau, rimmed with cedar forests, as well as the arid scrubland to the north where thorn trees mark the course of river beds and people dig in the sand for water. Closely related to the better-known Maasai, the Samburu speak a dialect of the same Maa language, and they probably splintered off after their joint migration southward from the Sudanese Nile. They refer to themselves not as Samburu, but *il-Oik*op (see page 217).

This dusty landscape, speckled with cattle, ostrich and gazelle, may seem monotonous. But it has its tales to tell. The road passes through the town of **Baragoi** and winds on, flanked by Koitokol Mountain on the right and the saw-toothed Kowop Range on the left.

From there, it's on to **South Horr** ❹, sandwiched between Ol Doinyo Mara Mountains to the right and the Nyiru Range on the left. This lush valley grows bananas and paw-paws (papaya), which are brought in to the

TIP

Short of mounting a costly private expedition, the best way to explore the north is Gametrackers' (www.game trackersafaris.com) well-organised 'Turkana Truck', whose eight-day itinerary to the Jade Sea includes Marsabit and the Chalbi Desert.

Samburu woman wearing a mporro necklace to signify her married status.

towns. The Catholic mission also sells lemons to thirsty travellers. Towering above the village, on Nyiru's flank, is **Kosikosi**, a brown, fissured outcrop of rock gleaming in the sun.

Before reaching South Horr, there is a road to the left that leads to **Tuum**, a seldom-visited village nestling against Nyiru's western slopes. There is a popular two- to three-hour mountain climb up Mount Nyiru from Tuum with spectacular views of Lake Turkana, Suguta Valley and Lake Logipi. The secluded **Desert Rose Lodge** (http://desertrosekenya.com) has made Tuum and the mountain more accessible to visitors, and it is also a useful base for camel safaris into the surrounding badlands.

Tuum is also the gateway to the **Suguta Valley**, an alien moonscape originally moulded by erupting volcanoes on the approach to the southern end of Lake Turkana. A track from the village leads down to the tiny settlement of **Parkati** – 'the place of no water' – on the valley's edge. Here, amidst jagged black lava scarps the height of office blocks, live the Turkana, tending

Gabbra herdsman and camels, Chalbi Desert.

their goats and camels, alongside silver-backed jackals and Grant's gazelle.

On the floor of the valley is **Lake Logipi ❺**, framed by an amphitheatre of rust-red hills. Logipi Hill, ringed by silver, rises from its centre like a shining Excalibur. This shallow soda pan is visited seasonally by thousands of flamingos, which form a shimmering cerise carpet as they sift the waters with upside-down beaks.

Lake Turkana, the 'Jade Sea'

Logipi's northern neighbour, **Lake Turkana ❻**, is the final destination for every safari in this area – after a journey of at least two days from Nairobi. The lake, which is about 300km (185 miles) long and 50km (30 miles) wide, has its northern tip in Ethiopia, where it is fed by the broad Omo River that rises in the Ethiopian Highlands near Addis Ababa. Lake Turkana is a place of spellbinding beauty. The algae that abound in the lake change their colour from charcoal grey to Delft blue as clouds scud overhead. But most often its surface dances deep green in the sunlight, giving it the nickname 'Jade Sea'. Soon, this charm may vanish into the thin air as the lake is likely to start drying up when Gibe III, a brand new Ethiopian hydroelectric dam, becomes fully operational in 2016. One of the possible impacts of the controversial project is that the lake shrinks and then splits into two if incoming water is limited.

In the hottest months, Lake Turkana's cool depths may look tempting, but note that the bitter alkaline waters can never quench your thirst, and swimming is a pastime to be treated with a certain amount of caution. The lake supports the world's largest population of crocodiles, which can be seen basking along the shore, seldom venturing far from the beaches. For the most part, the crocs of Turkana are fish-eaters, but they do eat large mammals too, even humans, albeit rarely.

Sportsmen appreciate the lake for its fishing possibilities and almost invariably have this in mind when they head for either the **Lake Turkana Lodge** ❼, at Ferguson's Gulf on the western side, or the **Oasis Lodge** ❽ (www.oasis-lodge.com) at Loiyangalani on the eastern shore. For keen anglers who don't want to endure a two-day overland trip for a spot of fishing, there is a kilometre-long airstrip nearby.

Anglers in search of sport try for the great Nile perch (*Lates niloticus*), an enormous fish that can attain a length of 2 metres (6.6ft) and tip the scales at 200kg (440lb). As an angling challenge, however, it is a disappointment, providing about as much fight as an outsized goldfish. Less spectacular, but more exciting are the ferocious tigerfish that can be reeled in from the shore.

Three national parks associated with Turkana – with a collective area of around 1,600 sq km (415 sq miles) – were designated as a Unesco World Heritage Site in 1997. The volcanic **Central Island National Park** (tel: 054 21223; www.kws.go.ke; daily) ❾, most easily reached by boat from Ferguson's Gulf, hosts a large crater lake nested at by an extremely large number of crocodiles and many water birds. Once you're on the island, the ascent to the crater rim has to be undertaken on foot, which can be very strenuous in the heat of the day.

South Island National Park (tel: 054 21223; www.kws.go.ke; daily) ❿ is the bird-watcher's and Nile perch fisherman's paradise of Lake Turkana. Care must be exercised if you are camping rough since the large population of crocodiles can be dangerous. The airstrip on the island is a twisted, rock-strewn horror – a challenge for every bush pilot in Kenya.

Sibiloi National Park

The third component of the Lake Turkana World Heritage Site is **Sibiloi National Park** (www.kws.go.ke; daily 6am–7pm) ⓫, on the eastern lakeshore north of Loiyangalani. Ironically, given that Lake Turkana is now a place where people and animals struggle for survival, this park may also have been the birthplace of the human race itself. Since the 1970s, the pioneering Kenyan palaeontologist Richard Leakey, followed by a succession of local and international scientists, have painstakingly exposed

Lava rocks and alkaline water at the southern end of Lake Turkana.

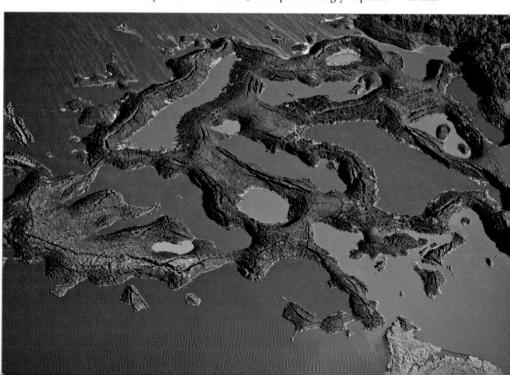

a treasure trove of hominid bones and stone tools demonstrating that hominids inhabited the lake shores as far back as 4 million years ago.

At the heart of this palaeontological wealth, the ridge known as **Koobi Fora** ⑫ – a Gabbra name meaning 'Place of the Myrrh Tree' – first burst into the public arena in 1972 when Bernard Ng'eneo, a member of the Leakey team, caught a glimpse of the first of 300 tiny skull fragments that were eventually reconstructed to form the 1.9 million-year-old *Homo habilis* skull known simply by its archaeologists' index number of '1470'. Since then, hominid remains assigned to five different species have been uncovered at Koobi Fora, ranging from the 4 million-year-old *Australopithecus anamensis* to the 1.4 million-year-old *Homo ergaster*. Some of the fossils found on the site can be seen at the local branch of the National Museum of Kenya (www.museums.or.ke; daily 8am–6pm).

Although it is best known for its significance in tracing early human evolution, little-visited Sibilio is also a wildlife sanctuary where visitors can watch lion, cheetah, oryx, zebra and topi in almost guaranteed solitude. Just before the park's entrance, on the right, is **Sibiloi Mountain**, where giant petrified trees 125cm (4ft) in girth are strewn like building blocks of the gods. Seven million years ago, these junipers stood at 15 metres (50ft) and could have flourished because of high rainfall.

Mirages in the Chalbi

To vary the return journey to Nairobi, turn right at North Horr and then take the track to the left, to drive southeast across the **Chalbi Desert** ⑬. Here, in this stretch of true desert, mirages play tricks on the traveller. Dark triangular blobs drifting through ribbons of water evaporate as you approach. In their place are a string of several hundred dusky camels in the care of Gabbra tribesmen who will raise their rifles in friendly salute. In the middle of nowhere, at the site of a fresh-water spring, the small village of Kalacha is the site of a self-catering community lodge and campsite.

On the far side of the Chalbi is **Marsabit** ⑭, perhaps the most fascinating of the myriad volcanic mountains in the north. Long extinct, it is capped with mist forests where elephant and greater kudu live. Just 4km (2.5 miles) from the town, in **Marsabit National Park** (tel: 069 210 2028, 020 250 2005; www.kws. go.ke; daily 6am–7pm), Marsabit Lodge (www.marsabitlodge.com) overlooks a pretty forest-fringed crater lake that is usually studded with birdlife and regularly visited by thirsty elephants. Further up the mountain, the enchanting and tranquil spot known appropriately as **Lake Paradise** is another water-filled crater, one whose rim provides a breathtaking view over several hundred miles.

The road south from Marsabit to Isiolo, at the foot of the Mount Kenya massif, is best driven in convoy. This may not allow the traveller to linger by the Mathews Range on the right. But, at this stage, it won't matter too much. The rest of the northern safari will have been more than enough.

Lake Logipi.

The Turkana

Hardy desert-dwellers, the staunchly traditionalist Turkana of northern Kenya practice a pastoral lifestyle similar to that of the related Maasai and Samburu, but in an even harsher environment.

Nilotic-speakers, whose ancient ancestry is sometimes controversially traced to North Africa or even the Arabian shore of the Red Sea, the Turkana inhabit the whole northwest of Kenya, from Lake Turkana west to the escarpment marking the Uganda boundary. Numerically, they are the third-largest Nilotic-speaking group in Kenya, after the Kalenjin and the Luo, with a population of almost one million – 2.5 percent of the national total – according to the 2009 census. There are 20 or so Turkana clans, all who speak the Turkana language. Communities are classified as 'forest people' (Nimonia) or 'plains people' (Nocuro), a distinction divides all territorial districts in areas they inhabit.

Family life

A Turkana homestead *(awi)* comprises a man and his wife and their children. Sons remain within the family group, while daughters leave their homestead as soon as they get married. A family *awi* usually consists of the principal enclosure for the head of the family and a secondary enclosure where additional wives and their children and married sons live.

For the Turkana, marriage is a three-year ceremonial process. Not until the first child has been weaned and has reached walking age can the marriage process be completed. Considerable numbers of stock (cattle or camels) are required to meet the bride price, and these the suitor obtains from his own herds and those of his father, his uncles and bond-friends. The important position of the wife in the *awi* is reflected in the close ties that will be perpetuated between her husband on one hand, and her father and brothers on the other.

The Turkana have evolved a material culture peculiar to themselves. They carve water troughs and containers from wood and decorate them with poker work; fat, butter and milk containers are made from hides (particularly camel) decorated with beadwork and cowries. Traditional weapons are a 2.5-metre (8ft) leaf-shaped spear, knobkerrie fighting stick, wrist knife, finger hook and, for defence, a shield of buffalo, giraffe or hippo hide. The women wear enormous quantities of beads around the neck, a neck-ring of brass or aluminium, and a distinctive lip plug.

Milk and blood are the main diet, and cattle also provide hides to make sleeping mats and sandals, and to cover the huts against rain. Their horns are used for snuff containers. Camels are also important in the Turkana economy, while goats and sheep are killed for guests, minor rituals or meat. Donkeys are used solely as pack animals, with hides cut into strips for panniers. Dried milk is made by boiling large quantities of fresh milk and drying it on skins. Wild berries are crushed and made into cakes with blood or ground into a dried meal. Women cultivate their homelands near watercourses in the rainy season where they grow millet and gourds.

Fishing is not practised traditionally, though fish now form an important protein supplement in periods of drought. However, all previous attempts to revitalise the Turkana region through fishing have failed. It remains to be seen how the northern lakeshore economy will be transformed by the planned irrigation scheme on the Lower Omo in neighbouring Ethiopia and the full opening of the Gibe III hydropower dam. Environmentalists fear the lake's water level will drop by some 20 metres, with a disastrous affect on the 300,000 locals who depend on it.

Turkana woman wearing beaded necklaces.

Fishermen on Lake Turkana.

A mother and her calves.

AMBOSELI NATIONAL PARK

Amboseli is everyone's picture of Kenya: open plains, woodlands and swamps, with an abundance of wildlife, all set against the spectacular backdrop of Mount Kilimanjaro.

A mboseli National Park (tel: 020 802 9705, 0716 493 335; www.kws.go.ke; daily 6am–6pm) is normally best viewed around dawn. The animals are up and Mount Kilimanjaro, which straddles the border with Tanzania, is usually exposed for an hour or so before it vanishes behind a blanket of cloud. Alternatively, Amboseli at sundown can be as unreal as a pantomime set. On the vast stage, the mammals are lit by strong pink and amber hues, with the mountain a gradually darkening cycloramic backdrop. Looming above that is perhaps a necklet ruff of cloud, the black hump of high moorlands and the speckled edge of the icy Kibo summit at 5,895 metres (19,340ft).

Park history

Amboseli is one of the oldest protected areas in East Africa, having been accorded game reserve status by the British colonial administration as early as 1899. It was originally part of the Southern Maasai Reserve, which also encompassed the **Kajiado** and **Narok** area where several clans of the nomadic Maasai people lived. It became the Amboseli Game Reserve in 1948, when the right of the Maasai people to live there was recognised and a special area for wildlife was set aside. In 1961,

it became a Maasai Game Reserve, together with the much larger Maasai Mara, and administration was ceded to Maasai Tribal Control.

However, by 1970, competition for grazing had become such a problem that a sanctuary around the reserve's swampy core was preserved for game only and local pastoralists were not allowed to enter. This aggrieved the Maasai so much that they killed many of the rhino population without even taking their horns. Consequently, a portion of the swamp was

A marabou stork.

A spotted hyena pup.

President Kibaki declared that the national park should be downgraded to become Amboseli National Reserve, and control should be decentralised from the Kenya Wildlife Service to the local Olkejuado County Council. This controversial decision was proclaimed illegal and reversed by the High Court of Kenya in 2010.

Amboseli elephants

The national park is famous for its tranquil beauty and easily approachable wildlife. The elephant population of greater Amboseli, currently 1,600 strong and on the rise, is one of the few in Africa that was left unravaged by poachers in the 1980s. Thanks to the **Amboseli Elephant Research Project ❶** (www.elephant trust.org) founded by Cynthia Moss in 1972, it is also the world's longest studied and best researched elephant population. Indeed, Cynthia Moss and her colleagues know every elephant resident in the ecosystem by face and name, and have written about them in the book, *Elephant*

given back to the Maasai in exchange for an area to the north, and a ring of boreholes was created around the reserve to make life easier for the pastoralists.

In 1974, Amboseli achieved full national park status, as the comparatively small 392-sq-km (160-sq-mile) core of an 8,000-sq-km (3,100-sq-mile) ecosystem that spreads across the Kenya-Tanzania border. In 2005,

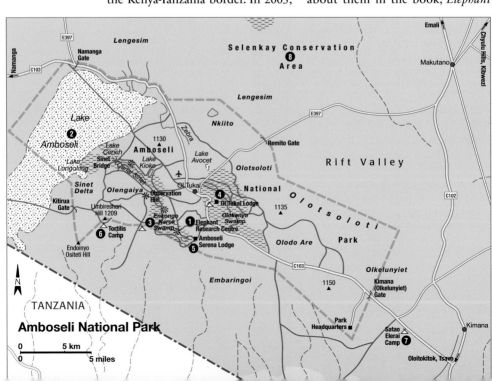

Memories. The project may be visited by arrangement (staff sometimes give lectures); enquire at the lodges in the park.

Lake Amboseli

Lake Amboseli ❷, from which the park takes its name, is a dry lake, some 10km by 16km (6 by 10 miles), and is flooded only during the rare occasions when there are heavy rains. The maximum depth in the wettest years is about half a metre (18ins), but the surface is more usually a dry, caked expanse of volcanic soil – boring to look at, if it were not for the frequent appearance of a phantom lake in a genuinely spectacular mirage. The entire horizon seems liquid, with perhaps a file of wildebeest reflected on itself in a shimmering mirror image. Mirages aside, the lake's fine, alkaline dust has a habit of creeping into every crevice, so photographic equipment should be protected in plastic bags.

The clouds of dust that blow up from the perennially dry bed of the lake provide a stark contrast to the lush vegetation of the marshy areas such as Enkongo Narok, which form the heart of the ecosystem. These swamps are fed by melted ice and spring water from Kilimanjaro, which percolates through the porous volcanic soil to form underground streams that rise close to the surface in the ancient lake basin.

Where the water reaches the surface, the desert is suddenly green, sprouting with wild palms and enough grass cover to attract the fauna for miles around. Forests of towering yellow-barked acacias (fever trees) used to surround the Amboseli swamps, but their numbers have decreased in recent years. Initially, this was blamed on the park's plentiful elephant population, which love to strip off and eat the bark. However, it was subsequently discovered that the naturally rising water table, induced by a period of good rains, was causing toxic salts to rise to the surface and pickle the trees' roots, so that they couldn't absorb enough water to compensate for moisture loss through

The bateleur's name comes from the French for 'tightrope-walker'.

African elephant.

The area of Kilimanjaro's iconic snowcap decreased by 85 percent between 1912 and 2007, sparking fears that it would vanish altogether. As of 2015, however, it seems that the ice-cap has built up and it's not likely to disappear anytime soon.

transpiration. Overall, however, the park has a varied habitat with open plains, umbrella acacia woodland, swamps and surrounding marsh areas.

Park life

Due to the open nature of most of Amboseli, wildlife is generally easy to spot, even from a distance. The main stock grazers are wildebeest, zebra and gazelle, numbers of which declined by as much as 90 percent in 2009 as a result of severe drought, but have subsequently recovered, through both immigration from adjacent areas and recruitment. Zebra numbers are now back to pre-drought of 6,000. Buffalo are also common, especially in the swamps, while herds of giraffe are often seen gliding between the acacias in more densely wooded areas. Hippos live in the open water and connecting swamps and channels, while elephants penetrate deep into the water to feed on aquatic vegetation, often emerging with a high tide mark on their flanks. For years, ecological and

Zebra and wildebeest make compatible grazing companions.

behavioural studies of these beasts have been carried out in the park, so animals are accustomed to cars, and visitors will be able to observe these large mammals at close range from inside their vehicles.

The density of visitors has had negative impacts on wildlife. Cheetahs, for example, have been so harassed by crowding vehicles that they have abandoned their usual habit of hunting in the early morning and late afternoon, and have taken to hunting at midday, when most tourists are back at the lodge having lunch and a siesta. Since this is not the best time of day to hunt, the result has been a reduction in the cheetahs' reproductive success.

Likewise, the park's once abundant lion population has suffered greatly in recent years, largely through conflict with the local Maasai, whose stock they frequently raid, but also as a result of prey shortage in the 2009 drought. Lions are still resident in the park, but sightings are infrequent by comparison to, say, the Maasai Mara. By

contrast, spotted hyena, although uncharacteristically timid, are plentiful, having benefited both from lack of leonine competition and the abundant carrion associated with drought.

Practical facts

Amboseli can be reached from Nairobi by two main routes, the most common being along the main Kajiado-Namanga road, turning left at **Namanga**, and then entering the park through the main gate about two-thirds of the way along the rutted 75km (45-mile) road to the park's wooded centrepiece **Ol Tukai**. The second access point is along the main Mombasa road, turning left just beyond the railway bridge past **Emali** and then following the Oloitokitok road for approximately 65km (40 miles), taking another right turn near the flat-top **Lemeiboti hill** and following this road for 32km (20 miles) before reaching the lodge. This route is shorter than the 240km (150-mile) Namanga road, and – resurfaced in 2011 – it is also

now in far better condition. Daily internal flights from Nairobi are also available.

The most productive game runs are normally around the main swamps of **Enkongo Narok** ❸ ('black and benevolent'), where icy water bubbles out of fissures in black lava. Another favourite run is up the solitary Observation Hill, which is a great place for long-range

Golden palm weaver.

Marshland.

wildlife spotting, especially when Kilimanjaro obligingly emerges to form a spectacular backdrop.

Of diminished significance since the headquarters were relocated close to the southwest park boundary, the patch of fever tree forest known as Ol Tukai remains an important Amboseli landmark, set in the swampy heart of an area known for its high concentrations of elephants. The first camp in Amboseli was built here in 1948, as an amenity for movie *The Snows of Kilimanjaro*, and though the original huts have been demolished, it remains the site of **Ol Tukai Lodge** ❹ (www.oltukailodge.com), where informal buildings of wood, stone and slate offer first-class accommodation and panoramic views of Kilimanjaro. The only other lodge inside the park is **Amboseli Serena Lodge** ❺ (www.serenahotels.com), built in the style of a Maasai *manyatta* (village) near one of the springs feeding Enkongo Narok.

A number of smaller and more luxurious camps lie within private or community conservancies bordering the national park. These include **Tortilis Camp** ❻ (http://tortilis.com), just outside the southeast boundary; **Satao Elerai Camp** ❼ (www.sataoelerai.com) to the east of the park; and **Amboseli Porini Camp** (www.porini.com) in the **Selenkay Conservation Area** ❽. The latter is a particularly good option for serious wildlife-lovers, as visitors have exclusive traversing rights over a 150-sq-km (58-sq-mile) tract of plains and woodland that supports several species seldom observed within the national park, notably gerenuk and lesser kudu. The conservancy is also very good for lion and cheetah, and longer game drives into the national park can also be undertaken, as the boundary is only an hour's drive from camp. There are several other advantages to staying in accommodation outside the core national park: visitors are not restricted by game-park regulations, and so you are allowed to take game walks and night drives (both of which are forbidden within national parks and reserves).

VULTURES AND EAGLES

Amboseli supports a varied birdlife, with more than 420 species recorded to date. Birds of prey are represented with more than ten types of eagle, as well as kites, buzzards, goshawks and harriers, and six species of vulture, which might be seen squabbling over kills or gliding on hot up-drafts from the desert. Of the plentiful water birds that frequent the park's swamps, no less than 12 species of heron have been recorded, but the kingfishers are perhaps the most photogenic, especially when caught making a strike. Of special interest to dedicated birdwatchers is the beautiful Taveta golden weaver, which is endemic to reed beds and swamps along the eastern border region of Kenya and Tanzania. The male bird has vivid golden yellow plumage.

African jacana.

The Akamba

Skilled craftspeople, the industrious, Bantu-speaking Akamba have a strong economic presence in the capital.

Occupying the Machakos and Kitui districts of Eastern Province, the Akamba (singular Kamba) are a people of the plains east of Nairobi. Numbering over four million, they constitute the fourth-largest ethnic group in Kenya. Like the neighbouring Kikuyu, their language Kikamba is part of the Bantu linguistic group, with four distinct dialects being recognised.

The Akamba account for their presence in the region with the myth that Ngai Mulungu (the Supreme Being) planted the first Kamba man and woman on Mount Nzaui. In reality, they probably migrated north to their present homeland from Kilimanjaro.

Hunters, who also kept some livestock and cultivated millets and sorghums, the Akamba probably settled four centuries ago at Mbuni, taking advantage of the higher rainfall and fertile soils to adopt a more sedentary life as agriculturalists. From Mbuni they colonised the whole area.

At first they traded in arrow poisons and iron implements with the neighbouring Kikuyu, Embu, Tharaka and Mijikenda. Then came a second stage in the growth of the Akamba economy. By 1840, Akamba caravans loaded with ivory were reported almost weekly at the coast. In return they traded glass beads, copper, blue calico and salt for barter in the interior.

But late in the 19th century, rinderpest seriously attacked the Akamba herds, and with the building of the Uganda Railway and the ban on further expansion, the Akamba were soon in economic trouble. Their land was no longer fertile. Their refusal to reduce their herds and the erosion of the impoverished soil led to periods of famine.

Akamba handicrafts

Skilled craftsmen, the Akamba use iron and copper wire to make bracelets, necklets, arrowheads and spears. The same skills serve to create inlaid stools of exceptional beauty: their traditional art of wood-carving is the basis of a major handicraft industry. Clay cooking pots are made by the women, as are the finely plaited baskets fashioned from the fibres of the baobab and wild fig trees.

The basic unit of Akamba life – economic, political, religious and social – is the extended family.

Little distinction is made between one's children and one's nieces and nephews, and as a result, children move easily between the households and are made to feel at home by their aunts and uncles. The naming of children according to Akamba tradition is very important, and a couple's first two boys and first two girls are always named after their maternal and paternal grandparents.

Traditionally, both sexes undergo circumcision, although female genital mutilation has been outlawed in Kenya. In some parts there are two stages: the 'small' ceremony at four or five, and the 'big' ceremony at puberty with a long initiation and scarifying of the chest and abdomen for purposes of ornamentation.

Unlike the Kikuyu, the Akamba were slow to adopt progressive agricultural methods, preferring to serve in the police and King's African Rifles. Drought and famine still plague the Akamba, especially in Kitui. There are government and *harambee* (self-help) water schemes and integrated development projects. But the further desiccation of Akamba country (Ukambani) as a result of poor agricultural practices, and deforestation arising from charcoal production, continues to militate against successful economic development in the area.

Akamba man pressing sugar cane for juice, Ngomongo Village.

Lone giraffe, Tsavo East
National Park.

TSAVO EAST AND WEST

Tsavo is one of the largest wildlife sanctuaries anywhere in the world. Once famous for its man-eating lions, it now provides luxury accommodation for viewing wildlife of all kinds.

Nairobi

Split into its separately administered western and eastern components by the Nairobi-Mombasa Highway, Tsavo is Kenya's largest and second-oldest national park, gazetted in 1948 to protect a wilderness area larger than Wales. Although the two parks form one contiguous 21,812-sq-km (8,425-sq-mile) ecological unit, they are quite different in character and are seldom visited in conjunction. The smaller and hillier Tsavo West is one of the largest wildlife sanctuaries anywhere in the world. Once famous for its man-eating lions, it is generally incorporated into a southeastern safari circuit that also includes nearby Amboseli, while the flatter and more arid Tsavo East tends to function in isolation as a popular target for short safaris out of the coastal resorts of Malindi and Watamu.

Tsavo undoubtedly has more of a wilderness feel than any other major Kenyan public reserve, thanks to its vast area and relatively sparse tourist development. Wildlife tends to be a little more skittish than in certain other reserves, though Tsavo East is very productive for dry country species such as cheetah, gerenuk and oryx, while Tsavo West is a genuine hotspot for black rhino. Otherwise, both parts of Tsavo support a similar selection of big game, including the

country's largest elephant population, estimated at around 11,000 based on an aerial survey undertaken in 2014 (down from 12,600 in 2011), and large numbers of lion, which tend to be quite elusive.

Approaching Tsavo

The most widely used route to Tsavo West from Amboseli (about 130km/80 miles) is out through Kimana village on a straightish southeasterly line of dirt roads and tracks to the Chyulu Entrance Gate, and on to Kilaguni,

Main Attractions
Ngulia Rhino Sanctuary, Tsavo West
Mzima Springs, Tsavo West
Lake Chala
Taita Hills Sanctuary and Salt Lick Lodge
Tsavo East National Park

Kirk's dik-dik, Tsavo West National Park.

the traditional centre of the park. As a useful point of reference, a high-folded range of green hills – of an unusually vivid, velvety green – stays on the left, but gets gradually closer. This is the **Chyulu Range** ❶, which is incorporated within the **Chyulu Hills National Park** (tel: 020 262 6174, 0711 574 766; www.kws.go.ke; daily 6am–7pm) and may be among the world's youngest mountains, having formed as a result of volcanic activity as recently as 500 years ago – as evidenced by the naked black, cauterised pumice that forms its more exposed spurs.

Overall, the range is approximately 80km (50 miles) long, 7km (4 miles) wide and just over 2,200 metres (7,000ft) at its highest point. A track on the crest offers scenic views over the expanse of Tsavo Park, but is seldom used and becomes downright dangerous when the mists descend. In among the hills lie a few small remote luxury camps – **Ol Donyo Lodge** ❷ (http://greatplainsconservation.com/ol-donyo-lodge), for instance, or **Campi ya Kanzi** ❸ (www.maasai.com) – where,

Black-headed Lapwing, Tsavo East National Park.

within view of Kilimanjaro, you can experience the wilds of East Africa away from the main tourist circuit and without a set programme.

Tsavo West

Much of **Tsavo West National Park** (tel: 020 238 4417, 0720 968 527; www.kws.go.ke; daily 6am–6pm) is of recent volcanic origin and is therefore very hilly. Entering through Tsavo Gate, on the main Nairobi-Mombasa Highway, you come across the palm-fringed Tsavo River, from where the country rises through dense shrub to the steep, rocky **Ngulia Hills** that dominate the area. Of the many volcanic cones, rock outcrops and lava flows that scar the landscape, the most famous – situated near Kilaguni Serena Safari Lodge – is Shetani ('Devil' in Swahili), a 200-year-old jumble of rough black lava blocks that looks as if it has only just cooled.

The Ngulia range peaks at close to 1,800 metres (6,000ft) and on the southern side drops a sheer 600 metres (2,000ft) to the Tsavo River valley. Apart from the permanent spectacle,

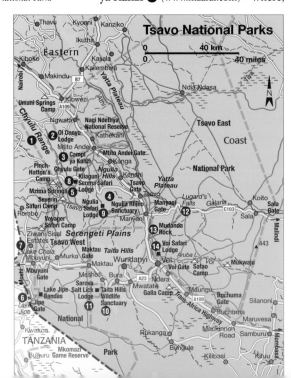

Ngulia stages a special nocturnal show towards the end of the year. Thousands of birds appear out of the nightly mountain mists. They are palaearctic migrants, flying out from the European winter, and about 40 species have been recorded. More than 60,000 birds have been netted and ringed – some subsequently tracked back as far north as St Petersburg.

Another key attraction associated with these hills is the **Ngulia Rhino Sanctuary** ❹ (www.awf.org/projects/ngulia-rhino-sanctuary; daily 4pm to 6pm), an electrically fenced 56-sq-km (35-sq-mile) block of scrub set aside in 1986 to protect the few black rhinos that survived the intensive poaching of the previous ten years. The original population of around 20 rhinos, protected by a dedicated anti-poaching unit, has increased to around 70 individuals today, so there is a good chance of sighting a black rhino, though the bush here is very thick, and the sanctuary is open for only two hours to ensure these endangered creatures get some peace. This sanctuary within a sanctuary also

supports a dense incidental elephant population of around two individuals per square kilometre.

The famous **Mzima Springs** ❺ are found in this volcanic zone. The springs gush out an incredible 225 million litres (50 million gallons) of water a day, of which 30 million litres (7 million gallons) are piped down to provide Mombasa with water. The rest of the water flows into the Tsavo and Galana rivers. The water originates on the icecap of Kilimanjaro and in the Chyulu Hills as rain, which percolates rapidly through the porous volcanic soils to form underground rivers.

Hippos, accompanied by shoals of barbels and crocodiles, can be watched from an underwater **observation chamber** at Mzima Springs. The best time for viewing is early in the morning; during the day hippos move to the shade of the papyrus stand and remain out of sight. It is also worth exploring the short walking trail through the surrounding fever-tree forest, which is alive with birdsong, and also often attracts antelope and other grazers to drink.

FACT

Finch Hatton's luxurious camp (http://finchhattons. com) at the foot of the Chyulu Hills is named after Denys Finch Hatton, the beau of Karen Blixen – played by Robert Redford in the movie *Out of Africa*– who died in May 1931 when the Gypsy Moth he piloted crashed near Voi.

Mzima Springs, Tsavo West National Park.

FACT

Kilaguni Lodge was the first wildlife lodge built in a Kenyan national park. It was opened in 1962 by the Duke of Gloucester and is now operated by Serena Group (www.serena hotels.com).

Sarova Salt Lick Lodge, Taita Hills Wildlife Sanctuary.

East of the springs (downstream) is a stand of wild date and raffia palms, the latter with fronds of up to 9 metres (30ft).

North of the Mzima Springs are numerous extinct volcanoes, rising cone-shaped from the plains. Mount Kilimanjaro dominates the western horizon. To the south is a beautiful picnic site at **Poacher's Lookout** on the top of a hill. The view across the plains to Kilimanjaro is worth the trip.

Tsavo West stretches further south to the **Serengeti Plains,** which despite their name, have nothing to do with the Serengeti National Park, although the landscape is similar. This part of the park, lying at the foot of Kilimanjaro, is crossed by the road and railway from Voi to Taveta.

Birds and baobabs

Tsavo West has spectacular baobab trees, which used to be far more numerous. In the mid-1970s, there was an enormous and as yet unexplained attack by elephants on baobabs. Some claim it was because of the drought, others claim that there were 'too

many' elephants. Whatever the reason, the remaining baobabs are quite safe today.

Aside from elephants, which remain numerous, having largely recovered from the intensive poaching of the 1980s, wildlife densities in Tsavo West are low compared to the likes of Amboseli or the Maasai Mara – and it can be difficult to spot anything much shorter than an elephant in the dense vegetation, particularly after the rains, when the grass grows very long. Nevertheless, lion, spotted hyena, buffalo, warthog, Maasai giraffe, waterbuck, klipspringer, impala, Grant's gazelle and plains zebra are all reasonably common, as is the black rhino, though it is all but confined to the sanctuary near Ngulia.

The variety and sheer numbers of birds in Tsavo are incredible. **Lake Jipe** ❻, which straddles the Tanzanian border at the southwest tip of the park, is surrounded by tall reeds and is one of the most important wetlands in Kenya, providing a sanctuary for a number of water and marsh birds, including migrants from Europe. Some of the more interesting birds commonly seen here include African pygmy goose, pied kingfisher, palm-nut vulture, and African skimmer.

Another interesting spot situated on the Tanzania border is **Lake Chala** ❼, which lies about 8km (5 miles) north of Taveta and only 10km (6 miles) outside the national park's western border. Chala is a gorgeous sunken crater lake with a diameter of 3km (1.8 miles); brilliant turquoise water enclosed by steep walls, and a superb setting on the southeast footslopes of Kilimanjaro. Swimming in Chala's clear water, though tempting, is not advised, as crocodiles have taken at least one life in recent years.

Of the several lodges dotted around the park, **Kilaguni Serena Safari Lodge** ❽ (www.serenahotels.com) is worth a visit even if you are staying elsewhere, as the waterhole attracts an incredible variety of animals in the dry

season, and it also offers impressive views towards Kilimanjaro. Nearby **Ngulia Safari Lodge ❾**, sited on the edge of a great escarpment, also overlooks a waterhole and salt lick, where elephants converge to within touching distance and dig at the salt-bearing earth with their tusks.

If waiting for the wildlife to come to you appeals more than long dusty game drives, then a worthwhile alternative – or addition – to a Tsavo safari is the private 110-sq-km (44-sq-mile) **Taita Hills Wildlife Sanctuary ❿**, which shares an unfenced border with Tsavo West, and is frequented by a similar selection of wildlife. The centrepiece of this small reserve is **Sarova Salt Lick Game Lodge ⓫**, a bizarre stilted construction overlooking a small waterhole where Kenya's most photogenic elephants sometimes gather in their hundreds. There is also the **Sarova Taita Hills Game Lodge**, which offers luxury accommodation. Both lodges are operated by Sarova Hotels (tel: 0728 608 765; www.sarovahotels.com). For dedicated birders, this sanctuary, situated along the main road between Voi at Taveta, also offers the closest tourist-quality accommodation to the Taita Hills, an isolated range whose forests provide the only known refuge for the endemic Taita thrush and Taita white-eye.

Tsavo East

Tsavo East National Park (tel: 020 2608 488; www.kws.go.ke; daily 6am–6pm) can be approached from three directions. A direct 115km (70-mile) dirt road links the northeastern Sala Gate to the coastal resort town of **Malindi** on the coast north of Mombasa. Alternatively, the two main access points from the Nairobi–Mombasa Road are the entrance gates at the towns of Mtito Andei (closer to Nairobi, and also the site of a gate to Tsavo West), and Voi (a much larger town, and closer to Mombasa). Even closer to Mombasa, but somewhat in the middle of nowhere, is the Buchuma Gate, which lies alongside the Mombasa–Nairobi Road about 50km (31 miles) southeast of Voi.

Lake Chala.

The outstanding physical feature in Tsavo East is the **Yatta Plateau**, which runs almost parallel to, and is easily seen from, the Nairobi–Mombasa Road. The plateau, which is between 5–10km (3–6 miles) wide and about 300 metres (1,000ft) high, originated as a lava flow from Ol Doinyo Sabuk east of Nairobi. Natural erosion over the millennia has exposed the flow to form the striking plateau seen today.

Around Voi, close to the road boundary, extends flat, dry, semi-desert thorn-bush country stretching as far as the eye can see. The road running northeast from here to Sala Gate offers the most reliable game viewing in the park. For much of its length, this road follows the seasonal Voi River, which meanders slowly to **Aruba**, where a large man-made dam (the remains of a defunct fish-farming scheme) makes an oasis for both animals and birds, and is also now the site of a recently opened lodge. Along the banks of the river is the dependent riverine woodland, with numerous wildlife paths leading down to waterholes. The road between Aruba Dam and Buchuma Gate is heavily populated with weavers, starlings and lilac-breasted rollers with iridescent wings. This road between also provides access to the superb **Satao Camp** (www.sataocamp.com), which overlooks another waterhole where elephants frequently congregate in their hundreds.

Running for more than 200km (124 miles) through the heart of Tsavo East, where it effectively forms the northern boundary of the part of the park freely open to the public, is the perennial Galana River, which in its early stages borders Nairobi National Park. One of the most spectacular sights along the river is **Lugard's Falls** ⑫, 40km (25 miles) north of Voi. Here the water rushes through water-worn coloured rock, which you can reputedly step across at its narrowest point; the crocodiles downstream doubtless look forward to meeting those who try. A good spot to see these prehistoric reptiles, alongside numerous hippos, is **Crocodile Point** further along the river. Otherwise, wildlife along the Galana

Voi River outside Tsavo East National Park.

is rather scattered, though elephant and lesser kudu frequently emerge from the dry bushland along the river banks.

Situated between Voi and Manyani Gate, the scenic **Mudanda Rock ⑬**, a 1.5km (1-mile) long inselberg run through by striking quartzite striations, is a water catchment area that supplies a natural dam at its base. It is a vital watering point for animals and birds during the dry season and therefore one of the best wildlife viewing areas in the park, often attracting large numbers of elephants. Visitors can leave their cars at the rock and climb up to overlook the dam.

Tsavo East wildlife

Tsavo's lions were made famous by Colonel Patterson in his book, *The Maneaters of Tsavo*, which records the havoc caused by marauding man-eating lions to the imported Indian labour brought in to build the Mombasa–Nairobi railway during the last years of the 19th century.

Grant's gazelle, zebra, impala, kongoni, giraffe, elephant and lion rank among the most conspicuous large mammals in Tsavo East. Large herds of buffalo can also be found, numbering several hundred or even as many as a thousand. Some of the more rare and unusual animals include fringe-eared oryx, lesser kudu and klipspringer; the latter can be seen standing motionless on rocky outcrops. Rock hyraxes, the improbable first cousins of elephants, spend the days sunning on rocks and chasing one another in and out of rocky crevices.

As for birds, the white-headed buffalo weaver (more striking for its red rump than white head) is conspicuous here, while the riverine habitats harbour the likes of palm-nut vulture, African skimmer, and red bishop. But the real attraction for birders here is some handsome and colourful dry-country birds, for instance pale chanting-goshawk, northern carmine bee-eater, red-and-yellow barbet, golden pipit, golden-breasted starling, red-winged lark, and rosy-patched bush-shrike.

The roads north of the Galana River and east of the Yatta Plateau are closed to the public, except when special permits are granted by the park warden. The country is wild and woolly, and spotted with outcrops such as Jimetunda and seasonal rivers such as the Tiva.

The main focal point for accommodation is along the road between Voi and Sala Gates, which is also the best game viewing circuit, following the Voi River Lodge. At Voi Gate, it is well worth stopping at **Voi Safari Lodge ⑭** (www.voiwildlifelodge. com), which clings to the side of a hill overlooking the vast expanse of Tsavo and is literally built into the rock. This lodge overlooks two busy waterholes, and even during the hottest times of the day various wildlife, such as impala and warthog, come to drink. There are also several smaller camps along the Galana River, an area stronger on atmosphere than on game viewing.

FACT

The Galana is the second-longest river in Kenya, after the Tana. Almost 400km (249 miles) long, it rises as the Athi River outside Nairobi and enters the Indian Ocean near Malindi (where it is also known as the Sabaki River).

Grant's gazelle, Tsavo East National Park.

Fort Jesus, Old Town Mombasa.

Cannon and shot at Fort Jesus.

MOMBASA

The final few chapters explore Kenya's coast – with its beautiful beaches, spectacular coral reefs and fascinating Swahili towns, some dating to medieval times.

A Swahili proverb sums up the pervasive atmosphere of the Kenya coast: *Haraka haraka haina baraka* – 'Haste, haste brings no blessing'. Here, the gentle philosophy of the Swahili people spawns a leisurely pace of life, as might be expected at zero altitude on the Equator. It's hot, humid and yet tempered all the time by the northeast or southeast monsoon, the trade winds of the Indian Ocean determining the seasons.

Coastal climate

The northeasterly *kaskazi* blows from October until March, with its rainfall peak in November. This is the warmer of the two monsoon seasons, with the hottest months occurring on the coast in January and February. In times past, mercantile sailing dhows from the Arabian Gulf followed this wind south to East Africa, sometimes continuing from there across to India. The southeasterly *kusi* blows from April until September, and its rainfall peak is from May until July. It's the stronger of the two winds, the cooler and the less comfortable, but this is relative since the climate stays mostly benign. The trading dhows from Arabia used to sail home on the *kusi*, carrying with them a cargo of goods such as gold, ivory, frankincense, acacia gum and tortoiseshell – as well as slaves sourced from the Africa interior.

One might expect Kenya's beaches – facing winds blown across several thousand miles of ocean – to be wild, dangerous playgrounds, constantly battered by surf. But they are not. For almost the entire length of the coast, the shallows and sands are protected by a coral reef about a mile offshore, stretching from Vanga in the south to Lamu in the north. The only breaks in this protective reef lie opposite the creeks at Mombasa, Mtwapa and Kilifi, or at the mouths of the Sabaki and Tana River, cut by an outpouring

Main Attractions
Mombasa Old Town
Fort Jesus
Nyali Beach
Haller Park

Fruit vendor, Mombasa.

QUOTE

'The aspect of Mombasa as she rises from the sea and clothes herself with foam and colour at the approach of the ship is alluring, even delicious.'

Winston Churchill, 1908

of freshwater past or present, and millions of tons of silt.

Between the fringing coral reefs and the shoreline are shallow, safe waters. There are few or no sharks, only scores of species of spectacular coral fish easily observed in the clear, warm ocean. As for the beaches, they are often miles on end of fine white sand, edged in dunes and serried ranks of coconut palms and wispy casuarina trees.

Mombasa Island

The main gateway to this exceptional coastline is **Mombasa ❶**, which is the second largest city in Kenya, and vies with Dar es Salaam in Tanzania as the busiest port in East Africa. The island-bound town centre is the commercial gateway to a vast interior, stretching

west into the Congo, northwest into Sudan and southwest into Zambia. Countries without a seaport, such as Rwanda and Uganda, depend to a large extent on Mombasa for imports and exports of their cash crop commodities.

According to some sources, Mombasa in its most ancient incarnation was called 'Tonika', a fitting description for Kenya's main seaside town and the major centre for rest and relaxation. Just the sight of it, from an escarpment above the island, is instant relief for the weekender from Nairobi and the upcountry interior. It is just as attractive to arrivals from further afield – hundreds of thousands of visitors fly in every year from Britain, Germany, Italy, France, Scandinavia and elsewhere.

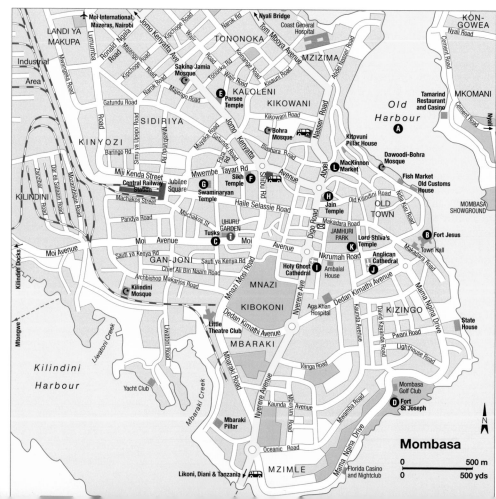

Mombasa

0   500 m
0   500 yds

Mombasa is often described as a melting pot, and for good reason. One of the most important trade centres on the East African coast since medieval days, it is – like so many seaports – home to a rich and diverse blend of indigenous and exotic cultures. These include the coastal Mijikenda and Swahili, long-established settlers from Arabia and India, more recent arrivals from Europe, and of course large numbers of upcountry migrants from the Maasai and Samburu to the Akamba and Kikuyu. Despite this, Mombasa comes across as a far more culturally cohesive and integrated whole than the upstart Nairobi, with its focal point being the characterful old town below Fort Jesus.

The Old Town

Joined to the mainland by a trio of bridges and causeways, central Mombasa is spread over a small coral island, flanked by the two creeks, Tudor and Kilindini (deep water), which provide its natural harbours. The **Old Harbour** Ⓐ grew up beside the eastern Tudor inlet, but

as trade grew in the early part of the 20th century and when the harbour capacity became overstretched, a new port was built at Kilindini on the western side of the island.

Thus the traditional and interesting waterfront of the Old Town was spared demolition and redevelopment, although in 2014, it was announced that in order to boost the country's fish exports, it would be transformed into a fishing port equipped with processing facilities. For the time being, however, it remains as a 'period piece' attraction. An intertwining maze of alleys, many too narrow to allow motor traffic, it sprawls out either side of the main thoroughfare Ndia Kuu Road, lined with two- and three-storey buildings, whose overhanging fretwork balconies and carved Zanzibari doorways are still recognisable from photographs taken 100 years ago. Displaying a mix of British, Indian, Arabian and Swahili architectural influences, these venerable buildings mostly date to the period 1870 to 1930, and many have been lived in by the same family since Victorian times.

Fort Jesus was used as a prison by the British until 1958, when the Gulbenkian Foundation provided £30,000 for its restoration and the establishment of a museum.

Mombasa Old Town.

TIP

Mombasa's buses and *matutus* are both overcrowded and risky, being a favourite workplace of skilful pickpockets. If you don't mind sharing a cab, group taxis can be found at the bus station, or your hotel will order you a taxi to yourself.

By the close of the 20th century, the Old Town had acquired a somewhat dishevelled and down-at-heel appearance. More recent years have seen something of a rejuvenation, partly as a result of active conservation and partly due to a growing influx of tourism custom. Traditional craftsmen such as goldsmiths and silversmiths are still active in the Old Town, and many traders still conduct a substantial import-export business behind quaint and unpretentious storefronts, but the area is also now studded with craft and antique shops specialising in Swahili, Indian and Arabian furniture, as well as all manner of local handicrafts.

At the Old Harbour, flanking Government Square, the city's commercial hub back in the 1890s, are a couple of historic buildings and the **Fish Market** (its planned renovation was announced in 2015). Even until the late 20th century, small coastal dhows from Lamu and Somalia still anchored in the harbour here seasonally, to trade in fruit, dried fish and similar commodities. From December to April – the *kusi* monsoon season – these were sometimes joined by larger ocean-going booms and *sambuks* from further afield, most with diesel engines to supplement the traditional lateen sailing power. Now, however, the old harbour is all but disused, and what few boats are docked there form little more than a picturesque remnant of the dhow fleets of the port's heyday.

The Old Town also boasts several mosques of antiquity. The oldest is Basheikh Mosque, founded in the 13th century and topped by a tall curved minaret. There is also the 16th-century Mandhry Mosque on Sir Mbarak Hinawy Road, situated opposite a well that was connected to it by an aqueduct prior to 1901, when its ornate seat-like front was built. In both cases, however, the mosque itself has been rebuilt several times since it was originally founded, and the site is of greater religious than architectural significance. The brooding bulk of **Fort Jesus** Ⓑ (www.museums.or.ke; Mon–Sat 8.30am–5.30pm), which overlooks the Old Town, is thus the oldest extant building in Mombasa.

Mombasa's best-known landmark, the tusks spanning Moi Avenue.

Central Mombasa

The 20th century saw the rapid expansion of Mombasa beyond the Old Town. Today the city contains administrative buildings dating from the early colonial days; street markets offering souvenirs, fruits and colourful cloth for sale; a jostle of pavement vendors selling coffee, coconut milk, roasted maize and cassava; and, in sharp contrast, new office blocks, the smart post office and modern shops stocking goods from all over the world.

Docks and temples

Moi Avenue links the old and new port areas and supports most of the travel and shipping agencies, local tour operators, curio shops, and the better hotels, bars and restaurants. The dual carriageway is spanned by the city's best-known modern landmark – four crossed elephant **Tusks** **C**, made of aluminium and erected to commemorate Queen Elizabeth's visit in 1952. They lie close to Uhuru Garden, site of the National Freedom Monument.

Enthusiasts may continue on to visit **Kilindini Docks**, which are modern, efficient and still expanding. A distant view will suffice for most visitors, however, and this is particularly attractive at night, as the ship and shore lights reflect on the waters of Kilindini Creek. A slow drive at dusk along Mama Ngina Drive, past the insubstantial ruins of **Fort St Joseph** **D** and through the course of the Mombasa Golf Club (www.mombasagolfclub.com), also provides a chance to breathe the cool sea air and join the colourful promenade of the city's cosmopolitan populace.

Mombasa is notable for its great variety of churches, mosques and temples. Travelling south from Makupa Causeway on Jomo Kenyatta Avenue, you'll see the **Parsee Temple** **E** on your left, then, on Mwembe Tayari Road to the right, the **Sikh Temple** **F** and **Swaminaryan Temple** **G**.

If you continue to the main thoroughfare, Digo Road, you'll find the Khunzi Mosque and, nearby on Langoni Road, the beautiful **Jain Temple** **H**, with its marble pillars, elephants flanking the solid silver doors, and domes and pyramids on the roof. South along Digo Road is the Roman Catholic **Holy Ghost Cathedral** **I** and, on Nkrumah Road, the curiously Moorish-looking **Anglican Cathedral** **J**, which was erected as a memorial to Archbishop Hannington, who was killed in Uganda in 1885. It lies virtually opposite **Lord Shiva's Temple** **K**, the religious centre for the city's Hindus, with the tallest spire in town, topped by a crown of solid gold. The Baluchi Mosque on Makadara Road is the successor to the original built by the Baluchis who migrated here from the Makran coast (now Pakistan).

Mackinnon Market

Mombasa is essentially a casual place and visitors will soon be as relaxed as the residents, especially if they wear the right clothes: cool cotton prints, such as the *kikoi* sarong, the

FORT JESUS

Inscribed as a Unesco World Heritage Site in 2011, Fort Jesus is one of the oldest European buildings on the eastern coast of Africa, constructed by order of King Philip I of Portugal in 1593, and designed by the Italian architect Joao Batista Cairato. The ultimate in indestructible fortresses, it stands 15 metres (50ft) high on the seaward side, where it overlooks the entrance to the Old Harbour, and its stone walls are up to 2.5 metres (8ft) thick. For most of its existence, Fort Jesus has been the most significant building on the coast north of Ilha do Moçambique (which lies about 1,000km/600 miles further south) and despite its apparent impregnability, it changed hands at least a dozen times prior to the colonial era. The longest and most violent struggle for Fort Jesus was the 33-month Omani siege that claimed at least 6,000 lives between 1696 to 1698, and resulted in Portugal being ousted from Mombasa.

Fort Jesus was used as a prison by the British until 1958, when the Gulbenkian Foundation provided £30,000 for its restoration and the establishment of a museum. Entered via an arched passage that has been in place since the 16th century, the museum houses some fine examples of imported ceramics, carved doors and other artefacts relating to the history of Mombasa, as well as displays about Swahili and Mijikenda culture.

*Traditional dhow on
the Mombasa River.*

*Spice stall,
MacKinnon Market.*

strikingly patterned *kanga* or white full-length *khanzu*, bought perhaps after a happy haggle with the laconic (and experienced) shopkeepers of Biashara (Bazaar) Road. Nearby, the famous **MacKinnon Market ⓛ**, also known as Marikiti Market, sells a tempting selection of fresh fruits and vegetables, along with a variety of spices and basketware.

At night the city shakes off its languorous daytime air and offers its visitors a lively nightlife, ranging from sophisticated dining and dancing at smart beach hotels to the uninhibited atmosphere of cabaret clubs and sailors' bars. There are a number of casinos and cinemas, while the **Little Theatre Club**, set in a historic building on Mbaraki Road, has put on regular amateur productions since its foundation back in 1947.

A wide variety of good food is available in Arabian, Chinese, Indian, Pakistani and European styles. In addition, seafood is inexpensive as well as plentiful. One *touristique* but enjoyable diversion, bookable through any hotel or safari operator, is the Dhow

Sundowner Cruise along the shores of Mombasa Island. As darkness falls, the dhow docks and visitors proceed to Fort Jesus, its main entrance 'guarded' by 'Arab and Portuguese' men with blazing torches. Inside, a sound and light presentation of the turbulent history of the East African Coast is followed by a candelabra-lit dinner.

Moi International Airport

Trade is essential to life in Mombasa, as it has been for at least two millennia. Exports of tea, coffee, pyrethrum, potash and many other commodities pour out of the interior, through acres of warehouses and on to the quays. Tankers discharge crude oil into Kenya's refinery, almost the sole source of processed fuel for the East African region. Bulk cement carriers load cargo from the Bamburi silos north of Mombasa, one of Africa's largest cement works. Apart from the vast array of export and import operations, Mombasa has its own industrial complex which manufactures anything from pins to hull plates for ocean-going ships.

An indicator of the importance of Mombasa to the Kenya economy, **Moi International Airport**, a few miles to the west of the island, is now serviced by several scheduled and chartered international flights from Europe and elsewhere. Kenya Airways and a number of private carriers also operate flights from here to Kenya's other main tourist attractions, including Nairobi, the coastal resorts up to Lamu, and most key national parks and reserves. For a taste of more old-fashioned travel, the railway terminus in the town centre is connected to Nairobi by a comfortable overnight rail service, as are bus and taxi stops for departures to the beaches and beyond, north and south of Mombasa Island. The town is to become a major transport hub for East Africa when a new railway line running from Mombasa through Nairobi and Kisumi to Kampana in Uganda and Kigali in Rwanda opens in 2018–2020.

Mainland suburbs

In recent decades, Mombasa has spilled beyond the island and on to the mainland in all directions. The only link between the city and its southern suburbs is the **Likoni Ferry**, which plies across the mouth of the deepwater Kilindini Port throughout the day. To the east, the connection is via the **Nyali Bridge**, which spans the upper reaches of Tudor Creek. To the northwest, Makupa Causeway carries road, rail and fuel arteries to Nairobi and up-country Kenya.

At **Mazeras** ❷, about 19km (12 miles) along the Nairobi Road, are the small municipal Botanical Gardens, which contain a wide range of tropical shrubs, flowers and trees – many of which are eventually used to beautify the city streets, parks and public places. The mission stations of **Rabai** and **Ribe**, established by Lutheran pastors in the mid-19th century, are situated a few kilometres inland, and near **Mariakani**, 16km (10 miles) further on, you can visit a traditional *kaya* or stockaded settlement of the Giriama tribe.

Freretown

Leaving central Mombasa via Nyali Bridge, the first main intersection on the mainland is Kongowea Junction,

Mosque minaret, Old Town.

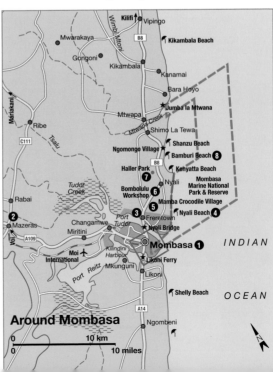

Around Mombasa

which lies in the area formerly known as **Freretown ❸**. Sir Bartle Frere founded this settlement in the 1870s as a refuge for freed slaves (many of whose descendants still live there) and it is the site of the Emmanuel Anglican Church, one of the oldest churches in East Africa, constructed in 1889.

A right turn here leads to the legendary **Tamarind Restaurant** (www.tamarind.co.ke), whose reputation for excellent seafood is complemented by a fine breezy situation overlooking the Old Harbour and city centre. The nearby **Krapf Memorial**, a stone cross dedicated to Dr Johannes L. Krapf – the first Christian missionary to work in Kenya (after the Portuguese) – is situated opposite the graves of his young family, who died 'of the fever' there in 1844.

Nyali Beach

Just to the north, **Nyali Beach ❹** is Mombasa's premier coastal strip, dense with private properties and swish hotels, of which the doyen is the Nyali Beach Hotel (www.nyali-international.com) – for many years the trendsetter for standards of excellence.

Another important landmark here is the **Nyali Golf and Country Club** (www.nyaligolf.com), whose superb golf course is the only 18-holer along the coast north of central Mombasa. Nearby, the **Mamba Crocodile Village ❺** (tel: 0729 403 670; daily 8am–6.30pm), claims to be the largest crocodile farm in Africa, containing over 10,000 crocs, from tiny hatchlings the size of your hand to ancient behemoths such as Big Daddy, a 120-year-old, 5-metre/yd-long male captured on the Tana River in the 1980s. Though the compound is a little rundown, it's impressive to see giant crocs at such close quarters, and there are also interesting collections of snakes, spiders and epiphytic orchids.

About 7km (4 miles) north of Nyali Bridge is the **Bombolulu Workshop ❻** (tel: 020 239 9716; http://apdkbombolulu.org; Mon–Sat 8am–6pm, Sun 8am–3pm; free), which was set up by a German philanthropist to give homeless and disabled people an opportunity to work and support themselves. Visitors can look around the workshops where the handicrafts, jewellery, furniture and

Women carrying makuti (dried palm fronds).

clothing are produced, and follow this up by visiting the on-site shop where these goods are sold.

Haller Park

Next, the road passes the **Bamburi Cement Factory**, one of the largest producers of its kind in Africa, producing upwards of a million tons of cement annually from the coral limestone that underlies the coastal plain. The factory grounds are of interest to tourists for **Haller Park** ❼ (tel: 041 548 5901; www.lafarge.co.ke; daily 8am–5pm), which has been transformed from an unsightly quarry once thought to be too saline to support vegetation, to an exemplary private nature reserve under the guidance of its namesake, the award-winning Swiss agronomist René Haller. One of the most remarkable environmental rehabilitation projects in the world, the park can be explored along a 90-minute nature trail that passes enclosures grazed by giraffe, zebra and antelope, as well as patches of indigenous woodland, rattling with coastal birdlife. The park also features fish and crocodile farms, a reptile park, a butterfly pavilion and a restaurant.

A mile further on is **Kenyatta Beach**, where the late President had his coastal home, and **Bamburi Beach** ❽, which has a number of excellent hotels, restaurants and nightclubs. The Bamburi Cement Factory, supported by the Kenya Wildlife Service, has launched an initiative to help conserve the marine turtles that breed naturally at Bamburi Beach. Locals are hired to collect the eggs from the beach, before they can be poached, and deliver them to an artificial hatchery where they are protected until they hatch, then released back into the ocean. As a result, local turtle populations are now stabilising after years of decline.

A short distance further north, inland of Shanzu Beach, the educational **Ngomongo Village** (daily 9am–5pm) is another reclaimed quarry, planted with indigenous trees, and dotted with 'traditional villages', each of which comprises a few traditional homesteads and crops associated with one of Kenya's many tribes.

Mamba Crocodile Village.

Diani Beach.

THE SOUTH COAST

Palm-fringed beaches stretch south from Mombasa like a string of pearls. The resorts range from glamorous Diani Beach to laid-back Wasini Island.

Nairobi

Main Attractions
Diani Beach
Shimba Hills National Reserve
Mwaluganje Sanctuary
Kisite-Mpunguti Marine Park

Kenya's South Coast has a more rustic feel than Nyali or any of the other suburban beaches immediately north of Mombasa, partially due to its logistical dislocation from the island-bound city to which it is connected not by a road bridge, but by the steady-and-slow Likoni ferry service. South of the ferry, the surfaced A14 sticks to within 2–3km (1–2 miles) of the seashore for most of its length, veering further inland only as it approaches the Lunga Lunga border with Tanzania, about 120km (72 miles) south of Mombasa.

Tiwi and Diani

The best beaches on the South Coast, and the main concentration of tourist development, runs along the coast between the townships of Tiwi and Diani – a 21km (13-mile) stretch of seafront starting about 20km (12 miles) south of Mombasa. In this sector, hotels, campsites and private properties line the entire length of the shore.

To reach **Tiwi Beach ❶**, turn left 6km (4 miles) after the turning to Kwale. Tiwi has many quiet beaches and self-catering bungalows. If you're heading for **Diani Beach ❷**, it is impossible to miss the turning: cross the Mwachema River estuary and continue a few kilometres further south to **Ukunda**, then turn left at a junction

where several of the beach hotels are signposted. Little more than a junction village in the 1980s, Ukunda has expanded rapidly to become a thriving small town with numerous small guesthouses, restaurants, shops, filling stations and other facilities catering to the families whose breadwinners are employed at one or other of the nearby beach hotels.

Diani is a ribbon of flawless tropical beach, straight for over 13km (8 miles) and probably 75 metres/yards wide at low tide. The sand is white,

Fisherman on Diani Beach.

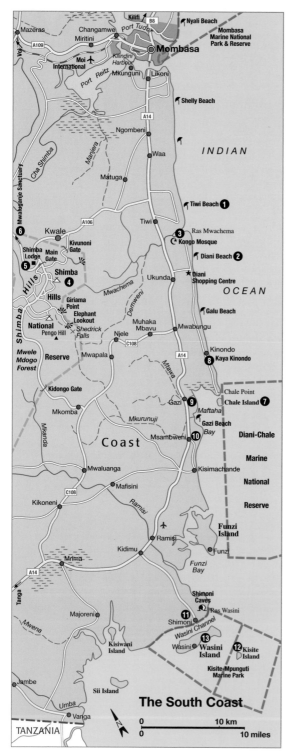

fine-grained, gently cambered to the ocean and shaded with palms and casuarinas. The ocean at Diani, or rather the inshore shallows, are entirely protected by the fringing reef, massive and solid like a seawall. Nothing can penetrate – no sharks, no other large marine life, and very little pollution. The ocean scenery also seems on a larger scale than anywhere else on the Kenyan coast, subtle and infinitely varied. When the tide goes out, a half-mile stretch of coral and sand between the reef and shore is exposed as a mosaic of rock pools.

A narrow lagoon at the outlet of the Mwachema River, at the northern end of the beach, is a decorative pattern of islands. At high tide it's all covered, but to no great depth. The coral formations show on the mirror-flat surface as a vast abstract colour wash, with changing warmer tints around dawn and in the early evening. Occasionally the coral is scoured out into deep caves, some with black felt-like ceilings of countless bats. They peel off and erupt in the evenings, great clouds of them against the sunset.

The land immediately behind the beach is scenic and only partially developed, mostly with coconut, banana and citrus cultivation. Elsewhere there are patches of indigenous forest, lush green tracts of woodland where Angola colobus and Sykes' monkeys share the canopy with forest birds such as the aptly named trumpeter hornbill and beautiful Fischer's turaco.

Situated in a grove of flat baobabs at **Kongo Creek**, between Tiwi and Diani on the Mwachema estuary, is the **Kongo Mosque** ❸, built by 16th-century pilgrims. The vaulted prayer room is intact and still used by worshippers, but its historic walls are now obscured behind several more modern additions including a rather ugly tin roof that detracts from its sense of antiquity. It is a pretty spot, nevertheless, and the creek's sand flats support a variety of terns, gulls and other shorebirds. Be warned that the site has a reputation for muggings, so don't visit it carrying valuables.

Amenities on the Diani Strip

Development on the Diani Strip has been fairly intense, not only in terms of tourist accommodation, which includes dozens of large resorts and several smaller beach hotels, but in a whole range of ancillary services. There's a number of shopping centres, several banks and ATMs, a hospital, restaurants, hairdressing salons, laundromats, DVD rental stores, craft stalls, internet cafés, vehicle hire, training facilities and equipment for snorkelling, scuba diving, windsurfing, glass-bottomed boating and deep-sea fishing. Hotels here range from air-conditioned concrete and glass to vintage, open villa-style fanned by breezes off the ocean. All offer assorted water sports and deep-sea fishing, have good restaurants, and arrange day tours to Mombasa's old town and other sites along the

south coast, such as Shimba Hills or Wasini Island, a popular option with those on extended beach package holidays.

Coastal safaris

A few miles inland of Tiwi and Diani beaches the upper reaches of the Shimba Hills – gentle, rolling downs rising to 450 metres (1,500ft) from the coastal plain – are protected within the 250-sq-km (97-sq-mile) **Shimba Hills National Reserve** ❹ (tel: 0774 935 374; www.kws.go.ke; daily 6am–7pm). This pretty reserve used to be the last Kenyan stronghold for the handsome sable antelope, less than 100 of which inhabit the reserve now, but can still be observed in areas of open grassland. Shimba also supports substantial populations of buffalo, elephant, zebra, warthog and seldom-seen leopard. The birdlife is also profuse and includes several coastal specials, including Fischer's turaco, black-and-white casqued hornbill, Kenya crested guineafowl, and the country's only population of the beautiful green-headed oriole.

Kikois for sale, Diani Beach.

TIP

Wasini Island is the one place in Kenya where the spectacular coconut crab – the world's largest terrestrial crustacean – is reasonably common. To stand a realistic chance of seeing this impressive nocturnal creature, however, you would need to spend the night on the island.

An easy drive from any of the beach resorts, Shimba Hills not only provides visitors with an excellent safari opportunity, but also offers a refreshing climatic change from the humid coastal strip. In addition, there are long-range ocean views from the eastern escarpment, from where the pretty Sheldrick Falls can be reached on a guided walk that also offers the possibility of exciting wildlife encounters on foot. **Shimba Lodge ❺**, overlooking a water hole in the middle of the forest, is a beautifully sited tree lodge noted for its night-time game viewing.

Effectively a northern extension of Shimba Hills National Reserve, the **Mwaluganje Sanctuary ❻** (daily 6am–6pm) is an admirable community ecotourism project set on 36 sq km (14 sq miles) of baobab- and cycad-studded hills, volunteered for conservation purposes by 200 Mijikenda families. Elephants are far more easily seen here than in Shimba proper, as they frequently gather at the waterhole in front of the Mwaluganje Elephant Camp, the only accommodation within the sanctuary.

Shimba Lodge.

South of Diani

Officially, the immediate ambit of the Tiwi-Diani holiday comes to an end at the speck of coral known as **Chale Island ❼**, now the site of an exclusive lodge, The Sands at Chale Island (http://thesandsatchaleisland.com). This is a stopover for boat trips at the south extreme of the beach. Beyond that, down to the Tanzanian border at Vanga, is what the Diani planners describe as a 'remote area' for longer excursions out of the beach hotels. In 1994, the Diani-Chale Marine National Reserve was created to protect these fragile coral reefs, which incorporate 36 recognised diving sites.

About 13km (8 miles) south of Diani, the time-lapsed fishing village of Kinondo is the site of **Kaya Kinondo ❽** (tel: 0722 446 916; www.kaya-kinondo-kenya.com; 9am–4pm except on the local Chipalata holiday, every fourth day) – a community-based ecotourism project protecting one of the many forests (*kayas*) held sacred by the Digo Mijikenda people. These are essentially ceremonial shrines, where ancestral spirits are consulted and medicinal plants collected, but no hunting or cultivation is permitted. Kaya Kinondo itself is home to around 50 bird and several mammal species, including spotted ground thrush, Ader's duiker and Zanj elephant shrew. A 45-minute or two-hour guided trail through the forest can be followed by a visit to a traditional Digo medicine man.

A short distance further south, the now unassuming village of **Gazi ❾** was once the headquarters of Mbaruk bin Rashid, the slave trader who masterminded the ill-fated 1895 Mazrui Rebellion and died shortly afterwards in exile in what is now Tanzania. Mbaruk's abandoned palace, built in the 1850s, still stands on the outskirts of the village. Of greater interest perhaps is the community-managed 300-metre (975ft) **Gazi Women Mangrove**

Boardwalk (daily 8am–6pm), where six different species of mangrove can be seen, along with habitat-specific wildlife such as the mudskipper crab and dazzling mangrove kingfisher.

Just to the south of Gazi, **Msambweni ⑩** has a fine, empty beach, a large hole in the ground reputed to be an old slave pen, holiday hotels and a small number of self-catering villas for a get-away-from-it-all stay. The village is also the site of the superb **Msambweni Beach House** (http://msambweni-beach-house.com), a sumptuous Swahili-style boutique hotel overlooking the idyllic baobab-studded beach from tall coral cliffs.

At the far end of the South Coast, about 80km (50 miles) from Mombasa and only 10km (6 miles) from the Tanzania border as the crow flies, **Shimoni ⑪** was once the headquarters of the Imperial British East Africa Company. The former District Commissioner's residence still stands (just about), and close by is the grave of Captain Lawrence, who died while trying to suppress the 1895 Mazrui Rebellion. The town's best-known site is the **Shimoni Caves** (daily 8.30am–6pm), a coral and limestone labyrinth used as a holding pen for slaves in the 19th century. Chains and hooks dating from the slaving era are still embedded in the cave, which also contains a natural well of semi-saline water from which its inmates once drank.

Kisite-Mpunguti Marine Park

Shimoni hosts the headquarters of the **Kisite-Mpunguti Marine Park** (tel: 020 3549 520; www.kws.go.ke; daily), which comprises 40 sq km (16 sq miles) of open sea and reefs centred upon **Kisite Island ⑫**, a remote coral outcrop unrivalled on the Kenya coast both for the clarity of its water and for the variety of marine life present. Most day trips from Diani incorporate a session of snorkelling at one of the many excellent reef sites around Kisite, which lies 8km (5 miles) from Shimoni by boat. Bottlenosed dolphins can frequently be seen during the ride out. Schools of yellowfin tuna can often be seen in the area, and sightings of mantas, humpbacked whales and whale sharks have become more frequent in recent years.

Day tours from Diani almost always include a lunch stop on **Wasini Island ⑬**, which lies on the opposite side of the narrow sea channel in front of Shimoni town. The island is named for the Chinese (Wa-Cini in Swahili), who once traded with the islanders, a link evidenced by the presence of an ancient pillar tomb inset with Ming porcelain. Wasini is best known as the site of the legendary Charlie Claws Restaurant, and its gargantuan seafood buffet lunches. A less superficial attraction is the **Coral Garden Boardwalk**, managed by a local women's group, that runs through a patch of exposed coral outcrops and sand flats inhabited by hermit crabs, mudskippers and the coconut crab.

FACT

Kisite Island lies close to the edge of the Pemba Channel, which drops to a depth of more than 300 metres (1,000ft) to form one of the finest deep-sea fishing and diving areas on the East African coast.

Mangrove swamp, Wasini Island.

NORTH TO MALINDI

The coast north of Mombasa is home to many exquisite beaches, not to mention medieval Swahili ruins, wildlife reserves and a sultry town that was a favourite with Ernest Hemingway.

Nairobi

S ituated 115km (70 miles) north of Mombasa, and of comparable antiquity, the smaller port of Malindi ranks among the busiest resort towns along the East African coast, thanks to its superb beaches, fine opportunities for game fishing, and proximity to the pristine reefs protected within the Malindi Marine National Park. Malindi is situated a mere 20km (12 miles) northeast of the smaller resort town of Watamu, which offers equally good swimming, fishing, snorkelling and diving, but also lies alongside the impressive ruined medieval city of Gede, in the heart of the wildlife-rich Arabuko-Sokoke Forest.

North from Mombasa

Coming from Mombasa, the gateway to the cluster of attractions associated with Malindi and Watamu is the bridge that spans **Mtwapa Creek**, an old river course cut deep into the coral limestone some 20km (12 miles) north of Nyali Bridge. Water sports centres and marinas line both sides of the creek, and the small town of Mtwapa, set on a coral cliff above its northern bank, boasts a few popular restaurants and nightclubs, but facilities are aimed squarely at the Mombasa weekender crowd rather than international tourists.

About 4km (2 miles) along a side road running towards the ocean east of Mtwapa lies the ruined city of **Jumba la Mtwana ❶** (www.museums. or.ke; Mon–Fri 9.30am–6pm), a Swahili trade outpost founded in the 14th century and abandoned about 100 years later. Set right on the beach, the brooding ruins were totally engulfed by jungle prior to being excavated by James Kirkman in 1972, and the three mosques and four other buildings that remain are overgrown, but otherwise well-preserved.

Main Attractions
Mnarani National Monument
Arabuko-Sokoke National Park
Gede National Monument
Watamu Marine National Park
Malindi
Marafa Depression

Malindi Beach.

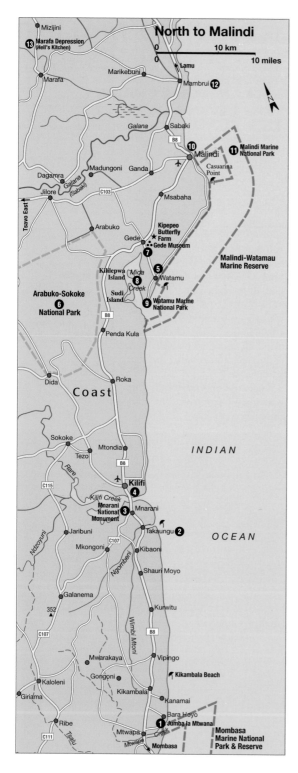

North to Malindi

A further 20km (12 miles) north is the sandy track leading to **Takaungu ❷**, a modest fishing village that served as a important slave trading centre, and the main base of the ruling Mazrui dynasty, after Fort Jesus fell into Omani hands in 1828. Relics from this period include the grave of a sultan who died there in the 19th century, the old slave market, and an overgrown mosque of unknown antiquity. This stretch of road also passes through the **Vipingo Sisal Estate**, Kenya's largest, where lines of the sharp-pointed plants – whose leaf fibre is used to make course string – stretch to the horizon.

Ten kilometres (6 miles) beyond the Takaungu turn-off is **Mnarani**, on the south side of Kilifi Creek, where there are several hotels with water sports facilities. It is also the site of the **Mnarani National Monument ❸** (www.museums.or.ke; 9.30am–6pm), a Swahili ruin notable for its 13th-century pillar tombs and a pair of mosques inscribed in a mysterious Arabic script known elsewhere only from one site in Tanzania. Reached via a steep flight of 104 stairs, the monument is shaded by a giant baobab claimed to be 800 years old and the largest tree of its type in Kenya.

The bridge across the creek leads to the small town of **Kilifi ❹**, the administrative centre of a district that stretches to the borders of the Tsavo national parks. Of all the coastal centres, Kilifi has held out most strongly against the uncontrolled development of tourism. Most of the seafront land is privately owned, much of it in the hands of retired farmers from the highlands. But the presence of sleek, ocean-going yachts and powerful fishing cruisers attests the attractions of Kilifi to upmarket visitors.

Watamu

The popular resort of **Watamu ❺**, 55km (33 miles) north of Kilifi, runs along **Turtle Bay**, a striking enclosed beach named for the turtle-shaped coral outcrops that erupt from its clear turquoise waters. The resort is endowed with several excellent upmarket hotels catering mainly to international visitors, as well as a few deep-sea fishing and water sports centres, and it is arguably the finest diving and snorkelling destination in the country.

Watamu is a favourite watering place for locals, and it hosts what is perhaps the most frantic New Year's Eve party in the country. The small town is also the site of the superb **Bio-Ken Snake Farm** (tel: 042 233 2303; www.bio-ken.com; daily 10am–noon, 2–5pm), which is populated by snakes acquired through the free 'remove-a-snake' service it offers to locals, and hosts the most varied collection in the country.

A short distance inland of Watamu, the **Arabuko-Sokoke National Park** ❻ (daily 6am–7pm), which extends over about 400 sq km (155 sq miles) west from the main coastal road between Mombasa and Malindi, protects Kenya's largest surviving tracts of coastal *Brachystegia* woodland

and lowland rainforest. In addition to small and seldom-seen populations of elephant, buffalo and leopard, the forest is home to a number of rare and/or endemic mammals, including Aders' duiker, Sokoke bush-tailed mongoose, and golden-rumped elephant shrew – the latter, measuring up to 50cm (20ins) long and is among the largest members of a peculiar African family named for their elephantine snouts.

Arabuko-Sokoke is the haunt of many endemic and other localised forest birds including Sokoke scops owl, Retz's helmet shrike, Amani sunbird, Sokoke pipit and Clarke's weaver. A memorable sight here is the thousands of butterflies that drink along the pools near the forest tracks. The Visitors' Centre, close to the main road, is the starting point for several guided and unguided trails, and the more remote reaches of the forest can be explored in a 4x4. Birders seeking rarities such as Sokoke scops owl and Clarke's weaver are best served taking a knowledgeable local guide, as these

The Mnarani ruins.

Malindi is the big-game fishing centre of the Kenya coast and hosts a number of large fishing competitions between September and April.

Larger striped swordtail butterfly, Watamu.

birds have quite specific habitats within the forest.

Set in a stand of dank, jungle-like forest between Watamu and the national park, **Gede Museum** ❼ (tel: 042 32065; www.museums.or.ke; Mon–Sat 8.30am–5.30pm) comprises the substantial and haunting ruins of a once-prosperous Swahili trade city that was suddenly and inexplicably abandoned, probably in the 17th or 18th century. Although an invasion of trees and bush engulfs the old town, there are many well-preserved relics of mosques, houses and palaces built in the traditional Swahili style. It is something of a mystery how, presumably, the sea receded to leave the port high and dry. It is curious, too, why there is no contemporary mention of a town that might correspond to present-day Gede (also sometimes spelt Gedi) in any of the ancient maritime literature, when Arabic or Portuguese logs detail most other coastal ports from Lamu to Vanga. The site takes at least an hour to explore properly, and the small site museum and neighbouring **Kipepeo Butterfly Farm** (tel: 042 32380; www.

kipepeo.org; daily 9am–5pm; free) are also worth a look. The forest footpaths to the outer limits of the abandoned town are a good place to look for monkeys and the endemic golden-rumped elephant shrew, which is a little more habituated to visitors here than in the national park.

At the southern end of the Watamu Peninsula, the 6km (4-mile) -long **Mida Creek** ❽ is surrounded by tidal mudflats covered in mangrove trees. The creek is known for the large numbers of waders – including curlew, whimbrel, sanderling, ruddy turnstone, and various sandpipers and plovers – that break their journey here between March and May on their way north during the annual migration. Osprey, several species of tern and the rare crab plover are resident in the creek, along with half a dozen species of heron and egret. In the mangroves, flocks of the brilliant carmine bee-eaters flash in the sunlight. At the western tip of the creek, reached via a track that branches from the main Mombasa–Malindi Road opposite the Arabuko-Sokoke National Park,

GHOST CITIES OF THE SWAHILI COAST

Three well-preserved ruins of abandoned medieval Swahili cities lie along the road between Mombasa and Malindi, namely, Jumba la Mtwana, Mnarani and Gede. Archaeological evidence indicates that the history of these coral-rag settlements is broadly similar: all were founded in or around the 13th century, all were clearly Islamic and boasted at least one large mosque, and all thrived on maritime trade with ships from Arabia and Asia.

It remains unclear, however, why these cities were abandoned at around the same time. Clearly, the arrival of the marauding Portuguese in the early 16th century was a factor, but archaeological evidence suggests that most of the city-states were still occupied towards the end of the 16th century. It may also be that the partial collapse of centuries-old maritime trade routes during the Portuguese occupation led to a more gradual decline, one exacerbated by the centralisation of trade on larger ports. Meanwhile, a grisly local legend, supported by several contemporary chronicles, attributes the demise of many old Swahili ports to the southward sweep of a mysterious cannibalistic tribe called the Zimba.

Today, these ruins offer an insight into the advanced architectural techniques that characterised the medieval Swahili Coast and give some idea of how ports such as Mombasa and Malindi would have looked in pre-Portuguese times.

a community project has constructed the **Mida Creek Boardwalk and Bird Hide** (daily 6am–6pm) to facilitate birdwatching in the mangroves.

Watamu Marine National Park

Stretching north from Mida Creek, via Watamu, through to Malindi, the **Malindi-Watamu Marine Reserve** extends out to sea for 5.5km (3 nautical miles) and the landward boundary is 30 metres (100ft) from the high-water mark. The first conservation area of its sort to be established in Kenya, it incorporates the Malindi and Watamu Marine National Parks, which are arguably the finest snorkelling and diving sites in Kenya.

Watamu Marine National Park ❾ (tel: 020 2335 459; www.kws.go.ke), designated a UN Biosphere Reserve in 1979, protects a channel that runs inside the reef wall for the length of the bay, on the eastern edge of which are the scattered coral heads of much-visited coral gardens. One of the best snorkelling sites in the area, and easily the most accessible,

is Turtle Bay itself, whose wealth of coral gardens are accessible from the shore, but are more commonly visited on formal snorkelling excursions in flat glass-bottomed boats operated by most of the hotels as well as numerous private operators.

The fish in these coral gardens are marvellously colourful, perhaps the most common being the blue surgeon fish with its built-in 'scalpel' at the base of the tail. This is a defence mechanism – the fish extends the very sharp spine when it feels threatened. Although it's not poisonous, the scalpel can inflict a severe wound, and the fish is generally treated with caution by fishermen emptying their nets.

Many varieties of butterfly fish occur, including the coachman with its long trailing dorsal fin. This fish is often mistaken for the similar Moorish idol, which is also very common. Angelfish abound, their immature colouration being so different from the adult that identification is not easy for the beginner.

Holes and crevices in the coral are hiding places for the shy reef

The ruined Gede palace.

residents, including moray eels, soldier fish, barbel eels, octopus and turtles. Needless to say, it is an offence to collect turtles' eggs, of which many hundreds at a time are laid and buried in the sand above the high-water mark.

South of Turtle Bay, the most exciting area of the marine park is at the entrance to Mida Creek, where the **Big Three Caves** are home to a resident school of rock cod *(tewa)*, giants that weigh up to 200kg (450lb). To the north of Turtle Bay is the shallow, sheltered **Blue Lagoon**, sandy bottomed and free of currents. At low tide, woolly-necked storks can often be seen foraging for food, and the cliffs at the southern end are heavily populated with multicoloured crabs, skittering over the sharp terrain. Further afield, world-class diving schools at several hotels in Watamu can arrange fully equipped excursions to prime dive sites such as Hancock's Hole or Ed's Caves – well known by the local diving fraternity, but not marked on any maps.

Coral outcrop, Turtle Bay.

Malindi

With its sultry old town and sweeping beaches, **Malindi** , is the most northerly of Kenya's main coastal resorts, having gained fame after Ernest Hemingway visited there in the 1930s to enjoy the big-game fishing. It has been developed to cater for both local and foreign tourism, with Italy and Germany being particularly important markets, and its lively hotels, nightclubs and bars mean it is well set up for the hedonist on holiday.

Daily flights from Nairobi, Mombasa, Lamu and the game parks arrive at the small airport situated 2km (1 mile) outside town on the Mombasa Road. The main road forks at a roundabout – turn right for the south end of Malindi and its beautiful beaches and hotels, left for the main town on the Lamu Road. This is Malindi's main shopping area – four shopping plazas, each with its own open-air bar/restaurant. Southwards along the seafront, the former **District Commissioner's Office**, built by the Imperial British East

Africa Company in 1890, is a gazetted building but decidedly rundown all the same.

You are now on the outskirts of the **old town**, an interesting Swahili quarter dating from 1930–1950, with a large and busy market. Here, the **Juma'a Mosque** (reputedly built on the site where slaves were auctioned weekly until 1873) stands alongside a pair of 15th-century pillar tombs of a type unique to the Swahili Coast. Opposite this lies the Malindi Tourist Market, one of Kenya's best spots for craft shopping with more than 50 stalls to browse, though most sell a pretty similar selection of goods at similarly negotiable prices.

On the waterfront less than five minutes walk south from here, opposite the main jetty, is the **Malindi Museum** (tel: 042 31479; www.museums.or.ke; daily 8am–6pm), whose displays include several rare wooden totems as erected by the Gobu sub-tribe of the Mijikenda, housed in a colonnaded three-storey building that started life as an Indian trading centre in 1891. Further on stands East

Africa's oldest church, the small Portuguese **Chapel of St Francis Xavier**, built in 1542 and surrounded by a small but very old cemetery. Opposite, on the headland, but only possible to visit if you already have a ticket from the museum, is the Vasco da Gama Pillar, a cross carved from Lisbon stone marking the navigator's visit in 1498.

The modern town centre lies to the north of this, and is dominated by the tourist-oriented **Galana Shopping Centre**, where there are several craft shops, restaurants, bars and even a nightclub. About 500 metres/yds inland, **Falconry of Kenya** (daily 9am–5.30pm) provides temporary or permanent refuge to a variety of injured and orphaned raptors, ranging from snake-eagles to eagle-owls. A small reptile park is attached.

Part of the Malindi-Watamu Marine Reserve, **Malindi Marine National Park ⓫** (tel: 020 2335 684; www.kws.go.ke) extends about a mile out from the shore between Point and Leopard Point, where it offers equally good diving to Watamu, as

Vasco da Gama called in at Malindi on his way to India in 1498. Before he left, he raised a memorial cross beside the Sultan of Malindi's palace. It was moved to its present location in the 16th century.

Locals at Malindi's busy market.

The Portuguese Chapel, Malindi.

The Marafa Depression.

well as some great snorkelling. The main area of interest within the park is **North Reef**, which lies roughly parallel to the shore. Low tide exposes much of this reef, leaving numerous shallow pools. The southern part comprises the coral gardens, which slope off on the seaward side into **Stork Passage**, some 15 metres (50ft) deep. On the shore side, the coral is flanked by the slightly shallower **Barracuda Channel**.

Malindi Bay suffers from the seasonal dumping of brown silt, caused by up-country flooding, from the Sabaki River, which has its outlet at the north end of the bay. However, the beaches south of Vasco da Gama Point are protected by coral reefs and are largely unaffected by this. The bay, on the other hand, is not protected by reefs, and so produces remarkably big waves for surfing, especially when the *kusi* monsoon comes in May and June.

Mambrui and the Marafa Depression

About 5km (3 miles) north of Malindi, the road that eventually

leads to Lamu crosses the Sabaki River over a concrete bridge, constructed after the previous suspension bridge was swept away by a massive flood in the 1990s. Another 5km (3 miles) further on is the turning to **Mambrui** ⑫, which is strongly Muslim in character. It has a fine mosque and pillar tomb, as well as access to a vast expanse of beach stretching up a spit of sand dunes. The coastal strip north of the town has recently been subjected to large-scale tourist development, and there are a number of hotels and restaurants situated on Sheshale Beach.

A worthwhile deviation in the area is to the **Marafa Depression** ⑬, about 35km (23 miles) from Malindi. From the village of Marafa, a short footpath runs down into the depression, a spectacular gorge of eroded sandstone pinnacles and cliffs that looks like a miniature version of the Grand Canyon. Also known as 'Hell's Kitchen', it is most spectacular in the early morning and late afternoon light, when the sandstone assumes striking colours.

Offshore Assets

The marine parks and reserves that line the Kenyan coast support a diverse set of colourful creatures, and offer some fantastic diving and snorkelling.

Stretching for more than 500km (300 miles) between the Somali and Tanzanian borders, Kenya's Indian Ocean coastline is lined by a series of offshore reefs that cover a total area of around 500 sq km (193 sq miles) and comprise almost 200 species of hard coral. The most biodiverse and pristine of these offshore coral gardens are now protected in a series of six marine reserves and four marine national parks and reserves, the oldest of which (at Malindi and Watamu), was established in 1968.

Protecting a total area of almost 1,000 sq km (386 sq miles), Kenya's marine parks and reserves are alive with colourful reef fish, with hundreds of species being represented, while the open waters host a diversity of larger marine creatures, ranging from dolphins and whales to turtles and manta rays. It is forbidden to spear-fish in these protected areas, or to remove shells or coral, or to disturb the occupants of a balanced but highly sensitive ecosystem in any other way. One of the main purposes of these rulings is to combat the serious threat of over-exploitation of shells by souvenir hunters. Efforts have been made to control the number of shell dealers, who must obtain a costly licence, but sadly it is still common to see illegal collectors on the beach.

Coral gardens

The marine reserves are also a major tourist attraction, and for a small fee, it's possible to snorkel or dive in the gardens of coral, whose diversity comes close to matching the more fêted reefs of the Red Sea. The best dive sites lie along the fringing reef that runs parallel to the entire coastline, apart from breaks at *mlangos* (Swahili for 'doors') at the outlets of extinct or extant rivers. The shallows and lagoons between the reef and the beach vary in width and depth. In places, it is possible to wade out in ankle-deep water half a mile to the reef; in others, you have to swim or take a boat. Incidentally, it's very safe in these inshore waters, since sharks generally stay outside the fringing reef, fearing that they could be trapped and possibly beached by the receding tide.

The best time of year to explore the marine world is October to March, when the northeast monsoon blows. Conditions are best for snorkelling or diving at low tide. If this is in the early morning, the water surface will not be too disturbed by wind. In between tides, currents can be strong and the water tends to be murky. Snorkellers should take basic precautions against sunburn, ideally wearing a T-shirt while they are in the water, and should also take great care when walking in rock pools and swimming. Wear stout shoes, and avoid sea urchins, whose mildly toxic spines often break off in a hand or foot, resulting in discomfort for days.

Particularly in areas of dead coral, keep an eye open for stone fish, masters of camouflage whose dorsal fins can inject a dose of venom that is excruciatingly painful and, sometimes, fatal. Stinging coral can cause minor discomfort, a fern-like hydroid that grows abundantly on hard corals. Other potential nasties are jellyfish and cone shells, and several other fish have poisonous defence mechanisms. All in all, it is safest – and most responsible – to leave the underwater world exactly as you find it, and touch nothing at all.

The delicate coral off the coast of Kenya is protected by marine parks.

THE SWAHILI

A unique blend of indigenous African and exotic Arabic influences has bequeathed the Islamic Swahili people their distinctive cultural heritage.

Inhabiting the coast and oceanic islands of Kenya and Tanzania, the Swahili are the most culturally distinctive of East African people, thanks to their long history of maritime trade with Arabia and Asia. The KiSwahili language, like many in Kenya, is classified as part of the Bantu linguistic group, but its enduring importance as a lingua franca – initially of coastal trade, later along caravan routes into the interior – has led to a relatively simplified grammar and a liberal peppering of Arabic words.

Culturally, the Swahili display strong Arabic influences. An obvious example is the near-universal adoption of the Islamic religion, which has dominated along the Swahili Coast since medieval times (the oldest known Islamic structure in East Africa being an 11th-century mosque on the Lamu Archipelago). And the very name Swahili derives from an Arabic word meaning 'coastal.'

Dhows – their design adapted from Arabian vessels – are used widely along the Swahili Coast, not only as fishing vessels, but also as the main mode of transport between the mainland and the islands, and for shipping goods between ports. Best known is the graceful *jahazi*, with its distinctive billowing triangular sail. There is also the all-purpose keel-less *dau la mwao*, while a dugout canoe or double-outrigger canoe may be used in creeks and harbours.

The ocean is integral to the Swahili way of life. In addition to maritime trade, fishing features prominently in the local economy, with spears, hand lines, nets and basket traps all commonly used for this purpose. Also of considerable economic importance is the ubiquitous coconut palm, various parts of which are used for food, drink and oil, as well as forming the raw material for building, thatching, rope-making and plaited basketwork.

Henna painting, though traditionally reserved for special occasions, is now accepted as an everyday adornment by women along much of the Swahili Coast. Both the hands and feet can be painted, often in patterns that are unusually ornate and floral for an Islamic culture.

The ornate wooden doors typical of Lamu and other ancient Swahili settlements were traditionally the first part of a house to be erected. The heavy spikes were not originally mere adornment but were borrowed from mediaeval India, where they provided protection against war elephants used to ram down doors.

Although many Swahili women now dress in a quite modern style, or wrap up in the colourful vitenge (cloths) ubiquitous in East Africa, the all-black veiled bui-bui is still conventional in more traditional towns such as Lamu.

The music of the coast, known as Taarab or Tarabu, fuses Swahili lyrics with Arabic-style melodies, and traditional instruments such as the udi (lute), darbuk (drums) and gannon (zither) with more recent imports such as guitar and violin.

ARTS AND ARCHITECTURE

The most conspicuous manifestation of the rich Swahili artistic tradition is the stone architecture of ruined cities such as Gede (also known as Gedi), or living ports like Pate or Lamu, which are notable for their tall narrow designs, gracious arches, and features such as mangrove pole ceilings and multiple niches. While the Arabic influence on Swahili architecture is easily detected, innovations include the mediaeval pillar tombs that still stand in the likes of Gede and Malindi – tall narrow grave markers whose closest counterparts are overtly phallic medieval stelae erected in parts of southern Ethiopia.

The Swahili also have a substantial poetic literary tradition, one whose origins are rather obscure since the earliest works were not written down but passed between generations orally. Certainly, the tradition is hundreds of years older than the earliest extant Swahili document, an epic poem called *Utenzi wa Tambuka (Story of Tambuka)*, written in Arabic script in Pate in 1728.

Like so many aspects of coastal culture, the traditional *taarab* music is something of a hybrid, fusing Swahili lyrics with Arabic melodies. Traditional *taarab* instruments include the lute-like *udi*, the zither-like *gannon*, and a type of drum called a *darbuk*. However, many modern performers supplement these traditional instruments with the likes of guitar, violin and keyboards, while others have taken the fusion a step further by assimilating elements of Bollywood, R&B, and hip-hop production.

Islam has been a presence on the Swahili Coast for more than a thousand years, and the region is studded with historic mosques such as this handsome example built in 1829 at Shela on the island of Lamu.

Unlike most traditional Kenyan food, which tends towards the bland, traditional Swahili dishes tend to be quite spicy, reflecting centuries of trade with Asia and Arabia. Crabs and other seafood are central to the coastal kitchen, and rice or stews are usually flavoured with grated coconut or coconut milk.

The main form of maritime transport along the Swahili Coast is the dhow. Although an increasing number of these boats are motorised, their large billowing sails are still a characteristic sight off Lamu and other traditional Kenyan ports.

Muslim women in the old fort, Lamu.

TO LAMU AND BEYOND

The fascinating old town of Lamu, set on the remote sleepy island of the same name, is Kenya's most evocative bastion of traditional Swahili culture.

●Nairobi

R emote from the mainstream resorts of Kenya's south-central coastline, the Lamu Archipelago lies almost 250km (150 miles) northeast of Malindi by road (and ferry), closer to the border with Somalia than to any other Kenyan town of substance. Studded with medieval ruins and time-warped Swahili ports whose commercial heyday passed several centuries ago, it is one of the most compelling destinations on the East African coastline, offering a vibrant and culturally stimulating alterative to the sort of conventional beach holiday associated with the likes of Diani and Malindi.

Overland from Malindi

Few tourists travel to Lamu by road. Not only is the overland route from Malindi rough and dusty, but outbreaks of banditry, and more recently of terrorist attacks, associated with the area's proximity to Somalia, have been a cause for serious concern. In 2011, several kidnapping incidents took place in northeast Kenya, and in 2014, Al-Shabaab attacks in the region, most notably in Mpeketoni, claimed at least 89 lives. At the time of writing, travel advice from governments such as Britain, the US and Australia was advising against all but essential travel to areas within 60km (37 miles) of the Kenya-Somalia

border, including all of Lamu County and northern part of Tana River County. Before making plans to head to this region, consult the travel advice on the website of your country's foreign office.

A few buses trundle along the road up to Lamu daily, and it is possible to drive through in half a day, ideally with a 4x4 and a reasonably early start, although this is not recommended. Having crossed the **Sabaki/ Galana River Mouth** immediately outside Malindi, the road continues

Main Attractions
Tana River National Primate
  Reserve
Lamu Town
Shela Beach
Takwa Ruins
Pate Island
Kiunga National Marine
  Reserve

Riyadha Mosque, Lamu.

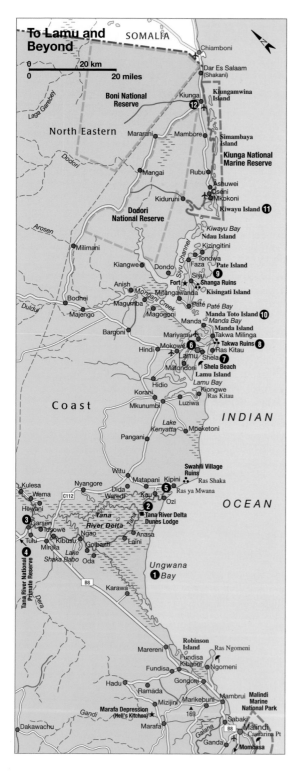

north for 25km (15 miles) to the village of **Gongoni**, after which it is flanked by extensive salt works, interspersed with areas of cultivation and coastal thicket, all the way to Garsen, which lies at the end of the tarmac, another 110km (65 miles) to the north. About halfway along this road, **Karawa** is the junction for an adventurous side trip east to see the sand dunes of **Ungwana Bay ❶**, the largest beach on the whole East Africa coast, undeveloped, deserted – and virtually inaccessible. Situated at the north end of this bay, on the south bank of the Tana River mouth, the blissfully isolated **Tana River Delta Dunes Lodge ❷** (www.deltadunes. co.ke) sits on the dunes, in the shade of the thick riverine forest, a remote and totally unspoiled area.

Back on the main road, about 7km (4 miles) before Garsen, a recently surfaced causeway veers westwards to cross the Tana River en route to Lamu. Near here, a small hill affords the only view in the entire lower Tana basin – a hazy vista of endless dry bush country, broken only by the green ribbon of the riverine strip. Although this new route to Lamu bypasses it, **Garsen ❸** is worth a minor diversion. Set on the banks of the Tana, it's an important local trading centre, and Waldei Gabbra (Somalis), Orma and Pokomo people crowd the street on any morning. It's a good place to buy a cool, refreshing drink, and sit and watch the scene.

Tana River National Primate Reserve

One of Kenya's least visited but most intriguing wildlife destinations, the **Tana River National Primate Reserve ❹**, runs for about 35km (20 miles) along the forested course of the country's largest waterway, some 50km (30 miles) north of Garsen. Gazetted in 1976 and then degazetted in 2007 due to legal issues, this reserve is the only known home of the Tana River red colobus and Tana mangabey, a pair of endangered monkey species whose closest evolutionary relatives live hundreds of kilometres away. The area also supports the Critically Endangered hirola, and is the only known locality for two birds, the Tana river cisticola and nominate race of the white-winged apalis, which have not been observed for so long they may well be extinct.

Back on the Lamu Road, after crossing the Tana, the tarmac gives way to a more erratic dirt surface that can be rather treacherous after rain. After another 50km (30 miles), the road emerges at **Witu**, a sleepy village bearing few signs of having once been the centre of an important sultanate and capital of the short-lived state of 'Swahililand'.

Just beyond Witu is a turn-off to the beach, about 19km (12 miles) away at the village of **Kipini ❺**. This is at present the mouth of the Tana and was the district headquarters until this was subsequently moved well upriver to Hola. Like Witu, the village is Swahili in character with stone-walled houses and *makuti* (palm-leaf) thatched roofs. The river outlet to the sea has been there only since the 1860s, when the Sultan of Witu had a canal dug between the old course of the river and a small stream called the Ozi. Kipini still has a sultry and rather time-warped atmosphere, and there are several old Swahili ruins to the east, the best being 11km (7 miles) away at **Ras ya Mwana**.

Beyond Witu the road passes through the edge of **Witu Forest**, once much more extensive than it is now. The surrounding area is largely a parkland of doum palm and bush interspersed with grassy *ziwas* – shallow depressions that flood during the rains. Baboons, topi and elephants can be observed in this area. At the village of Mkunumbi, the road turns inland for some distance to go around the creeks and

mangrove swamps that lace the area. Eventually, it reaches the sea again at the village of **Mokowe**, from where regular passenger ferries run across the channel to Lamu town.

The Lamu Archipelago

Comprising the islands of Lamu, Pate (pronounced 'pâté') and Manda, together with a number of smaller islets, the Lamu Archipelago is protected in a sheltered bay that once formed part of the same riverine delta as the mainland Mongani Creek. The islands are separated from the mainland by a narrow channel – in parts little more than 1km (0.6-mile) wide – yet they retain a distinctive old Swahili character epitomised by such historic ports as Pate, Siyu and of course Lamu itself. Arriving by light aircraft, as most visitors do, provides a wonderful overview of the historic archipelago, and it is a spectacular sight of shimmering azure channels offset by lush mangrove forests and blindingly white beaches.

The main tourist focus here is the port of **Lamu ❻**, a Unesco World

Swahili women selling silver jewellery, Lamu.

Aerial view of Lamu town.

TIP

Lamu is pleasant at any time of year, but some tourist-class hotels close over May and June for renovation and holidays.

Heritage Site whose 19th-century appearance makes it the most substantial survivor of an urban civilisation that has existed on this part of the coast for at least 1,000 years. Settlements in the archipelago were first noted in the 2nd century AD although no evidence of habitation earlier than the 9th century has yet been excavated. The settlements of Weyuni and Hedabu date back at least to the 13th century. Hedabu, once a principal township, was finally engulfed by sand dunes probably 500 years ago and these shifting sands are now threatening Shela, a picturesque village and fabulous tourist beach at the southern tip of the island.

Lamu itself was a thriving port by 1505, though there were frequent troubles between it and the sultanates of Mombasa, Zanzibar and Pate, the dominant island port to the north. At this time, the Lamu economy was slave-based. Like most other states in the archipelago, its production was mainly grain and fruits, and its exports included ambergris, mangrove poles, turtle shells, rhino horn and ivory. These highly profitable commodities were shipped on dhows to Yemen, Arabia, the Persian Gulf and India.

During the 17th century, nomadic Oromo tribes invaded the coast from the north and sacked most mainland settlements, but bypassed the Lamu Archipelago. The effect was a spate of migration to Lamu, Pate, Siyu and Faza, all of which developed rapidly, with Pate becoming pre-eminent by the 18th century.

Culture flourished at this time; a great tradition of poetry was developed and architecturally ambitious houses were built, some with hot-and-cold plumbing systems, which made European ablutions primitive by comparison. Clothing was elegant and jewellery ornate, with gold and silver cloth woven in Lamu and furniture inlaid with silver and ivory.

But paradise was not complete. The island states warred with each other until 1813, when the people of Lamu trounced an army from Pate at the battle of Shela. From then on, Lamu began its golden age, which

Lamu waterfront.

lasted more or less until 1873, when Britain forced Zanzibar to sign an anti-slaving pact. The Royal Navy patrolled the coast and prevented the Sultan's attempts at slipping slave dhows past the blockade. By 1897, there were fewer than 10,000 slaves on the island and 10 years later slavery was abolished for good.

The first tourists

The cheap labour on which Lamu's prosperity depended was gone and the island plunged into decline. An American visitor at the time wrote: 'The freeing of the slaves has reduced most of the freeborn inhabitants to a state of poverty and, moreover, those with property and coconut *shambas* find it difficult or impossible nowadays to find sufficient labour. I fear there is, then, little hope of their ancient prosperity returning to them, for they have no arts, large industries or resources on which to fall back.'

He was among the island's first 'tourists', who also included Henry Morton Stanley. A few years later,

the Germans moved in to establish the short-lived 'Protectorate' around Witu on the mainland, and opened the Lamu Post Office, the first established outside Germany. For 70 years, Lamu merely jogged along, half comatose – isolated from developments within the new British East African Protectorate and later the Kenya Colony. The technology of Europe's industrial revolution was not imported, nor was the competitive ambition and materialism of the 20th century. The island is still largely untouched by 'civilisation', which accounts for its unique charm.

Then, in 1962, shortly before Kenya's Independence, Lamu's economy began to rally, principally from a new role as shipper of Somali cattle to Mombasa. Tourism arrived in 1967 with an initial eight beds at the Peponi Hotel in Shela Village. Since then, dozens of hotels have been built, and scores of lodging houses opened by the local people. Communication with the island has also been improved, with the upgrading

Boy selling coconuts for drinking, Lamu.

TIP

Most upmarket beach resorts around Lamu will arrange dhow trips for the clients. For independent travellers, the best place to do this is along the old town's waterfront, where numerous guides and captains hang out, waiting for custom. Prices are negotiable, and it is a good idea to ask other travellers for recommendations.

of the Malindi Road and of the airport on Manda Island. Yet, following the recent outbreaks of violence the tourism industry is struggling, travel business has gone down, many hotels have closed and the unemployment has risen sharply.

Old world intact

Lamu's old-world ambience remains its major attraction. The approach to the town is still exclusively by sea – usually by creaking diesel-powered launches from the road-head at Mokowe, or by motorised dhow from the airstrip on Manda Island. A strong sea wall runs the length of the town, decorated in places with black, defunct cannon. Many buildings facing the sea have Swahili-style pillars and castellated walls, or verandas, and behind them is a maze of narrow streets no wider than the span of the donkey carts that remain the main haulage vehicle. The oldest of Lamu's 22 mosques is the **Pwani**, whose *qibla* (dome) dates back to 1370. The **Friday Mosque** was started in 1511, but almost all other buildings date from the 18th or 19th century.

Since very little architectural development has taken place since the late 19th century, Lamu's narrow cloistered pre-colonial town plan is intact. Inset in the unbroken lines of tall buildings are heavy, ornately carved timbered doors and shuttered windows precluding a glimpse of often attractive courtyard gardens inside. There are tiny shops in alleyways, always thronged with strollers – the men in white full-length *khanzu* and *kofia* caps, the woman in black cover-all dresses, called *bui bui* in Swahili.

Lamu Museum

One of the main landmarks along the handsome waterfront, the excellent **Lamu Museum** (tel: 042 633 073, www.museums.or.ke; daily 9.30am–6pm), converted from a colonial governor's residence built in 1891, has several worthwhile displays relating to the region's rich history. Behind it, the main town square is flanked by the **Old Fort**, built with the

LAMU'S FUTURE

The low-key tourist industry that used to thrive on Lamu's idyllic old world ambience currently faces two major threats. The first is the turn-away of international tourism in the wake of recent terrorist attacks in the region. Following two separate incidents in 2011 where westerners were kidnapped and killed by Somali pirates, Kenyan troops entered Somalia to curb Al-Shabaab Islamist fighters, allegedly behind the abductions. In response, Al-Shabaab militants have mounted unprecedented retaliatory attacks against Kenya. In summer 2014, nearly 100 people lost their lives on the northeastern coast, including in Lamu and neighbouring villages, while 2015 saw one of the deadliest attacks in the country's history, when 148 were killed in siege of a college in Garissa, 250km (155 miles) northwest of Lamu. While security has been beefed up, it will be a long time before tourism resumes as normal.

Another threat to Lamu's cultural integrity is the construction of a modern port at nearby Magogoni, a small town in Manda Bay, north of Lamu. The port is intended to serve as the oceanic outlet of the Lamu Port and Southern Sudan-Ethiopia Transport Corridor (LAPSSET) project. This ambitious US$24 billion initiative aims to create a trade corridor and railway linking Lamu to the rich oilfields of South Sudan and agricultural land of southern Ethiopia, and would be the first phase in the construction of a planned pipeline connecting Lamu to Uganda, and one day to Cameroon.

This will form Kenya's second transport corridor – the first running between Mombasa and Uganda – and key features will include a new two-lane highway, an expansion of the existing railway, and three airports. The construction of the port's first three berths was launched in 2015. Although sceptics point out that grand and costly schemes of this sort have a long history of failure in Africa, this time the authorities seem to be fully committed to the infrastructure development plans, which were accelerated by the discovery of crude oil in 2012. While further exploration continues, the country is gearing up to become an oil producer by 2017.

Undoubtedly there are clear potential economic benefits to LAPSSET, but there are also some concerns: about its environmental and cultural impact, its bulldozer approach to sensitive land ownership issues, and a lack of consultation with local communities and their leaders.

assistance of the Sultan of Oman in 1821, as well as the aforementioned Pwani Mosque, and the more imposing **Riyadha Mosque,** built by a Yemeni settler in 1901.

Running north from the square, **Harambee Avenue**, which ran along the waterfront prior to a reclamation programme dating to the mid-19th century, is the town's most important trade thoroughfare, lined with small boutiques and a selection of cafés and other eateries. Behind this, on rising ground, are some of the larger houses of the town, many of which span the streets and create mysterious cloisters of light and dark. They give way to a mosaic of Swahili mud-and-wattle houses, thatched with *makuti*, leading to the viewpoint summit of the hill. On the high ground is the old town hospital.

The beach tourism sector of Lamu is at **Shela ❼** village on the east side of the island, where the Peponi Hotel (www.peponi-lamu.com) marks the beginning of a 13km (8-mile) beach of uninterrupted, empty sand flanked by high dunes. Founded by 17th-century refugees from Manda Island, this small settlement is the site of a striking Friday Mosque, built in 1829, and famed for its 18-metre (60ft) minaret. At the far end of Shela Beach is the village of **Kipungani**, noted for its mango orchards and two old mosques. On the west side of the island, the nearest settlement to the mainland is **Matondoni**, whose people are friendly and addicted to music and dance festivals.

These celebrations or *ziaras* give special eminence to Lamu in the Muslim world. The most important of them is the *Maulidi al Nebi* (birthday of the Prophet). This is a week of religious festivals, feasting and dancing that draws thousands of pilgrims from East and North Africa, Arabia and the Arabian Gulf to inundate the town for the event. They sing and dance in the square before Riyadha Mosque and there is an impressive evening worship in the open air under the stars.

Among the many visitor attractions of Lamu are the typical souvenirs of Arab silver jewellery, carved chests, model dhows and Swahili furniture.

Excursions from Lamu

Manda Island, directly opposite Lamu and Shela towns, houses the **Takwa Ruins ❽** (www.museums.or.ke; 9.30am–6pm), a medieval Swahili trade city that was abandoned in the 17th century and compares in interest and state of preservation to Gede (see page 266). The town ruins at Manda's north end are completely overgrown and buried, but archaeological work has determined them to date from the 9th century – making them the oldest on the Kenyan coast. The site of the main airport serving Lamu Island, Manda is a short dhow ride away from either Lamu or Shela. The island was practically uninhabited throughout the 20th century due to its limited supply of drinking water, but subsequent development

Lamu town backstreet.

School children, Lamu.

Lamu Museum.

includes a string of luxury private villas and upmarket beach resorts along the shore facing Shela.

About 32km (20 miles) northeast of Lamu, **Pate Island** ❾ has been the archipelago's most important cultural and trade centre for much of its long history. Here, the historic village of **Siyu** – once a renowned centre of Islamic scholarship supporting a population of 20,000 – is the site of a well-preserved 19th century fort, and can be visited at any time. Accessible only when tides are suitable, the town of Pate, a small enclave of three-storey buildings set in bizarre isolation among the palms and mangroves, is surrounded by the crumbling ruins of its medieval predecessor.

The archipelago also offers some excellent snorkelling opportunities. The most popular sites close to Lamu is **Manda Toto Island** ❿ (Baby Manda), an uninhabited coral outcrop that lies close to its larger namesake and is frequently visited in conjunction with the Takwa Ruins. Further afield, there are several sites

in the vicinity of the narrow **Kiwayu Island** ⓫ – site of one remote lodge (www.kiwayu.com) – which forms part of the **Kiunga National Marine Reserve** (tel: 0721 686 034; www.kws.go.ke), together with a 60km (37-mile) stretch of the mainland coastline and more than 50 smaller limestone islets. In addition, a plethora of colourful reef, larger marine creatures such as dugong, whale shark and various dolphins and turtles are also resident in the reserve, which protects several vital nesting areas for migratory birds.

On the mainland, north of the Mundane Range, a low ridge of ancient sand dunes, at the village of **Kiunga** ⓬ is attractively situated, with a beautiful old district officer's house perched on a coral headland overlooking the islets of the marine reserve. Inland of this, the contiguous **Boni** and **Dodori National Reserves** protect a wildlife-rich tract of primeval forest that remains little developed, largely because of its proximity to the Somali border and associated security concerns.

Shela beach.

TRAVEL TIPS
KENYA

TRANSPORT

GETTING THERE AND GETTING AROUND

GETTING THERE

By Air

Airports

The Kenya Airports Authority (KAA) is in charge of the country's three international airports, as well as seven of its busiest domestic airports. The KAA's website (www.kaa. go.ke) includes a detailed overview of facilities at all airports operated by KAA, as well all airlines that use the airport, and up-to-the-minute information on scheduled departures and arrivals. Airport taxes are charged on all flights to Kenya, but these are now always included in the fare. For those who require them, visas can be bought at all three international airports.

The most important of the country's three international airports is Nairobi's Jomo Kenyatta International Airport (JKIA), which lies alongside the Mombasa Road, in the suburb of Embakasi, about 10km (6 miles) southeast of the city centre. One of the busiest airports in Africa, JKIA serves over 6 million passengers annually, and the modern facilities include 24-hour currency exchange, ATMs, a post office, internet cafés and numerous duty-free shops, as well as restaurants, coffee shops and bars. Terminal 1A, 1B, 1C and 1E are for international flights and Terminal 1D is for domestic flights. Recently built Interim Terminal, or Terminal 2, allows the handling of an extra 2.5 million passengers annually, while the state-of-the-art 20-million passenger capacity Greenfield Terminal (to be called Terminal 3) is scheduled for opening in 2018.

Mombasa's Moi International Airport, situated on the mainland about 8km (5 miles) west of the island-bound city centre (and linked to it by a road causeway) is a less popular point of entry than JKIA, but it has good facilities and it now receives quite a number of international flights, being particularly popular with charter beach packages.

Eldoret International Airport, in western Kenya, is currently international in name only, and while it does receive a few cargo flights from outside the country, it is seldom used by tourists.

International Flights

The award-winning national carrier Kenya Airways operates one of the best and most extensive intra-African networks, with regular flights to most of the continent's major capitals, and it also flies directly to several European cities, including London, Paris and Amsterdam. It also has good connections to the Middle East and Asia, but doesn't fly to the Americas or Australia. Full timetables, details of booking agencies within and outside Kenya, and a user-friendly online booking service can be accessed at www.kenya-airways.com.

Nairobi, and to a lesser extent Mombasa, are major regional transit and entry points, and JKIA in particular is serviced by most major European and African airlines. There are no direct flights to Kenya from the Americas or Australia, so most visitors route through London, Amsterdam, Johannesburg or Addis Ababa.

By Rail

There is no viable train route into Kenya. A line constructed in the colonial era connects Nairobi to Kampala (the capital of Uganda) and to Dar es Salaam and Arusha (the two main urban tourist hubs in mainland Tanzania) but neither route has operated commercially in years. A new railway line running from Mombasa through Nairobi and Kisumi to Kampana in Uganda and Kigali in Rwanda is currently under construction, and is expected to be completed by 2020.

By Sea

Long gone are the days when a leisurely cruise to Mombasa was an everyday event. It is conceivable that a passenger berth can be found and negotiated on a cargo ship out of London or one of the European ports, but you'll have to work hard to find a passage. Most people who arrive in Mombasa by sea are on a luxury cruise liner and stop over for just a few days. These visits can include short safaris around the country.

It is also possible to take a dhow or catamaran to Mombasa from the

International Airlines

Major carriers to Nairobi include the following airlines:
British Airways www.british airways.com
Egypt Air www.egyptair.com
Emirates www.emirates.com
Ethiopian Airlines www.ethiopian airlines.com
KLM www.klm.com
Lufthansa www.lufthansa.com
South African Airways www.fly saa.com
Swiss International Air Lines www.swiss.com

Traffic passing under Mombasa's famous elephant tusks.

Tanzanian ports of Tanga, Zanzibar or Dar es Salaam, but be warned that dhows are often very uncomfortable, sailing times are unpredictable and fatal accidents happen regularly.

By Road

The only circumstance where you would be likely to enter Kenya in a private road vehicle is if you were driving there yourself, or catching an overland truck from Southern Africa or Europe. If you do drive yourself, note that the following paperwork will be required:
International touring documents: Carnet de Passage
International Certificate of Insurance
International Driving Licence (visitors may use their domestic licence for up to 90 days, after which they should apply for a Kenya driving licence).

Further advice can be obtained from the Automobile Association of Kenya (tel: 020 697 9000; www. aakenya.co.ke).

From the north: access by road is difficult because of problems of uncertain transit through northeast Africa. But it is not impossible, with the most viable route currently going through Sudan and Ethiopia. A handful of companies in London organise group overland safaris to Kenya, though such trips are designed for the adventurous. These include Truck Africa (www.truckafrica. com) and African Trails (www. africantrails.co.uk).

If you are tempted to organise your own private overland expedition, thorough advance planning is necessary, and you will need to consult with the embassies of countries on your chosen route. Bold travellers have done the journey solo by motorbike, but most people would be advised to travel with two or more 4x4 trucks, fully rigged for long desert crossings.

From the south and west: driving to Kenya from the south or west is less problematic. A popular route runs from South Africa via Zimbabwe, Zambia and Tanzania to Nairobi, variations on which might take you through Namibia, Botswana, Mozambique, Malawi, Rwanda or Uganda. For self-drivers, the main routes through this region are all surfaced, and can be driven in almost any saloon car, but a 4x4 is preferable, as it will allow better access to national parks and other game reserves. There are also plenty of overland truck trips between Southern Africa and Nairobi, typically starting or ending at Cape Town or Victoria Falls. Companies running these trips include African Overland Safaris (www.african-overland-safaris. com) and Getaway Africa (www. getawayafrica.com).

By Bus

It is possible to travel to Kenya by coach, bus and other local public transport, all the way from South Africa, via Tanzania, as well as from Kampala (Uganda) or Kigali (Rwanda). Buses in East Africa tend to be poorly maintained and dangerously driven, and while there are no absolute exceptions to this rule, the most reliable option is probably Scandinavia Express (www. scandinaviagroup.com), which has a network covering main routes in Kenya, Uganda, Tanzania and Zambia.

GETTING AROUND

The overwhelming majority of tourists are on bespoke or package safaris that include all transportation within the country, whether by air or road, or a combination of the two. Domestic flights are the quickest, easiest and (except in turbulent weather) the smoothest way of getting around, but

road travel tends to be a lot cheaper and allows you to see far more of the countryside, which is often spectacularly scenic. Flights aside, public transport (whether by road or by rail) tends to be slow, crowded and relatively unsafe, and it does not service the internal road circuit of any national parks or other reserves.

To and from Airports

There are no public bus or shuttle services to any airports in Kenya. However, most safaris are inclusive of all tourist airport transfers, failing which any upmarket hotel will offer an airport transfer or shuttle to their guests. In addition, plenty of taxi companies are represented at all urban and suburban airports, offering cabs at fixed or slightly negotiable fares. Typically, a taxi from JKIA or Wilson Airport to elsewhere in Nairobi will cost US\$10 to US\$30, depending on the exact distance. It is also worth noting that the appalling traffic in Nairobi means that it can take anything from one to three hours to get to the airport from elsewhere in town. From Moi International Airport, taxis to central Mombasa and beaches immediately north of the city cost around US\$20, while those to Diani and other destinations south of Likoni Ferry cost around US\$40 to US\$50.

By Air

An excellent network of domestic flights links Nairobi and other main centres to all parks and reserves, several of which have numerous airstrips allowing quick road access to all camps and lodges. Medium-sized planes tend to be used between Nairobi and Mombasa, but other routes are covered by light aircraft ranging upwards from five-seaters. Although there are several scheduled flights daily to all major reserves, the exact timing and the sequence of airstrips at which they land varies from one day to the next, depending on which camps the airline needs to drop passengers at, and collect them from. Note that the luggage restriction on most light aircraft flights is 15kg (33lbs) per passenger; this includes hand luggage and is strictly enforced.

With the notable exception of the national carrier Kenya Airways, whose domestic flights all leave from JKIA, most domestic carriers operate out of Wilson Airport (www.kaa.go.ke). Older than JKIA, this small but busy airport was established in 1933 as Nairobi

Aerodrome, and renamed in honour of the pioneering aviator Florence Kerr Wilson in 1962. It is situated about 4km (2.5 miles) south of the city centre and some 15km (9 miles) from JKIA, and it handles an average of more than 300 take-offs and landings daily, almost all of them light aircraft.

The main domestic carriers include the following:

SafariLink (tel: 020 6000 777; www.flysafarilink.com) – excellent domestic operator with extensive domestic network and user-friendly website booking. Daily flights connecting Nairobi, Naivasha, Tsavo West, Amboseli, Samburu, Shaba, Maasai Mara, Nanyuki, Lewa Downs, Kiwayu and Lamu, as well as Kilimanjaro International Airport in Tanzania.

Kenya Airways (tel: 020 327 4747; www.kenya-airways.com) – scheduled services from Nairobi to Mombasa, Malindi, Lamu and Kisumu.

Air Kenya (tel: 020 391 6000; www.airkenya.com) – operates regular flights from Wilson Airport to a similar set of destinations as SafariLink.

Mombasa Air Safari (tel: 073 4400 400, 020 204 0947; www.mombasaairsafari.com) – Mombasa-based company specialising in flights along the coast.

By Rail

Train travel is very good value and comfortable. The main line runs from Mombasa on the coast via Nairobi to Kisumu in the west. Trains run from Nairobi to Mombasa on Monday, Wednesday and Friday, and the other way on Tuesday, Thursday and Sunday, leaving at 7pm and arriving at 9.30am. The old-fashioned sleepers and dining car are all a bit shabby and trains are slow, but it's still a relaxing and enjoyable way to travel. First class tickets in two-bed cabins cost US$75 per person one-way. Second-class cabins, taking four passengers, cost US$65 one-way per person. These rates include dinner and breakfast. Tickets are best reserved in advance, either directly through the ticket office at Nairobi or Mombasa station, or through Kenya Train Travel (www.kenyatraintravel.com), a specialist operator that takes PayPal and credit cards.

By Bus/*Matatu*

Buses and coaches are the cheapest form of travel in Kenya, with a nationwide network wherever there are decent roads. The long-haul buses out of Nairobi and Mombasa are by no means excluded to visitors, but they are definitely rough and ready, and also often rather dangerously driven. Some of the recommended bus operators are Coast Bus Ltd (tel: 0722 206 446; www.coastbus.com) and Transline Classic Limited (tel: 0710 246 977; http://translineclassic.co.ke).

A popular alternative to buses are *matatus*, private minibuses that offer a cheap service around the urban centres and between towns. Legally, *matatus* are only allowed to carry 14 passengers and their speed is controlled by speed governors. Nevertheless, they are crowded, sometimes dangerous, and not recommended to visitors.

Taxis and Tuctucs

There are a number of properly organised taxi services operating in Nairobi and Mombasa, from the international airports to hotels or the suburbs. If you want to pre-book a cab, it is best to do this through your hotel reception. Alternatively, private taxis can usually be hailed down anywhere in central Nairobi or Mombasa. These are usually marked with yellow stripes, but otherwise are a decidedly motley collection of vehicles, in various stages of dilapidation, and none with meters. The fares are always negotiable, which presumes foreknowledge of reasonable rates.

Tuctucs are an inexpensive alternative to taxis. A type of modified motorcycle that takes up to three passengers, these were first introduced to Kenya in the late 1990s and are now ubiquitous in most urban centres. Because they are so much lighter on fuel, fares are typically about half the taxi equivalent.

Driving

Although the overwhelming majority of visitors to Kenya travel around on organised safaris, either flying between places of interest, or being driven by a local driver-guide, it is also technically possible just to hire a car and set off yourself. Be aware however, that driving conditions in Kenya are likely to prove quite challenging and stressful to visitors from Europe or North America. The two main cities, Nairobi and Mombasa, tend to be very congested, while the surfaced roads between larger towns are mostly single-carriageway and clogged up with slow trucks that tempt faster vehicles into kamikaze overtaking manoeuvres. Signposting is erratic at the best of times and non-existent in many reserves and parks, where dirt roads often become tricky in the rainy season. Because of this, rather than driving yourself you might want think about renting a vehicle with a driver – indeed, many companies will only rent a vehicle on that basis, blurring the line between car rental and a tailored safari.

If you do opt to rent a self-drive vehicle, a saloon car is fine for travelling between main towns and exploring the coast as far north as Malindi, but a 4x4 is more-or-less a prerequisite for most reserves and parks, especially in the rainy season. When you pick up the vehicle from your rental company, check it over carefully: make sure the tyres are not dangerously worn, that there is at least one good spare tyre (ideally two, if you'll be on safari), that a functioning jack and other tools are supplied, and the brakes are in good working order.

You will find things more relaxing if you limit travel distances to around 200–300km (125–185 miles) per day (depending to some extent on road conditions); pre-book your accommodation; and make sure you have sufficient maps, food and water (for yourself and the car). Be sure to fill your tank whenever you have the opportunity, since fuel stations tend to be few and far between in some areas. Driving at night is generally not recommended. In more remote areas, such as the road north to Turkana, you ideally want to drive in convoy with somebody with local experience.

Car Hire

Avis operates in Nairobi and Mombasa, together with numerous other local entrepreneurs offering everything from Range Rovers to small saloons. Recommended companies include:

Adventure Upgrade Safaris & Car hire
Tel: 020 228 725
www.adventureupgradesafaris.co.ke
Avis
Tel: 020 2386 420
www.avis.co.ke
Central Rent-a-Car
Tel: 020 2222 888
www.carhirekenya.com
Elite Car Rental
Tel: 020 358 1027
www.elitecarrentaltours.com

A – Z

A HANDY SUMMARY
OF PRACTICAL INFORMATION

A

Accommodation

Many visitors to Kenya spend most of their time on safari, where the choice of accommodation is enormous – at last count, more than 50 lodges and camps in the Maasai Mara alone – and the exact location of a lodge will often have a significant effect on the quality of game drives. Therefore, it is recommended to talk through your priorities and options with a knowledgeable safari operator.

Two broad types of accommodation are available in reserves. The more conventional of these, typically operated by chains such as Sopa, Sarova and Serena, and aimed largely at group tours, are large 'hotel in the bush'-style lodges whose packaged feel, high comfort levels and physical solidity are well suited to novice safari-goers and older travellers.

The alternative to these large lodges is an ever-growing choice of smaller (5- to 20-unit) bush camps that offer accommodation in en suite walk-in tents or bandas (huts or chalets) that blend into the surrounding bush to create a 24-hour safari experience. Many of these bush camps are surprisingly trendy in their style of decor, and are often genuinely luxurious, catering almost entirely to fly-in guests, for whom they provide all activities using their own experienced guides.

In Nairobi, and to a lesser extent in some small towns and along the coast, accommodation geared towards tourists tends to be dominated by multi-storey city hotels not far removed from what you would find anywhere in the world (the likes of Hilton, InterContinental and Fairmont are all represented in Nairobi) though often with an African twist to the decor. A welcome recent development has been the opening of several smaller suburban hotels, most famously perhaps Giraffe Manor, that fit somewhere between a bush camp and a boutique hotel in feel.

On the coast, most people stay in one of the numerous large resorts that line beaches such as Diani, Watamu, Malindi and the coast immediately north of Mombasa. These resorts are mostly very sumptuous, albeit in a rather stereotypical way, with palm-lined beaches, large swimming pool, great seafood and villa or hotel-like accommodation. However, there are also an increasing number of exclusive coastal properties that more closely resemble a bush camp in feel.

It is worth noting that almost all accommodation aimed at tourists is pricey by international standards, and there is very little in the way of mid-range accommodation that falls between expensive tourist hotels and the cheap but generally rather off-putting local guesthouses that proliferate in small towns. Indeed, the only place in Kenya where tourists regularly stay in small locally owned guesthouses is Lamu Town, which has the country's most compelling urban attractions.

For those willing to self-cater, it is also worth looking at the relatively inexpensive bandas (huts and cottages) operated by Kenya Wildlife Services (KWS) in and around many of the national parks and reserves. This usually takes the form of simple cottages with bed linen and towels provided, along with a gas cooker and cooking utensils. A full list is available on the website www.kws. go.ke, together with price and booking details.

Admission Charges

Daily entrance fees are charged for all national parks and reserves managed by the Kenya Wildlife Service (KWS). These are usually valid for a 24-hour period, and non-resident rates are quite high by international standards: US$80 per person for the Maasai Mara; US$80 for KWS's two 'premium parks' Amboseli and Lake Nakuru; US$75 for Tsavo East, Tsavo West and Meru; US$65 for Aberdare; US$50 for Nairobi National Park; and US$20–30 for most other parks and reserves. For climbing Mount Kenya, one-, four-, five- and six-day package rates are available, working out at around US$65 per day. Non-resident children and students pay about half-price, while resident rates amount to around US$10 for major parks.

Park entrance fees are normally included in the price of an organised safari. However, independent and self-drive travellers will need to pay them directly. In the case of Nairobi, Amboseli, Nakuru and both Tsavos, payment must be made with a 'safari card', which resembles a credit card and can be bought and loaded with cash at the KWS headquarters outside Nairobi National Park, as well as at the main gates to the four other parks where the card is recognised. Cash payments are not accepted for this quintet of parks, so visitors who enter through a minor gate without a loaded safari card will usually be given a temporary pass that needs to be paid for at one of the gates where safari cards can be loaded.

For all other parks and reserves, cash payments must be made at the entrance (neither safari cards nor other credit cards are accepted). Where possible, it is best to pay in US Dollars, but Kenya Shillings are also accepted at a poor exchange rate. Current fees for most parks and reserves, along with up-to-date details of the safari card system, are posted at www.kws.go.ke.

Most museums and archaeological sites fall under the auspices of the National Museums of Kenya (NMK, www.museums. or.ke), which charges non-resident entrance fees of Ksh800 (about US$8) for major museums and sites, and Ksh500 for minor ones. For anybody who plans to visit more than one museum, it's worth knowing that temporary membership of the Museum Society of Kenya, purchasable at the gift shop in Nairobi National Museum, only costs Ksh800 per month and includes free entrance to all NMK properties countrywide.

Private reserves and conservancies typically charge entrance fees comparable to the pricier national parks. Other private tourist attractions usually charge entrance fees equivalent to US$5–10 per person.

B

Budgeting for Your Trip

The majority of visitors to Kenya are on bespoke or package safaris/tours that typically include all accommodation, most meals (lodges and camps in reserves are usually bookable on a full-board basis only, while rack rates at most beach resorts include dinner and breakfast), all activities while on safari, domestic flights and/or transfers, services of a driver/guide and in some cases house drinks. This means that on-the-ground expenses are typically limited to a few meals, drinks, items of a personal nature, and tips.

To give an idea of average costs, a 500ml local beer typically costs around US$1.50 at a local bar and US$3–4 at more touristy places, while a glass of house wine (usually of the boxed variety) costs around US$4 and a bottle of wine anything upwards of US$20.

A main course at a local restaurant might cost US$2, while a smarter place catering to tourists would typically be in the ballpark of US$5–15 for a main course.

Most organised or bespoke tours include all transfers, but taxis are generally inexpensive: you shouldn't pay more than US$20 for a cab from Jomo Kenyatta Airport to a hotel in Nairobi.

For many visitors, particularly on bespoke tours, a significant on-the-ground cost will be tips (see page 297).

C

Children

A safari in Kenya is not ideally suited to younger children, who tend to get bored and possibly disruptive on long game drives. Indeed, many tented camps place a lower age limit on children staying at the camp and/or going on game drives. It is also the case that young children in unfenced camps require a high level of supervision for safety reasons. It depends greatly on the individual child, but a safari cannot generally be recommended to families that include children under the age of six. By contrast, most children over the age of ten, assuming some interest in nature, will love being on safari. Parents who are unsure about how their children will respond to the safari experience might consider booking a private vehicle, which will

Feeding a Rothschild Giraffe at the AFEW Giraffe Centre, Nairobi.

allow greater flexibility over game drive lengths without inconveniencing other tourists.

More pragmatically, babysitting services are not widely available at hotels in Kenya, so best check in advance if you plan on using them. Entrance fees are typically half the adult price, and many hotels charge discounted rates for children.

Climate

With an altitude ranging from sea level to 5,199 metres (17,057ft), the temperature, rainfall and humidity variations in Kenya are extreme. Overall, though, the interior tends to be pleasantly warm to hot by day, cooling off significantly at night, while the coast is much hotter, more humid, and offers less relief after dark. In relation to the four main physiographic zones, the climate and land-types can be generalised as follows:

Rift Valley and the Central Highlands

This highland region is generally fresh and invigorating, rather like a Swiss summer. The climate ranges from temperate in the Central Rift Valley to arctic on the Mount Kenya peaks.

The land here is the most productive in Kenya. In the uplands, between 1,500–2,000 metres (4,900–6,600ft), the greater part of Kenya's agricultural output is produced. In the Rift itself, production is mixed – arable, dairy and livestock.

The central massif of Mount Kenya and the high Aberdares form the country's main water catchment area, with rainfall of up to 3,000mm (120ins) a year on the mountains, producing run-offs to the main Rift lakes.

Statistics for Nairobi, at the centre of the region, are:
Altitude: 1,661 metres (5,450ft).
Rainfall: Minimum 20mm/0.8ins (July); maximum 200mm/8ins (April); average annual 750–1,000mm (30–40ins), mainly in two seasons March–May and October–December.
Sunshine: Averaging from maximum 9.5 hours daily in February to a minimum 5 hours (April).
Temperature: Minimum 10°C–14°C (50°F–58°F); maximum 22°C–26°C (72°F–79°F).

Western Kenya

Hot, wettish, with the rain spread fairly evenly throughout the year. Most of the rain falls in early evening. The climate at Kisumu, the centre of the

region, is fairly typical of Western Kenya:
Altitude: 1,157 metres (3,795ft).
Rainfall: Minimum 60mm/2.5ins (June); maximum 200mm/8ins (April); annually 1,000–1,300mm (40–50ins).
Sunshine: Between 7 and 9 hours daily throughout the year.
Temperature: Minimum 14°C–18°C (57°F–64°F); maximum 30°C–34°C (86°F–93°F).

Northern and Eastern Kenya

The land ranges from bleak lava desert around Lake Turkana, where west of the lake rainfall averages below 255mm (10ins) a year and temperatures rise to 104°F (39°C), to sand desert at the Chalbi in the north; from arid pastoralist bush, vast dryish grass and acacia rangeland, down to the baking soda lake of Magadi in the south, where again temperatures will be as high as 100°F (38°C). It is difficult to set an average climate for this vast T-section of the country, but one indicative example may be Garissa, at the eastern edge of the dry savannah belt:
Altitude: 128 metres (420ft).
Rainfall: Minimum zero (July); maximum 80mm/3ins (November); average annual, 255–510mm (10–20ins).
Sunshine: Averaging 9 hours a day over the year.
Temperature: Mean annual minimum, 22°C (72°F); mean annual maximum 34°C (93°F).

Coastal Belt

The coral beaches are hot with about 70 percent humidity, but tempered by sea breezes. Then comes a thin plain, suitable for agriculture (fruits, nuts, dairy, cotton), but this soon gives way to thorn scrub and semi-desert. The climate of Mombasa is typical of the region:
Altitude: 17 metres (57ft).
Rainfall: Average minimum 20mm/0.8ins (February) to 240mm/9ins (May); average annual 1,000–1,250mm (40–50ins).
Sunshine: Average maximum of 9 hours a day in March, 7 hours in May.
Temperature: Mean annual minimum 22°C (72°F); mean annual maximum 30°C (87°F).

When to Visit

There is no truly bad time to visit Kenya, but every season has its pros and cons. The worst time to visit the coast is over April and May, which together account for about 40 percent of the average annual

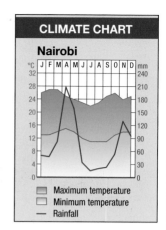

CLIMATE CHART
Nairobi

- ▢ Maximum temperature
- ▢ Minimum temperature
- — Rainfall

rainfall, while the most comfortable time of year is the relatively cool period from June to October. Inland, the long rains (late February to early June, peaking in April) are also a poor time to hike on Mount Kenya. As for wildlife viewing, the peak season is late July to October, when the wildebeest migration is centred on the Maasai Mara. However, game viewing is good throughout the year, and those who place a higher premium on a wilderness experience than on individual wildlife sightings might prefer to avoid those peak tourist seasons. For birdwatchers, the best time to be in Kenya is the northern winter (October to May), when many resident species are in full breeding colours, and 100-plus species of Palaearctic migrants are present.

What to Wear

If you'll spend most of your time on safari, bring a small, select wardrobe for all seasons. Light and casual is the clothing code for the coast and on safari. There is really no need to splash out on the full professional hunter khaki outfit – any light clothing in muted colours will do, plus, of course, a hat for protection against the sun. For the forest lodges, dress (almost) as for evening in a European ski lodge, or at least well wrapped up.

Drip-dry clothing is recommended, and plenty of it. Soil in Kenya is red and dusty just about everywhere, so clothes get grubby quickly. Don't bother bringing rainwear, even if the safari is timed for the rainy season. If necessary, a light waterproof can be picked up locally.

Women will probably find cotton dresses cooler and more comfortable than trousers, particularly for daytime. If you prefer to wear

TRANSPORT

A – Z

LANGUAGE

trousers, make sure they are baggy enough to allow plenty of ventilation. The local dresses or loose blouses are available in an infinite variety of designs and are good value. The *kikoi* and *kanga* – local wrap-around sarongs – are also useful.

For footwear, comfort should take precedence over style, as pavements are often uneven in the cities and towns – and non-existent, of course, in the bush. Take any specialised sports clothes you might want.

Crime and Safety

Kenya as a whole is considered to rank among the safest countries in Africa. In terms of common crime such as pickpocketing, confidence tricks and muggings, Nairobi – nicknamed 'nairobbery' – is the main hotspot, and it is probably unwise to explore the city centre without a local guide at any time, but especially after dark. Suburban Nairobi carries fewer risks for tourists, but it is advisable to use taxis to get around.

Some of the beaches around Mombasa have a bad reputation for snatch theft and muggings, so avoid isolated locations. Crime levels are less significant in smaller towns, but it remains a good idea to keep out of dark backstreets at night, wherever you are, and to avoid the sleazier bars and dance dives in the coastal towns. Don't carry valuables or too much money around, and avoid wearing expensive jewellery, whether you are walking in town or on the beach.

Theft from hotel rooms is uncommon and where it happens, it is most often a case of cleaning staff or similar helping themselves to unsecured valuables. Most hotel rooms have a combination-lock safe, and it is strongly advised to leave all your money, important documents and other valuables here instead of lying out in the open. If your room lacks a safe, then either secure any valuables in a locked suitcase, or leave them at reception.

Rape and sexual assault are uncommon. Should you be accosted, it is more likely that the villain is after your property than your body.

It's worth noting that street justice in Kenya can be harsh. If a victim shouts 'thief', a mob might well give chase and beat up – or, in extreme cases, kill – the perpetrator. So shout for help only if you think the situation warrants the severe beating the accused will receive.

Tourist Police

The rise in crime against visitors led to the formation of a Tourism Police Unit in 1992. This force is doing a good job, especially along the coast, and it has grown from an initial 50 officers to 300 today. Nevertheless, bag-snatching and muggings do happen, though crime against tourists seems to be far less common than it was in the 1990s. For further details about the police, see the website www.nationalpolice.go.ke.

Drugs

Marijuana is called *bhang* locally. Like most plants in Kenya, it grows wild and abundantly. Needless to say, smoking or dealing in it is against the law, and might be punishable by a jail sentence. Do not even think about exporting marijuana: the penalties are stiff and customs officers are wise to all the tricks.

The only other drug in common use is the mild narcotic known elsewhere as *khat* but called *miraa* in Kenya. It derives from the *Catha edulis* tree, which is grown extensively in the wet hills above Meru and Embu. Small sticks or leaves are chewed for an active ingredient called cathin, an amphetamine whose stimulating effect is comparable to strong coffee. It is legal in Kenya, where it is chewed mostly by the northern nomads as well as Muslims, whose religion forbids the consumption of alcohol. Mild though it is, *miraa* is proven to be harmful to the health of regular consumers, and it is illegal in many Western countries, so don't consider exporting any.

Until recently, hard drugs were almost unknown in Kenya. However, since about 2005, the country has grown in significance as a transit point between South America and Europe for hard drugs such as cocaine, opium and heroin. Usage of hard drugs remains relatively uncommon in Kenya, however, and it is highly illegal.

Terrorism and Kidnappings

Kenya's maritime proximity to Arabia and shared border with troubled Somalia make it unusually vulnerable to terrorist attacks. Past incidents included the bombing of the US Embassy in Nairobi in 1998 and a similar attack on an Israeli-owned hotel north of Mombasa in 2002. More recently, the northeast of the country has been subjected to a spate of kidnappings attributed to the Somali organisation Al-Shabaab (an affiliate of Al Qaeda). These include

Electricity

Mains electricity is 220–240V at 60Hz. British-style round or square three-pin plugs are in common use, so a travel adaptor is advised for electrical equipment with two-pin or other plugs. Most game lodges and camps depend on generators and/or solar power for their electricity, so there may be limited charging points and hours, and it is important you charge up regularly in order that batteries do not run so low they require immediate charging.

the killing of one British national and kidnapping of his wife near Lamu in September 2011, the kidnapping of a French National near Lamu in October 2011, and the kidnapping of two aid workers from the Dadaab refugee camp later in the same month. This prompted a Kenyan invasion of southwest Somalia in pursuit of Al-Shabaab, which since 2013 have carried out a spate of retaliatory attacks against the country, killing hundreds and injuring many more within the Nairobi area, along the coast, and in the Northeastern region. In April 2015, 148 people, primarily students, were killed in a massacre at Garissa University, the deadliest attack since the 1998 bombing of the US Embassy.

As a result, several governments currently advises their citizens against 'all but essential travel' to areas within 60km (38 miles) of the Somali border, Garissa County, the Eastleigh area of Nairobi, Lamu County and those areas of Tana River County north of the Tana river itself, and within 15km (9miles) of the coast from the Tana River down to, but not including, Watamu. One thing to remember is that this will render most travel insurance policies redundant within the affected zones. The situation will hopefully change for the better during the lifespan of this edition, so check the relevant websites (for example www.fco.gov. uk and http://travel.state.gov) for the latest advice when planning a trip.

Customs Regulations

Unused personal effects, unexposed film, cameras and accessories (except cine and slide projectors) may be temporarily imported duty-free.

Among items that must be declared, but will be admitted duty-free, are: 227 grams of tobacco, or 200 cigarettes or 50 cigars; one bottle of spirits or wine; and 250ml of perfume. There is no limit on the amount of local and foreign currency that visitors can import into the country or take out when they leave.

Refundable deposits may be required for the import of radios, tape recorders and similar equipment, musical instruments, etc. Firearms may only be imported if accompanied by a permit issued by the Central Firearms Bureau, PO Box 30263, Nairobi (tel: 020 272 5070).

The import of illegal drugs, hunting knives, meat products, plant products or pornographic material is forbidden.

D

Disabled Travellers

Although it doesn't measure up to most Western countries when it comes to facilities for disabled travellers, Kenya is one of the better-equipped countries in Africa. Most major tourist destinations have at least one lodge and hotel with disability-adapted rooms and tolerable level entry points, and there is a good awareness of the needs of mobility-impaired travellers within the industry. There is no official organisation that deals with disabled travel, but Go Africa Safaris (www.go-africa-safaris.com) is the leading regional specialist in safaris for people with disabilities, and Southern Cross Safaris (www.southerncrosskenya.com) also has a good reputation in this respect.

E

Eating Out

Many visitors go their entire time in Kenya without eating at a stand-alone restaurant. This is because tour itineraries tend to be focussed on national parks and other reserves where no stand-alone restaurants exist, driving after dark is forbidden, and it is customary for safari lodges and camps to include all meals in their rack rates. Likewise, most beach resorts in Kenya operate on a dinner, bed and breakfast or full-board basis, reducing the need for their clients to explore much further when it comes to mealtimes. Indeed, the only place where the average tourist is likely to have the option of eating out is Nairobi, or if they stay at a town hotel somewhere like Malindi, and even here a large

proportion of short-stay visitors will opt to eat in their hotel rather than explore further afield.

Despite this limitation, the standard of food is generally high. Larger lodges and beach resorts typically put on expansive buffets that are sometimes disappointing, but more often very good. Some beach resorts supplement this with one or two à la carte restaurants. At smaller camps, the usual offering is a three- to five-course set menu, typically comprising a starter and/or soup, a choice of one to three mains, a dessert, and coffee or tea.

Urban hotels almost invariably have at least one, and often several, à la carte restaurants. In Nairobi and to a lesser extent Mombasa, there is also a varied selection of world-class stand-alone restaurants, collectively specialising in pretty much every major global cuisine from Thai or Mexican to Italian and Ethiopian. There is also a good choice of restaurants in Malindi and to a lesser extent Kisumu, respectively tending to specialise in Swahili, Italian and Indian cuisine. In smaller towns, the choice is usually limited to local eateries (specialising in bland stews eaten with rice or ugali), mediocre western-style grills, and if you are lucky, an Indian restaurant or two.

What to Eat

The quality of fresh ingredients is exceptional. A lavish variety of tropical fruits and vegetables are available seasonally, and cost next to nothing at local markets. The coast specialises in seafood fresh from the Indian Ocean, ranging from line fish to prawns and lobsters, while the interior produces high quality beef and other meat, much of it sourced from free-range stock.

The most interesting local cuisine is Swahili, which dominates several restaurants along the coast, a speciality being mild to medium curries cooked in coconut milk. Elsewhere, a large and longstanding Indian population means that good Indian restaurants can be found in most towns. Otherwise, most lodges, camps and non-specialised restaurants tend to produce generic international-style food that is of a high standard but not really distinctive to Kenya.

Vegetarianism as a lifestyle choice is still a relatively unfamiliar concept to most Kenyans, even though few locals can afford to eat meat as regularly as most Western households would. Fortunately, however, most

Indian restaurants serve a good selection of vegetarian dishes, and a small proportion are exclusively vegetarian. Most lodge buffets and à la carte restaurants include a few vegetarian options. Smaller camps that do set menus will gladly provide a vegetarian option, or cater to any other special dietary requirements, but it is strongly advisable to ask your operator to give advance warning, and for you to confirm your requirements upon arrival.

Drinking

Although a limited amount of indifferent wine is produced in the Naivasha area, most lodges stick to superior imported stock, mostly, but not exclusively, from South Africa. It tends to be expensive in the context of the local economy, but not so much for European or American visitors.

Local lager beers are cheap and refreshing. Several brands are available, with Tusker being the best known and most popular with tourists. Most restaurants and hotels also stock a variety of imported and local spirits, as well as the usual brand name soft drinks. Tap water is generally unsafe to drink, but bottled mineral water is widely available.

Although some top end safari camps now include soft drinks, beers and house wines in the room rate, they are an extra at most lodges.

Embassies and Consulates

Foreign Embassies in Nairobi

Australia
ICIPE House, Riverside Drive (400 metres off Chiromo Road),
Tel: 020 427 7100
www.kenya.embassy.gov.au

Emergencies

The Police emergency numbers are 999 from a landline, or 112 from a mobile phone. These numbers can also be used to report a fire or to call an ambulance. Kenya Tourist Federation operates 24/7 tourist helplines at 020 6004 767 or 020 800 1000 (visit www.ktf.co.ke for more numbers). In the case of a medical emergency, a good first contact is Emergency Plus Medical Services (Emergency hotline: 0700 395 395; www.eplus.co.ke), which is owned by the Kenya Red Cross Society and offers 24-hour ambulance and medical services.

Canada
High Commission of Canada
Limuru Road, Gigiri, 00621 Nairobi
Tel: 020 366 3000
www.kenya.gc.ca

Ireland
Eden Square, Chiromo Road, 00100 Nairobi
Tel: 0729 000 353
www.dfa.ie

New Zealand
Room 2C, Mirage Plaza
Mombasa Road, 00200 Nairobi
Tel: 020 600 1074

South Africa
South African High Commission
Roshanmaer Place
Lenana Road, 00100 Nairobi
Tel: 020 282 7100
http://south-africa.embassies.nairobi.tel

UK
British High Commission
Upper Hill Road, 00100 Nairobi
Tel: 020 284 4000
http://ukinkenya.fco.gov.uk

USA
United Nations Avenue, Village Market, 00621 Nairobi
Tel: 020 363 6000
http://nairobi.usembassy.gov

Kenyan Embassies Abroad

Australia
43 Culgoa Circuit, O'Malley, ACT 2606
Tel: +61 2 6290 7100
www.kenya.asn.au

Canada
415 Laurier Avenue East, Ottawa
Tel: +1 613 563 1773
www.kenyahighcommission.ca

Ireland
11 Elgin Road, Ballsbridge, Dublin
Tel: +353 1 613 6380
www.kenyaembassyireland.net

It is wise to ask permission when taking photographs.

South Africa
302 Brooks Street, Menlo Park 0081, Pretoria
Tel: +27 12 362 2249
www.kenya.org.za

UK
45 Portland Place, London W1B 1AS
Tel: +44 20 7636 2371/5
http://kenyahighcom.org.uk

USA
2249 R Street N.W, Washington D.C 20008
Tel: +1 202 387 6101
www.kenyaembassy.com

Forms of Address

The masses in Kenya are known as the *wananchi* – the 'people' – and the word carries a connotation of respect. Do not use 'blacks' or 'coloureds'; the terms are 'Africans' or 'Asians'.

In addressing any man over 35, call him *mzee*, pronounced 'mu-zay'. It is a term of respect, meaning 'old man' or 'elder' and you can use it in shops, restaurants, anywhere. Call a mature woman (over 21) *mama* and a child *toto*. A word you will hear constantly is *wazungu*, meaning 'white people' (*mzungu* in the singular). A waiter is addressed as 'steward' or maybe *bwana*, which means 'mister'.

Etiquette

Kenya is a tolerant country and most people are pretty used to the ways of foreigners. All the same, visitors should show respect to the local people by exercising tact, tolerance, and common sense. A few 'don'ts' might be helpful:

Don't show disrespect for authority, starting with the President. Don't try to take his picture, or that of any of Kenya's other leaders, and don't tear up his portrait on a banknote: visitors have sometimes destroyed the last of their Kenyan

cash at the airport before their departure – and have got into trouble for doing so.

Don't photograph anyone without their consent, including tribesmen way out in the bush. A smile, waving your camera around and the offer of a few shillings is normally enough to get consent. These days, the Maasai are wise to the habits of tourists, and they may ask for up to US$10 for a photo of their handsome profile.

Don't make a show of your wealth anywhere. The obvious temptation is to relieve you of some of it in one way or another.

Don't transgress local dress codes, particularly on the coast, which is predominantly Muslim. Nude or topless bathing on beaches or even at public or hotel swimming pools is totally unacceptable anywhere in Kenya. Islamic port towns such as Lamu, Malindi and Mombasa are used to tourists wearing relatively scanty clothes, but even so it would be more respectful for men to wear knee-length shorts or long trousers, and for women to wear skirts or *kikois* that cover the knees, and to cover their shoulders in public places.

F

Festivals and Annual Events

Festivals do not form an important part of the tourist calendar in Kenya, the one major exception being the Swahili cultural festival held in Lamu every November (see the 'To Lamu and Beyond' section for advice on visiting this region). Otherwise, the most important annual events, though often quite festive in atmosphere, tend to be more sporty. A useful site for up-to-date listings and dates of festivals and other important annual events is www. kenyabuzz.com.

February

Kijani Trust Music Festival
www.kijanikenyatrust.org
Classical and choral music are the main focus of this annual charity festival, staged in Nairobi and which runs in two parts, one in February/March and the other in August.

July

Sigana International Storytelling Festival
www.zamaleoact.org
Held annually in Nairobi, this festival gathers together the finest oral storytellers, many of whom perform more regularly outside the country.

August/September

Slum Film Festival
www.slumfilmfestival.net
Founded in 2011 in Nairobi, the festival showcases documentaries and short films either made in slums or featuring stories about life in impoverished communities all over the world.

October

Nairobi Festival of Solos and Duets
http://danceforumnairobi.com
Annual dance festival organised by the Nairobi Dance Forum in partnership with The GoDown Arts Centre, Alliance Française and Goethe Institut.

November

Lamu Cultural Festival
www.magicalkenya.com
Kenya's most atmospheric old port is a fitting setting for this festival celebrating all aspects of Swahili and coastal culture.

G

Gay and Lesbian Travellers

Male homosexual behaviour is illegal in Kenya, and it carries a penalty of up to 14 years' imprisonment. The law currently makes no overt mention of lesbianism, but in 2010, Prime Minister Odinga confirmed that the new constitution 'is very clear on this issue and men or women found engaging in homosexuality will not be spared'. This attitude reflects popular opinion, as an overwhelming majority of Kenyans think homosexuality should be rejected by society. While in his 2015 visit to Kenya US President Barack Obama called for gay equality in Africa, President Uhuru Kenyatta replied that it is 'a non-issue for Kenya'. Despite this, discrete homosexuality is generally tolerated in Kenya, and formal gay rights are currently being promoted by Nairobi-based organisations such as the Gay and Lesbian Coalition of Kenya (www.galck.org) and Gay Kenya (www.gaykenya.com). In practice, travellers who happen to be gay or lesbian are unlikely to encounter any problems in Kenya, provided that they are discrete about their sexuality. That said, Kenya has a limited gay scene, and the country certainly cannot be recommended as a gay-friendly destination comparable with, say, South Africa.

H

Health and Medical Care

Malaria is a perennial hazard in most parts of Kenya below altitudes of 1,800 metres (6,000ft), and occasional outbreaks are recorded at slightly higher altitudes, such as Nairobi. Prophylactics are essential, and all prospective visitors are advised to consult a specialist travel clinic as to which pills are most appropriate for Kenya at the time you intend to travel. As an added precaution against the mosquito bites that spread the disease, wear long trousers, socks and long sleeves in the evenings, apply insect repellent to any bare skin and sleep under a mosquito net whenever possible.

Protection against yellow fever is an international requirement for entering Kenya, but cholera protection is not mandatory. Consult your doctor or a specialist travel clinic for advice.

Medical Services

Medical services are better in Kenya than in most other African countries. On the coast and in Nairobi there are some first-rate hospitals with specialist physicians and surgeons, as well as some fine dentists and opticians.

Medical Insurance

All visitors to Kenya are strongly urged to buy full medical insurance

Hospitals in Kenya

The Aga Khan University Hospital
3rd Parklands Avenue, Nairobi
Tel: 020 374 000
www.agakhanhospitals.org
Nairobi Hospital
Argwings Kodhek Road, Nairobi
Tel: 020 284 5000
www.nairobihospital.org
Karen Hospital
Langata Rd, Nairobi
Tel: 020 661 3000
http://karenhospital.org
Kenyatta National Hospital
Mbagathi Rd, Nairobi
Tel: 020 272 6300
www.knh.or.ke
M.P. Shah Hospital
Shivachi Road, Parklands, Nairobi
Tel: 020 4291 000
www.mpshahhosp.org
Aga Khan Hospital Mombasa
Vanga Road, off Nyerere Avenue, Mombasa
Tel: 041 222 7710
www.agakhanhospitals.org
Mombasa Hospital

Off Mama Ngina Drive, next to Treasury Square, Mombasa
Tel: 041 231 219
www.mombasahospital.com
Aga Khan Hospitals, Kisumu
Otieno Oyoo Street, Kisumu
Tel: 057 200 005
www.agakhanhospitals.org
Diani Beach Hospital
Diani Beach Road, Kwale
Tel: 040 3300 150
www.dianibeachhospital.com
Galana Hospital
Lamu Road, Malindi
Tel: 042 213 0575
Consolata Hospital Nyeri
Ururu Road, Nyeri
Tel: 020 353 6939
http://cmatharihospital.co.ke
Nakuru War Memorial Hospital
State House Road, Nakuru
Tel: 051 211 1990
Nanyuki Cottage Hospital
Nanyuki/Nyeri Road, Nanyuki
Tel: 062 203 2207
www.nanyukicotthosp.org

from a reputable organisation in their home country, ideally a policy that allows for repatriation where required.

Another worthwhile option is to buy inexpensive insurance from the famous **Flying Doctor Service** in Kenya. In the event of serious illness or accident on safari, a doctor will fly out from the service's headquarters at Wilson Airport and either treat the casualties on the spot or fly them to a hospital in Nairobi. For details call AMREF Flying Doctors (tel: 0733 639 088; www.flydoc.org).

AAR Healthcare (AAR; tel: 0730 655 000; www.aar-healthcare.com) sells visitors insurance packages that include the use of their service's health facilities throughout the country, including medical evacuation in conjunction with International SOS Assistance, mobile casualty units and air evacuation within Kenya.

Pharmacies

There is no shortage of pharmacies (chemists) in Kenya, all of which are staffed by qualified pharmacists.

Most drugs are available, although sometimes you may encounter unfamiliar brand names. If your specific prescription is not available, the pharmacist will often be able to prescribe a suitable alternative without the need of a visit to the doctor. Advice and treatment for minor ailments is always generously available.

Most pharmacies close on Saturday afternoon, Sunday and public holidays. When closed, the name and location of the duty chemist is usually posted on the shop door, or may be obtained at the nearest hospital. Weekend opening times are advertised in the local newspapers.

Public Holidays

1 January – New Year's Day
March/April – Good Friday
March/April – Easter Monday
1 May – Labour Day
1 June – Madaraka Day (anniversary of self-government)
20 October – Mashujaa Day (Heroes Day)
12 December – Jamhuri (Independence Day)
25 December – Christmas Day
26 December – Boxing Day
Variable – Id al-Fitr (Muslim holiday to mark the end of Ramadan)

Health Hazards

The Equatorial Sun

Tourists often feel that the sun in Kenya is no stronger than, say, on the west coast of America or on the European continent in the summer. But, being directly overhead in Kenya, the sun is unexpectedly powerful and pale skins must be exposed very gradually.

On the coast, the best practice is to start your sunbathing in the early morning and late afternoon, extending the exposure time each day as your skin begins to tan. Protection for your eyes, head, the nape of the neck and back (when snorkelling) are strongly recommended. Also, insist that children swim in T-shirts for peace of mind and peaceful nights.

Tap Water

In Nairobi, the water is drinkable, but the chances are that new arrivals are going to get diarrhoea anyway – from the change of diet as well as the water. Anywhere outside the city, the water should be boiled unless it has been drawn from ice-cold mountain streams. Bottled mineral water is widely available.

Altitude Sickness

It generally takes a couple of days to acclimatise to high-altitude locations such as Nairobi. The relatively thin air can cause new arrivals to feel tired around the middle of the day, or at least experience a certain light-headedness.

On the higher reaches of Mount Kenya, above 4,000 metres (13,000ft), there is a risk of pulmonary oedema, a capricious suffusion of the lungs that might bring down an athlete and yet leave an habitual smoker to go on blithely to the summit. The only antidote is a swift retreat back down the mountain; otherwise the consequences can be fatal.

HIV and Aids

Recent figures place the rate of HIV infection in Kenya at 5.3 percent of the adult population. While this is a significant improvement on the situation in the 1990s, it is still one of the highest infection rates in the world, and the risks associated with having unprotected sex in Kenya barely need stating.

If you have a pre-existing illness that may require hospital treatment, think twice before going to Kenya, because blood supplies in smaller

hospitals may be infected. Larger private hospitals are much more likely to have reliable blood supplies. You are advised to take a first-aid kit which includes syringes and so on, available from any good pharmacy or outdoor shop.

I

Internet

There are many internet cafés in Kenya's major cities and towns. Wi-fi and/or standard internet facilities are also available in most urban hotels, and even in some safari camps and lodges, though often at inflated rates. It is also possible to pick up internet on a mobile phone with a local SIM card. However, bearing in mind that connections tend to be erratic and slow in remote bush locations, it is probably wise to tell potentially concerned relatives and friends that you will be offline for the duration of any safari.

M

Media

Radio and Television

Domestic TV channels are shared between the Kenya Broadcasting Corporation (KBC) and Kenya Television Network (KTN). Other channels include Nation TV (local news) and STV, which carries a range of programmes including Sky News, CBS News and international sporting events. DSTV is available in some hotels and restaurants, broadcasting a range of news, sport and films. There are several FM radio stations, including Capital FM, BBC World Service, KBC Radio, Family FM and other local language broadcasters.

Newspapers

English-language dailies include *The Standard* (www.standardmedia.co.ke) and the *Nation* (www.nation.co.ke). The weekly *East African* (www.theeastafrican.co.ke) gives news from across East Africa. Foreign papers and magazines are commonly found in major towns around the country.

Money

The local currency is the Kenya Shilling (Ksh), which currently trades at around Ksh100 to the US Dollar, up from around Ksh85 in 2012–2014. Bank note denominations are Ksh50, 100, 200, 500 and 1000 shillings, while coins are in denominations of Ksh40, 20, 10, 5 and 1. Although this means the largest note in circulation is worth US$10, it can be surprisingly difficult to get change when you pay for an item with a larger denomination note, so try to carry a good stock of smaller bills.

Exchange rates are best at banks and exchange bureaux. Avoid changing currency at hotels unless you're desperate. However, most hotels, lodges and tented camps – even out in the bush – can change currency, though they may limit the amount you can change. Of course it is a bad idea to carry around a lot of cash, so plan accordingly.

Credit cards are widely accepted in Nairobi, Mombasa and at most tourist-oriented hotels, and they can also be used to draw local currency from ATMs in all urban centres of any substance. Visa is far and away the most widely accepted type of card in Kenya, though MasterCard and American Express are also accepted at some outlets.

Currency restrictions for visitors have been abolished, so there are no tedious currency declaration forms to fill out. But do not take a large amount of Kenya Shillings out of the country, since you will have trouble exchanging them when abroad.

Tipping

As far as tipping is concerned, the rules that you probably use at home should apply in Kenya. For instance, add 10 percent to a restaurant bill unless a service charge is included.

On a safari, it is conventional to tip the driver-guide around US$10 per person or couple per day, while at some upmarket camps, you might be looking at a minimum of around US$30 per day divided between the driver-guide, the spotter, and the general hotel staff.

O

Opening Hours

Working hours in Kenya are something of a movable feast: shops and so on open any time from 8am to 5.30pm, with some general stores or Indian shops (dukas) staying open well into the evening and also most of the weekend. In Mombasa, shops and businesses may open as early as 7am, shutting for a long siesta any time from 12.30 to 4pm, and then opening up again until after dark.

Normal banking hours are 9am to 3pm, Monday to Friday. Some banks open 9am to 11am on the first and last Saturday of each month. Banks at Nairobi's international airport run a 24-hour service. There are also 24-hour ATMs that accept Visa Cards outside most banks in Kenya.

P

Photography

Do not forget to always ask permission before attempting to photograph people.

If you are using a digital camera, take plenty of spare batteries – they can be hard to find outside of major towns. Rechargeable batteries can be topped up at hotels and lodges, but bear in mind that many bush camps operate on generator or solar electricity, so they may not always be able to charge batteries at the last minute.

The best light for photography is in the early morning and late afternoon. Midday vertical shadows tend to have disastrous effects. For further information, see page 205.

Postal Services

There is a post office in most major shopping centres in Nairobi, and the system is efficient. Mail can also be sent from major hotels, and from post offices in most other towns. International and local speed post and parcel services are offered by several independent operators.

R

Religious Services

The predominant religion is Christianity. About 23 percent of Kenyans are Roman Catholic, while another 47 percent adhere to one or other protestant denomination, be it Anglican, Presbyterian, Methodist, Baptist, Lutheran or one of several small Pentecostal churches. Churches are plentiful and well attended in all towns, and tourists are invariably welcomed. The other main religion is Islam, which is practised by about 11 percent of Kenyans, most widely along the coast. Minor religions include Hinduism and Baha'i, as well as various traditional faiths. As might be expected of such diverse country, the level of religious tolerance is high.

S

Shopping

Nairobi, Mombasa and (to a lesser extent) other large towns in Kenya are reasonably well endowed when it comes to shops, at least by African standards. The malls of suburban Nairobi are filled with trendy clothes boutiques, electronics emporiums, well-stocked bookshops, and delicatessens. Rest assured that if there is anything you really need to buy in Nairobi, you should be able to find it if you ask around.

Note that shopping opportunities tend to be very limited in the beach resorts and game reserves where most tourists spend the majority of their time in Kenya. The one exception to this is the hotel gift shops, stalls and other outlets selling handicrafts and souvenirs, which you'll find almost anywhere that is regularly visited by tourists.

The best chain of supermarkets is Nakumatt (www.nakumatt.net), the main branches of which – at least four in Nairobi, two in Mombasa and one each in Eldoret and Kisumu – are open 24 -hours, 365 days of the year.

What to Buy

A popular item with tourists is the **kiondo basket**, which is handwoven in sisal, often by old Kikuyu women, who can sometimes be seen weaving as they walk along the street. Some baskets find their way into stores in London, New York and Tokyo: bought locally, they are excellent value. **Soapstone carvings** from Kisii District are also popular with visitors. Some are polished black or red, but they are arguably better left in their natural greys and pinks. There are a few good local buys along the coast, such as the intricately carved, brass-bound and studded **Zanzibar chests**, varying in size from a small jewellery box to a steamer trunk. Coastal **jewellery**, in sterling silver, can also be very attractive. **Maasai beadwork** incorporated

Time Zone

Three hours ahead of GMT. Daylight is almost a constant twelve hours with fast sunrises and sundowns at around 6.30am and 6.30pm.

TRANSPORT

A – Z

LANGUAGE

Dialling Codes

Eldoret 053
Kisumu 057
Machakos 044
Meru 064
Mombasa 041
Nakuru 051
Nairobi 020
Nanyuki 062
Nyeri 061

into jewellery, belts, lampshades, tableware and clothing is beautiful, but quality can vary: look for good workmanship.

What not to Buy

Illegal Wildlife Products
Do not ever be tempted to buy any item that is made from a wild animal. It is illegal to hunt wildlife on Kenya, and also to sell any anatomical relics of wild animals, be it elephant-hair or giraffe-hair bracelets (which are sometimes offered by hawkers, and most likely made of plastic) or ivory, rhino horn or animal skins. Similarly, at the coast, the selling of seashells, corals and so on is illegal, a law that is haphazardly enforced, so that many hawkers openly try to sell them.

T

Telephones

Kenya has developed an excellent communications system for both domestic and international services. Direct dialling is available between most centres in the country, and overseas. Pre-paid calling cards for use with touch-tone phones and Telkom public phones can be purchased from any Telkom Kenya outlet, post office or authorised dealer.

The international dialling code for Kenya is +254. Main area codes are as listed, but with the leading zero dropped if dialling from outside the country. Telephone numbers beginning with '07' are invariably mobile numbers and once again the leading zero is dropped when dialling from abroad.

There are several mobile (cellphone) networks in Kenya, which makes communication throughout the country easier. Worldwide roaming services are now available with both networks. But, although the coverage is now widespread, it does not extend to many rural areas,

including many of the national parks and reserves. You can buy a local sim card – Safaricom (www.safaricom. co.ke) is recommended – and airtime vouchers for your mobile in many phone shops, supermarkets and hotels.

Toilets

Standard western flush toilets are the norm at all tourist-class hotels, lodges and restaurants, though some eco-conscious camps use biodegradable pit toilets. In most game reserves, toilets are restricted to a handful of public camping and picnic sites, so it's a good idea to go to the toilet before you leave on a game drive. Public toilets and facilities not aimed at tourists (filling stations, for instance, or markets) tend to be rather dirty and are best avoided.

Tourist Information

Before you Leave Home
The Kenya Tourist Board (KTB), Head Office at Kenya-Re Towers, Ragati Road, Upper Hill, Nairobi; tel: 020 2711 262; email: info@ ktb.go.ke; www.magicalkenya.com) is more concerned with marketing Kenya within the industry than with providing a standard tourist information service. Nevertheless, it has an informative website, and while it no longer maintains tourist offices outside the country, it is represented by marketing agencies in the UK, USA, Canada, Australia and several European countries (all listed on the website).

Once in the country, there are no official tourist offices or information bureaux whatsoever. Fortunately, however, most private tour companies scattered around the urban centres are fairly liberal with information and there are plenty of publications available – in the form of maps, guides of varying quality, brochures, pamphlets and Go Places magazine (www.goplaceskenya.com).

Tour and Safari Operators
Numerous operators, based either in or outside the country, offer group and/or bespoke tours and safari packages to Kenya. These are usually inclusive of all accommodation, as well as transfers, game drives and other transport, most meals and activities, and (at the top end of the price range) all house drinks.

The advantages of booking through an operator outside Kenya is that the safari price will usually include discounted international flights and you are in a stronger position when it comes to insurance, cancellations etc. However, booking your ground arrangements through a Kenyan operator tends to work out more cheaply overall, and it ensures that a greater proportion of your money goes directly into the local economy. There are literally hundreds of operators to choose from, and while no listing of this sort can be definitive, the selection below are all well-established companies with a good reputation:

Outside Kenya:
Abercrombie & Kent Ltd,
Tel: (USA) +1 800 554 7016 or (UK) +44 (0)1242 547 760
www.abercrombiekent.com
Now over 50 years old, this well-known upmarket operator, with offices in the UK and US, started life in Kenya and remains specialised in the country.
African Mecca Safaris
Tel: (USA) +1 866 527 4281 or (UK) +44 (0)161 870 6092
www.africanmeccasafaris.com
This award-winning American adventure travel company offers itineraries to more than 30 reserves in Kenya and Tanzania, as well as all the usual beach destinations.
Audley Travel
Tel: (USA) +1 855 838 8300 or (UK) +44 (0)1993 838 500
www.audleytravel.com
Award-winning UK operator specialising in top-end tailor-made tours all around Kenya.
Bench International
Tel: +612 9290 2877 (international)
www.benchinternational.com.au
One of Australia's oldest and best Africa specialists, with more than 45 years' experience arranging bespoke safaris in Kenya and elsewhere.
Naturally Africa Collection
Tel: +44 (0)1622 370 270
www.naturallyafricacollection.co.uk
Experienced agent offering tailor-made East African safaris for general and special interest groups.
Rainbow Tours
Tel: +44 (0)203 131 0780
www.rainbowtours.co.uk
Highly regarded UK operator specialising in bespoke itineraries to Kenya and elsewhere in East and Southern Africa.
Wild Frontiers
Tel: +27 (0)11 702 2035
www.wildfrontiers.com

Excellent South African-based specialist with 30 years' experience in East Africa, particularly good for multi-country safaris also taking in Tanzania, Rwanda or Uganda.

Kenyan Operators

Gametrackers Safaris
Tel: 020 222 2703
www.gametrackersafaris.com
A good choice for budget travellers, this well-established company runs regular overland truck camping safaris to Lake Turkana, the Maasai Mara and elsewhere in East Africa.

Gamewatchers Safaris
Tel: 0774 136 523
www.porini.com
This eco-conscious operator runs the four Porini Tented Camps, which lie in Maasai community reserves bordering the Maasai Mara and Amboseli, as well as in Ol Pejeta (Laikipia). It's a good contact for upmarket safaris that focus on superb game viewing in untrammelled areas away from the main game drive circuits.

Let's Go Travel
Tel: 020 444 1030
www.uniglobeletsgotravel.com
More booking agent than safari operator, this long-serving company is exceptionally knowledgeable and a good place for independent visitors to book accommodation or short safaris within the country.

Muthaiga Travel
Tel: 020 248 9985
www.muthaigatravel.com
This small hands-on company offers a good range of midrange group and bespoke safaris, and it also caters to business travellers in Nairobi and elsewhere.

Southern Cross Safaris
Tel: 020 807 0311
www.southerncrosskenya.com
One of Kenya's top safari companies since the early 1960s, Southern Cross has a large and varied fleet of 4x4s and other vehicles, and will tailor safaris and tours to suit all interest groups, from birdwatchers and honeymooners to family groups and corporate travellers.

V

Visas and Passports

All visitors must be in possession of a valid passport with an expiry date at least six months after the end of their intended stay in Kenya. Visas are required by everyone except citizens of some Commonwealth countries and certain countries with which Kenya has reciprocal waiver arrangements.

Citizens of the Australia, Canada, Ireland, New Zealand, UK, USA, and most European countries require visas. South Africans do not require a visa for a stay of less than 30 days, but do require one for a longer stay.

Until recently visas could be obtained upon arrival at any international airport and most overland borders to Kenya. Since September 2015 this has been replaced by an online application system. You can now apply for a visa at http://evisa.go.ke, and have your e-visa ready to be printed out within two to seven business days. This is a quick and straightforward procedure. Single entry visas cost US$51 and transit US$21.

For a multiple-entry visa (US$100) you should obtain an application form from the nearest Kenyan Embassy or High Commission, and allow at least a week for processing.

Since these arrangements may change, it is essential to double-check on visa requirements well ahead of the trip.

No visitor is permitted to take up work or residence in Kenya without the authority of the Principal Immigration Officer.

W

Weights and Measures

Kenya uses the metric system.

On safari in Maasai Mara National Reserve.

LANGUAGE

UNDERSTANDING THE LANGUAGE

Almost 70 different languages belonging to at least four different linguistic groups are spoken in Kenya. Of these, the majority are placed in the Bantu group, the most widely spoken set of languages in eastern and southern Africa, while others are placed in the Nilotic, Cushitic and Khoisan groups. The two official languages are English, which is spoken to a high standard by most educated Kenyans and by almost everybody associated with the tourist industry, and Swahili (or more correctly KiSwahili), a coastal tongue whose spread into the interior was initiated by the 19th-century slave caravans, but has also been officially encouraged in the independent era. Grammatically and in terms of pronunciation, Swahili is unambiguously a Bantu language, but the vocabulary includes a great many words of Arabic and English derivation.

BASIC RULES

Swahili is the official language of Kenya and Tanzania, and spoken as a second language almost universally in these countries. It is also widely understood in Uganda, Rwanda and Burundi, and in the north of Malawi and Mozambique. Although very phonetic and thus relatively easy to pronounce, Swahili does require some effort for the first-time speaker. Every letter in the language is pronounced, unless it's part of a group of consonants. If a letter is written twice it is pronounced twice. Word stress almost always falls on the second to last syllable. While English is widely spoken, it is worth learning the greetings and commonly used phrases.

PRONUNCIATION GUIDE

Vowels

a as in 'calm'
e as in the 'a' in 'may'
i as the 'e' in 'me'
o as in 'go'
u as the 'o' in 'too'

Consonants

dh as in 'th' in 'this'
th as in 'th' in 'thing'
gh like the 'ch' of the Scottish 'loch'
ng' as in the 'ng' of 'singer'
ng as in the 'ng' in 'finger'
ny as in the 'ni' in 'onion'
ch as in 'church'
g as in 'get'

Words and Phrases

Yes Ndiyo/ndio
No A-a/hapana
OK Sawa
Please Tafadhali
Thank you Asante (nashukuru)
Sorry Pole
You're welcome Karibu sana
Excuse me Hodi
I don't speak Swahili Sisemba/sisemi Kiswahili (sana)
How do you say … in Swahili? Unasemaje … kwa Kiswahili?
Do you speak English? Unasema Kiingereza?
Do you understand? Unaelewa?
I don't understand Sielewi
I understand Naelewa
A little Kidogo
I don't know Sijui
Please write it down Tafadhali niandikie
Wait a moment! Subiri!

Speak slowly, please Tafadhali sema polepole
Enough! Inatosha/Bas!
Good Nzuri
Fine Salama
Where is…? …iko wapi?
Where is the nearest…? …ya (la) karibu liko (iko) wapi?
…toilet Choo…
May I come in (s.o.'s home) Hodi!
Welcome! Karibu!
Reply: Salama/nzuri/safi/njema
Don't mention it Rica ederim
Pleased to meet you Nimefurahi
How are you? Hujambo (habari gani?)
Fine, thanks. And you? Sijambo, wewe? (nzuri, habari zako/yako?)
My name is… Jina langu ni (naitwa)…
I am British/American/Australian Natoka Uingereza/Marekani/Australia
Leave me alone Usinisumbue/niache
Go away! Hebu!/Toka!
What time is it? Saa ngapi?
When? Lini?
Today Leo

Emergencies

Help! Msaada (kusaidia)/saidia/njoo/nisaidie!
Fire! Moto!
Please call the police Mwite/muite polisi tafadhali
Are you all right? U mzima?
I'm ill Naumwa
I'm lost Nimepotea
(Get a) doctor (Umwite) daktari
Send for an ambulance Uite gari la hospitali
There has been an accident ajali/Pametokea ajali
He is (seriously) hurt Ameumia (vibaya)
I've been robbed! Nimeibiwa!
I'd like an interpreter Nataka mkalimani/mtafsiri

Tomorrow *Kesho*
Yesterday *Jana*
Now *Sasa*
Later *Baadaye*
Tonight *Leo usiku*
Why? *Kwa nini?*
Here *Hapa*
There *Pale*
Where can I find... *Wapi nawesa*
...a newspaper? *Gazeti?*
...a taxi? *Teksi?*
...a telephone? *Simu?*
Yes, there is *Ndiyo*
No, there isn't *Sivyo*

Days of the Week

Monday *Jumatatu*
Tuesday *Jumanne*
Wednesday *Jumatano*
Thursday *Alhamisi*
Friday *Ijumaa*
Saturday *Jumamosi*
Sunday *Jumapili*

Numbers

0 *sufuri/ziro*
1 *moja*
2 *mbili*
3 *tatu*
4 *nne*
5 *tano*
6 *sita*
7 *saba*
8 *nane*
9 *tisa*
10 *kumi*
11 *kumi na moja*
12 *kumi na mbili*
20 *ishirini*
21 *ishirini na moja*
22 *ishirini na mbili*
30 *thelathini*
40 *arobaini*
50 *hamsini*
60 *sitini*
70 *sabiini/sabini*
80 *themanini*
90 *tisiini/tisini*
100 *mia*
200 *mia mbili*
1,000 *elfu (moja)*

Months of the Year

January *Januari*
February *Febuari*
March *Machi*
April *Aprili*
May *Mei*
June *Juni*
July *Julai*
August *Agosti*
September *Septemba*
October *Oktoba*
November *Novemba*
December *Desemba*

Greetings

Courtesy is rated highly in Kenya, and greetings should not be rushed. Always shake hands if possible and pay attention to how people greet each other. If you learn nothing else in Swahili, try to master some of the following:
Good morning (literally, how's your morning been?) *Habari ya asubuhi?*
Good afternoon *Habari ya mchana*
Good evening *Habari ya jioni*
Goodnight *Lala salama*
Goodbye *Tutaonana/kwa heri, kwaheri (berphbk)*

Reply: The correct reply to all of these is '*Mzuri Sana*' (**very good**), which could be followed by '*Na Wewe?*' (**and you?**)
Greeting to an elder/authority figure: *Shikamoo...*
Reply: *Marahaba*
How are you...? *Hujambo...?*
Reply: *Sijambo* (or *Jambo* if you want to convert to English)
Hello *Salama/jambo* (*jambo* is mainly used for foreigners – reply *jambo* if you want to speak English, or *sijambo* if want to try out some Swahili phrases).

Health

Hospital *Hospitali*
Clinic *Zahanati*
First aid *Huduma ya kwanza*
Doctor *Daktari*
Dentist *Daktari wa meno/Mganga wa meno*
I am ill *Naumwa*
It hurts here *Inaumwa hapa*
I have a fever/headache *Nina homa/kichwa kinamua*
I am diabetic *Nina dayabeti*
I'm allergic to... *Nina aleji ya...*
I have asthma *Nina ungonjwa wa pumu*
I am pregnant *Nina mimba*
I was bitten by... *Niliumwa na...*

Sightseeing and Directions

Near *Karibu*
Far *Mbali*
Left *Kushoto*
On/to the left *Upande wa kushoto*
Right *Kulia*
On/to the right *Upande wa kulia*
Straight on *Moja kwa moja*
City *Mji*
Village *Kijiji*
Sea *Bahari*
Lake *Ziwa*
Farm *Shamba*
North *Kaskazini*
South *Kusini*
East *Mashariki*
West *Magharibi*
Is it near/far? *Iko karibu/mbali?*
How far is...? *Ni umbali gani?*

Travelling

Car *Motokaa*
Petrol/gas *Petroli*
Flat tyre/puncture *Pancha/kuna kitundu*
My car has broken down *Motokaa yangu imeharibika*
Bus stop *Bas stendi*

Bus *Basi/bas*
Train *Treni/gari la moshi*
Taxi *Teksi/taxi*
Airport *Uwanja wa ndege*
Port/harbour *Bandari*
Ferry *Meli*
Ticket *Tikiti*
What time does it leave? *Tutaondoka saa ngapi?*
Where do I go? *Nifikeje?*
Which bus do I take for...? *Niingie katika bas gani kwa kwenda...?*
Stop! *Simama!*

Shopping

How much (is this)? *(Hii) bei gani/ ni ngapi?*
Can I have? *Nipatie...tafadhali?*
Do you have any...? *Kuna...?*
Big *Kubwa*
Small *Ndogo*
How many? *Ngapi gani?*

Eating Out

Waiter/Waitress! *Bwana!/Bibi!*
Table *Meza*
Bottle (of) *Chupa (ya)*
Salt *Chumvi*
Black pepper *Pilipili*
Soup *Supu*
Fish *Samaki*
Chicken *Kuku*
Meat *Nyama*
Eggs *Mayai*
Vegetarian food *Wasiokula nyama*
Vegetables *Mboga*
Fruit *Matunda*
Bread *Mkate*
Water *Maji*
Beer *Biya*
Fruit juice *Maji ya matunda*
Wine (red/white) *Mvinyo/divai (nyeupe/nyekundu)*
Hot ginger drink *Tangawizi*
Coffee (black/with milk) *Kahawa (na maziwa/nyeusi)*
Tea *Chai*

TRANSPORT

A – Z

LANGUAGE

FURTHER READING

HISTORY AND SOCIETY

Dreams in a Time of War by Ngugi Wa Thiong'o. Autobiographic account of his Gikuyu childhood by Kenya's most renowned novelist.

Facing Mount Kenya by Jomo Kenyatta. Insightful account of traditional Gikuyu culture by the first president of independent Kenya.

Flame Trees of Thika by Elspeth Huxley. A collection of wonderfully told tales about the author's childhood in East Africa.

Imperial Reckoning: The Untold Story of Britain's Gulag in Kenya by Caroline Elkins. Controversial Pulitzer-winning account of the Mau-Mau era.

I Wish I Could Say I Was Sorry by Susie Kelly. Published in 2014, remarkable memoirs of a British woman's 1950s childhood in Kenya.

It's Our Turn to Eat by Michela Wrong. The story of the journalist John Githongo and his fight against corruption.

Kenya: A Country in the Making 1880–1940 by Nigel Pavitt. Absorbing collection of 700 monochrome photos from the early colonial era, enhanced by the lengthy and insightful captions.

The Life and Death of Lord Erroll by Errol Trzebenski. This vivid account of the murder documented in the movie *White Mischief* was reissued in 2011.

Lunatic Express by Charles Miller. The story of the building of the railway from Mombasa to Uganda.

Maasai by Tepilit Ole Saitoti and Carol Beckwith. Fascinating text and photos by one of the world's top ethnographic photographers add up to an illuminating and beautiful package.

Out of Africa by Karen Blixen. The famous autobiographic account of Blixen's life in Kenya during the early 1900s, which inspired the Oscar-winning film of the same name.

Unbowed by Wangari Maathai. Engaging autobiography of the Nobel Laureate and founder of the Green Belt Movement.

West With The Night by Beryl Markham. Fascinating memoirs of the legendary aviator.

FICTION

Discovering Home by Binyavanga Wainaina. This novella, written by Nakuru-born Wainana when he was still in his 20s, won him the Caine Prize for African Writing in 2002.

Going Down River Road by Meja Mwangi. Award-winning novel set in Nairobi's notorious River Road district following independence.

Petals of Blood by Ngugi wa Thiong'o. Controversial 1970s novel whose cutting political commentary is thinly veiled behind the trappings of a whodunnit set in a small village.

The River and the Source by Margaret Ogola. Published in 1995, this multiple award-winning novel

Send Us Your Thoughts

We do our best to ensure the information in our books is as accurate and up-to-date as possible. The books are updated on a regular basis using local contacts, who painstakingly add, amend and correct as required. However, some details (such as telephone numbers and opening times) are liable to change, and we are ultimately reliant on our readers to put us in the picture.

We welcome your feedback, especially your experience of using the book "on the road". Maybe we recommended a hotel that you liked (or another that you didn't), or you came across a great bar or new attraction we missed.

We will acknowledge all contributions, and we'll offer an Insight Guide to the best letters received.

Please write to us at:
**Insight Guides
PO Box 7910
London SE1 1WE**
Or email us at:
hello@insightguides.com

traces the story of three generations of Luo women.

Wizard of the Crow by Ngugi Wa Thiong'o. Arguably the crowning achievement of Kenya's greatest novelist, this hefty 700-page tome, set in the fictional republic of Aburiria, is a damning indictment of the hypocrisy and greed of many modern African leaders.

WILDLIFE AND NATURAL HISTORY

Birds of Kenya and Northern Tanzania by Dale Zimmerman, Don Turner and David Pearson. The best single-volume field guide to Kenya's birds.

Born Free: The Full Story by Joy Adamson. Expanded 50th anniversary edition of the classic account of Adamson's attempt to reintroduce the hand-reared lioness Elsa into the wild.

The End of the Game by Peter Beard. Dramatic photographs and story telling of the history – and uncertain future – of Kenya's wildlife, originally published in the 1960s but reprinted in 2008.

Field Guide to Common Trees and Shrubs of East Africa by Najma Dharani. Useful starter's guide.

Field Guide to the Birds of East Africa by Terry Stevenson and John Fanshawe. Another excellent field guide whose coverage extends to Tanzania and Uganda.

Field Guide to the Reptiles of East Africa by Stephen Spawls, Kim Howell, Robert Drewes and James Ashe. Magnificent albeit rather esoteric guide to every reptile species recorded in East Africa.

Kenya By Michael Poliza. Possibly the most stunning photography book about Kenya's wildlife ever produced.

Mara Serengeti: A Photographer's Paradise by Jonathan and Angela Scott. Lavish coffee-table-style introduction to the region's wildlife.

Pocket Guide to African Mammals by Jonathan Kingdon. A compact, authoritative field guide for novices.

The Safari Companion by Richard Estes. This informative guide covers most species likely to be seen on a Kenyan safari.

CREDITS

Insight Guide Credits

Distribution
UK
Dorling Kindersley Ltd
A Penguin Group company
80 Strand, London, WC2R 0RL
sales@uk.dk.com

United States
Ingram Publisher Services
1 Ingram Boulevard, PO Box 3006,
La Vergne, TN 37086-1986
ips@ingramcontent.com

Australia and New Zealand
Woodslane
10 Apollo St, Warriewood,
NSW 2102, Australia
info@woodslane.com.au

Worldwide
Apa Publications (Singapore) Pte
7030 Ang Mo Kio Avenue 5
08-65 Northstar @ AMK
Singapore 569880
apasin@singnet.com.sg

Printing
CTPS-China

First Edition 1985
Sixth Edition 2016

Every effort has been made to provide accurate information in this publication, but changes are inevitable. The publisher cannot be responsible for any resulting loss, inconvenience or injury. We would appreciate it if readers would call our attention to any errors or outdated information. We also welcome your suggestions; please contact us at:
hello@insightguides.com

www.insightguides.com

Editors: Kate Drynan; Tim Binks
Author: Philip Briggs
Head of Production: Rebeka Davies
Update Production: AM Services
Picture Editor: Tom Smyth
Cartography: original cartography Berndtson & Berndtson, updated by Carte

Legend

City maps

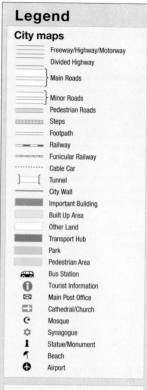

	Freeway/Highway/Motorway
	Divided Highway
	Main Roads
	Minor Roads
	Pedestrian Roads
	Steps
	Footpath
	Railway
	Funicular Railway
	Cable Car
	Tunnel
	City Wall
	Important Building
	Built Up Area
	Other Land
	Transport Hub
	Park
	Pedestrian Area
	Bus Station
	Tourist Information
	Main Post Office
	Cathedral/Church
	Mosque
	Synagogue
	Statue/Monument
	Beach
	Airport

Regional maps

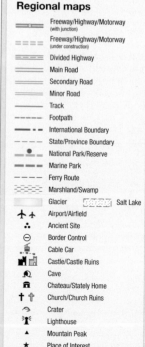

	Freeway/Highway/Motorway (with junction)
	Freeway/Highway/Motorway (under construction)
	Divided Highway
	Main Road
	Secondary Road
	Minor Road
	Track
	Footpath
	International Boundary
	State/Province Boundary
	National Park/Reserve
	Marine Park
	Ferry Route
	Marshland/Swamp
	Glacier / Salt Lake
	Airport/Airfield
	Ancient Site
	Border Control
	Cable Car
	Castle/Castle Ruins
	Cave
	Chateau/Stately Home
	Church/Church Ruins
	Crater
	Lighthouse
	Mountain Peak
	Place of Interest
	Viewpoint

Contributors

This fully revised edition was commissioned by Kate Drynan, updated by Katarzyna Marcinkowska and edited by Tim Binks. Many thanks to our wonderful author Philip Briggs, a South-African travel writer specialising in Africa. He first backpacked between Nairobi and Cape Town in 1986 and has been travelling the highways and byways of Africa ever since. He has written guidebooks to destinations all over Africa, including Insight Guides to South Africa, Tanzania and Zanzibar, Namibia and Gambia and Senegal. The on-the-ground research for this edition was facilitated by the assistance of three excellent local operators, Gamewatchers Safaris, Muthaiga Travel, and Southern Cross Safaris, whose contact details are all included on page 299.

Many of the images in this book were taken by Ariadne Van Zandbergen, a specialist in African wildlife and travel photography.

About Insight Guides

Insight Guides have more than 40 years' experience of publishing high-quality, visual travel guides. We produce 400 full-colour titles, in both print and digital form, covering more than 200 destinations across the globe, in a variety of formats to meet your different needs.

Insight Guides are written by local authors who use their on-the-ground experience to provide the very latest information; their local expertise is evident in the extensive historical and cultural background features. All the reviews in **Insight Guides** are independent; we strive to maintain an impartial view. Our reviews are carefully selected to guide you to the best places to eat, go out and shop, so you can be confident that when we say a place is special, we really mean it.

INDEX

Main references are in bold type